Kiwiosities

About the author

Gordon Ell ONZM is the author of many popular books about New Zealand's historic and natural heritage. His interest in New Zealand traditions has grown since boyhood in the Buller region, through many years of travelling through the country, often photographing aspects of the past for books and documentary films. Trained as a journalist, Gordon Ell worked also in radio and television production before becoming a wildlife film-maker and book publisher. He lives in Takapuna, Auckland, but spends a lot of time in the outdoors.

Kiwiosities

New Zealand traditions & folklore

GORDON ELL

First published in 2008 by New Holland Publishers (NZ) Ltd
Auckland • Sydney • London • Cape Town

www.newhollandpublishers.co.nz

218 Lake Road, Northcote, Auckland 0627, New Zealand
Unit 1, 66 Gibbes Street, Chatswood, NSW 2067, Australia
86–88 Edgware Road, London W2 2EA, United Kingdom
80 McKenzie Street, Cape Town 8001, South Africa

Publishing manager: Matt Turner
Editor: Jeremy Doyle
Design: Dee Murch
Cover design: Nick Turzynski

Ell, Gordon.
Kiwiosities : an A-Z of New Zealand traditions and folklore /
Gordon Ell.
Previously published as: A-Z of Kiwi fact & folklore. 2003.
ISBN 978-1-86966-233-2
1. National characteristics, New Zealand ‡v Dictionaries.
2. Popular culture—New Zealand—Dictionaries. 3. Folklore—
New Zealand—Dictionaries. 4. Legends—New Zealand—
Dictionaries. 5. Rites and ceremonies—New Zealand—
Dictionaries. 6. New Zealand—Social life and customs—
Dictionaries. I. Ell, Gordon. A-Z of Kiwi fact & folklore.
II. Title.
305.823—dc 22

10 9 8 7 6 5 4 3 2 1

Colour reproduction by Image Centre Ltd., Auckland
Printed in China at Everbest Printing Co, on paper sourced from
sustainable forests.

Table of Contents

The Making of Traditions

The traditions of this book have been gathered largely from experience; of living in this country for more than 50 years and also from reading a vast number of books that encompass the New Zealand way of life. The idea has been to recall some of the fascinating tales and idiosyncracies that are shared by New Zealanders.

My definition of a tradition is catholic, borrowed from the Oxford Dictionary as, in essence, the opinions, or beliefs, or customs handed down for posterity. In the case of New Zealand that includes some myths, a handful of legends and a lot of folklore, defined as commonly held beliefs. To this I have added popular allusions, words and phrases that are generally understood to have a special meaning to someone raised in New Zealand.

Some of these traditions are based in the cultures brought to New Zealand by immigrants, though they have often suffered a sea change on the voyage. Thus most New Zealanders celebrate Christmas with the menu of midwinter feasting, though Christmas dinner has to be eaten at midsummer. Most of the traditions, however, are based on our common experiences here.

In this summary of more than 700 traditions I have tried to capture, in outline, a folklore that is distinctively of New Zealand and New Zealanders. The entries, arranged alphabetically, begin with *A Good Keen Man* and end with the gowned glory of **Zealandia**. Between these quintessential figures are the popular assumptions and references that constitute the colour and character of New Zealanders.

The general approach has not been to define a culture but to bring together a sampler of popular beliefs and allusions. When I began the task, aiming for around 400 references, the job seemed finite. Only the economics of book production finally dictated a stop after some 600 entries. Yet the result remains very much a personal selection. The more I delved into our past the more there seemed to be worth recording. It is encouraging to find how rich our oral and written traditions are.

What I have looked for are good stories extending over a broad and common experience of New Zealand life. Some of the traditions are obvious, from the observance of **Anzac Day** to the singing of '**God Defend New Zealand**'. Yet there are many stories that will be less widely known, though in their district or time they have had considerable currency. For example the **Wreck of the *Endeavour*** in Fiordland will be unfamiliar to most yet in that region speculation about the bones of the ship sunk in Facile Harbour has fuelled a raft of legends over the past 200 years or so. The *Endeavour* finds its place in Fiordland tradition, among local legends of mythical beasts such as the **Native Otter**, and the people of the **Lost Tribe**. Other writers have investigated and recorded these stories in greater detail. This outline includes references to the fuller story for those whose curiosity is whetted by each anecdote.

The idea of New Zealand as a land of distinct traditions may seem strange to those of earlier generations who looked to Britain and elsewhere for the source of their culture. For those of us, however, who have grown to adulthood since the Second World War there has emerged a distinct New Zealand way of doing things: even when visiting the countries that gave rise to our Western outlook there is always a feeling of being among foreigners, people who look the same but behave differently in certain matters. Faced with a crisis New Zealanders will often act in a manner that sets them apart from people of other cultures; our assumptions about social behaviour reflect our own traditions.

These traditions were begun by pioneers, reflecting first a frontier society, then modified through the **Great Depression** and war, to be integrated in recent years into a mixed society, now chiefly urban. So the traditions of the founders have been modified and developed considerably through 200 years of social admixture and change.

Many of the ideas the pioneers brought here are still alive in community traditions and beliefs. The churches, for example, have kept alive their festivals though the interpretation here has sometimes taken on a native colour. **Easter**, springing from pagan times, retains its suggestions of seasonal rebirth, with Easter eggs and rabbits, though it is celebrated here in autumn. An observer armed with a folklore of European culture may make further connections: the use of **Finials** on gable ends, once placed to discourage witches from perching there, are in New Zealand a distinctive feature of **Wooden** Colonial-style homes.

A large number of our traditions spring from the founding cultures. The dancing of the kolo persists in Dalmatian communities while the Scots, particularly in the southern districts, mark hogmanay with haggis and first footing. The regional cultures of New Zealand have been deeply affected by the pattern of early settlement and their cultural inheritance. Christchurch is still referred to as the English city, Dunedin as the **Edinburgh of the South**. Rural Taranaki is rich in traditions of the cow **Cockies** while metropolitan Auckland assumes the title of **Largest Polynesian City in the World**, still holding within its multi-cultural diversity traditions from the Pacific and Europe. In the **Gold Rush** districts and among the high-country sheep stations the traditions of pioneer Australia are occasionally encountered. The material culture of the goldfields comes down through the **Forty-niners** of California and the Victorian fields, influencing how gold was sought and fought over. In the high country, New Zealand links with Australia are often reflected in common tales and practices, spread through pioneer settlers and the seasonal labour market which toured the **Stations** of both countries. Traditions flourish in the **Back Blocks**, as they do among returned soldiers and conservative communities, for they are kept alive wherever people accept a common culture and change is not too revolutionary.

This is not a book of Maori traditions, myths or legends: that subject has its own recorders. Yet Maori culture contributes a dimension to the definition of New Zealander and there are some things held in common as a product of living together. So some of the nature lore is shared – the full and early flowering of the **Cabbage Tree** portending a good summer for example. There is also a common use of customs such as **Hui** for discussion and the cooking of **Hangi**, though the meanings of such occasions may differ from group to group. There are also experiences common to most if not all of our cultures, such as the episodes of war in pioneer times. They find an expression here as reference points to our past and the impact they have made on popular belief.

I expect every New Zealander could add to this selection. To keep the length of this book under control I have had to do some choosing from the rich variety of material. A lot more could be said in detail about the traditions behind our place names, the phrases and slang that we use, our sporting traditions, the national icons (such as Marmite and Lane's Emulsion), the lore of the armed services and war, about disasters and politics. These topics have been, however, canvassed in specialist books, each one worth a volume in its own right. This collection draws together the broader strands of our common heritage, concentrating on the folklore that makes us distinctive as people.

As I worked through the traditions of this book I often felt how quickly Kiwi beliefs and attributes have changed in recent years. Ideas that had been central to our national consciousness, such as social security for all, have suddenly fallen to the margins of memory after a hundred years in the making. There has been a radical change in New Zealand since the determined destruction of the Welfare State began in the late 1980s.

Many of our traditional values have been challenged, some largely destroyed, in recent times. The presumptions of **Cradle to the Grave Social Security**, once central to New Zealand mores, have gone and with them the social patterns and concerns that, until recently, epitomised our way of life. Other traditions have perhaps been strengthened through this social change: our traditions of **Do-it-yourself** self-reliance, of Women's Suffrage, for example.

The restructuring of recent years has fundamentally changed our ways of doing things. It is challenging to consider whether such general pioneering ideals as **Mateship** and caring for others will reassert themselves in time or whether such traditions, dating back a century or more, can simply be destroyed by changing the social framework. In writing this book I felt privileged to have lived through the growing up of New Zealand and hope to have captured through these pages some of the values that we learnt along the way. Hopefully, the better part will still be with us now that the social revolution of the 1990s is over.

This book was originally published as *New Zealand Traditions & Folklore* some 14 years ago. In its new format, which emphasises the alphabetical approach to our heritage, a number of changes have been made.

The social revolution of the early 1990s has since settled, then changed again in many places, with widespread immigration from Asia, eastern Europe and even Africa. Burgeoning population has tended to concentrate on key cities; Auckland now has more than 1.1 million people. We are actually more urbanised than Japan and North America with 86 per cent of the population living in towns.

This urbanisation has radically changed attitudes to our pioneer and largely rural past. Whilst most city-dwelling New Zealanders a generation ago might have had direct personal links with the countryside, there now exists a flourishing urban society with its roots and recollections firmly in the city.

For someone who belongs to probably the last generation to come commonly from the country to the town, the experience of New Zealand and its traditions has changed radically in the past decade. Many of the stories and anecdotes in this book may no longer strike a first-hand chord with younger people: new settlers too have encountered only our urban society and may struggle to make a connection with our pioneer past as a largely rural society.

In a way, many of our traditions are now less accessible than they were just 10 years ago, and are therefore at risk of fading into a forgotten past. Compiling and updating this collection of facts and fictions I have endeavoured not to indulge in nostalgia but to make a popular record of attitudes and events that have helped to shape our country over the past 200 years.

Gordon Ell

Imperial–Metric Conversions

Books that touch on the past inevitably reflect its measures. The phenomenon of the quarter-acre section is less easy to appreciate when defined as .101 hectares and never, in fact, existed in this metricated form. The weight of a big trout may be similarly arguable. Pounds, shillings and pence along with half-pints of school milk, sea miles and 4" by 2" are further measures inextricably entangled with our past. Where obvious I have changed the measures in this book to metric but, for the rest, the poetry remains in its old imperial expression. For those who like to view things only in modern measures, and vice versa, here is a conversion table.

1 inch = 25.4 millimetres
1 foot = 30.5 centimetres
1 yard = 0.914 metres
1 mile = 1.61 kilometres
1 acre = 0.405 hectares

1 pint = 568 millilitres
1 gallon = 4.55 litres

1 ounce (oz) = 28.3 grams
1 pound (lb) = 454 grams
1 stone = 6.35 kilograms
1 ton = 1.02 tonnes

1 penny (1d) = 0.83 cents
1 shilling (1s) = 10 cents
1 pound (£1) = 2 dollars

In addition, there are 12 inches in a foot and three feet in a yard. There were 12 pence in a shilling, 24 pence in a florin, 60 pence in a half-crown, and twenty shillings or 240 pence in a pound.

How to Use this Book

The traditions and folklore that follow are listed in an alphabetical series. Care has been taken to use familiar expressions to identify each story. Some alternative names have been given as cross-references, however, to make it easier to locate particular subjects.

Stories beginning with 'a' or 'the' are usually listed by the word following, unless the definite article is part of a title.

Where there are related traditions and anecdotes, these have been referred to by a listing in bold type within each story. Thus it should be comparatively easy to trace several related traditions – for example those associated with the kauri tree – by following the words in bold type from one article to another. On the other hand it is hoped that the contrast and variety of the traditions themselves will make straightforward browsing pleasurable.

A Note on Sources

Writing about the past obviously requires a lot of research and reading; the author's indebtedness may go back over years of compulsive reading about New Zealand. Often I was at a loss as to how I came by a story and spent hours checking back to find confirmation in old books that are here mentioned in the text. In acknowledging sources for some traditions and anecdotes, I must thank all those who have taken the trouble over the years to record their experience for posterity.

Instead of listing the contents of the public library as a general source of references, I have instead mentioned useful books in the context of a particular article: not so much as the source, though this is acknowledged where it is the case, but to provide a starting point for anyone who wants to know more about a subject.

Such recommended reading is that of an enthusiast rather than an academic citation: to me looking back into New Zealand's past is still a source of enjoyment and recreation.

A Good Keen Man

Author Barry Crump began his extraordinary career as a popular novelist with a book of this name. In its first year *A Good Keen Man* sold 28,000 copies and set Crump to writing a chain of successful novels, amounting to some three million books in print over 30 years. In many of his popular expressions and some of his yarns, Barry Crump has captured the essential language of the laconic Kiwi countryman. Interviewed by the Wildlife Service at the beginning of the book, the young hero is sent into the bush as a trainee deer culler. He carries a letter of introduction to his field officer with the commendation, 'This is Barry Crump. He looks to me like a good keen man.' In those palmy days such qualities could take a man a long way in the back country. Read *A Good Keen Man*, by Barry Crump (A.H. & A.W. Reed, Wellington, 1960, reprinted many times). See also **Hang on a Minute Mate**.

A&P Shows, Agricultural and Pastoral Shows

Many rural communities and those larger ones that rely on them still hold Agricultural and Pastoral Shows. Stock and produce are judged, there are events for horses and their riders, sideshows and produce stalls bid for the farmers' interest. The show culminates in the grand parade of winning beasts and proud owners. The 'Royal Show' title is shared about the larger A&P associations, which take turns to host one. Show Day is still a public holiday in Canterbury.

Aerial Top-dressing

The idea of dropping fertiliser from the air was developed by State agencies in 1948 and became a commercial reality in 1949.

Former war pilots in twin-winged Tiger Moths pioneered the industry, dropping superphosphate and trace elements. In this way they rapidly improved the fertility of hill country previously impossible to top-dress. Aircraft were also used to spray weeds and scrub, preparing the way for re-seeding from the air. The industry led to the development of New Zealand-made specialist aircraft such as the Fletcher TU24 and the Te Kuiti AirTruk. Top-dressing planes operate from short airstrips in the hills where they often load within a minute on the ground.

Albertlanders

Non-conformist Christians from Britain made up the families who came to lower Northland in 1861 as 'Albertlanders' (named after Albert, the Prince Consort). Organised by William Brame, 500 settlers arrived in Auckland on the *Matilda Wattenbach* and the *Hanover*, but half stayed in Auckland when they faced the journey north. Most of the settlers boated to Riverhead on the upper Waitemata, walked overland to Helensville, then travelled by track or sea to the Albertland Settlement, on the Kaipara Harbour near present-day Wellsford. See *The Albertlanders* by Sir Henry Brett and Henry Hook, reprinted by Bush Press in 2003.

The All Blacks

The New Zealand representative rugby team. The name originated with the New Zealand touring side in Britain in 1905, but the etymology is arguable. Some relate the expression to the all-black shorts and jerseys with the **Silver Fern**, a reference used by J.A. Buttery of the *Daily Mail,* London, in his book *Why the All Blacks Triumphed*, following the tour. Another tale springs from the judgment that the New Zealanders, regardless of their position on the field, played as if they were all backs. A typographic error in an unspecified press report changed the headline ALL BACKS to ALL BLACKS. Regardless, the name persists while the uniform colours have been adopted by most other New Zealand sporting codes.

The All Whites

Soccer or association football puts its New Zealand team onto the field dressed in opposite colours to the **All Blacks**. The game received great support in the mid-1980s while the national game of rugby suffered from being found offside by many who objected to the social disruption of the 1981 Springbok Tour. With the dismantling of apartheid in South Africa, New Zealanders have now returned to supporting rugby, and soccer remains a secondary sport, along with rugby league. Professional competitions, however, keep it in the sports news.

The America's Cup

Competition for the world's premier yachting trophy for match racing, the America's Cup, captured popular interest among New Zealanders in the 1990s. In 1851, Col. John C. Stevens of the New York Yacht Club sailed his schooner *America* to race against the British and won the Royal Yacht Squadron's annual regatta around the Isle of Wight, taking home the One Hundred Guinea Cup. It was this trophy that became the America's Cup, first challenged for by the British in 1870 but held by the New York Yacht Club for 132 years. 'The Auld Mug' was then taken by the Australians in 1983. Won back by the Americans in 1987, it fell to New Zealand in 1995 when a team led by Peter Blake and skippered by Russell Coutts won the Cup 5–0 in San Diego. Its defence off Auckland in 2000 was also won 5–0. A tradition in the making emerged when Sir Peter Blake wore his 'lucky' red socks in the cup-winning series in San Diego. New Zealanders followed suit in the mass hysteria of support for the New Zealand defenders of the Cup. Unfortunately, in 2003, their hopes literally broke up on the Hauraki Gulf – and the America's Cup was taken 5–0 by a Swiss syndicate in which former Team New Zealand members, skipper Russell Coutts and tactician Brad Butterworth, played the critical roles. In 2007, NZL92 won the international Louis Vuitton Cup, giving New Zealand the right to challenge for the America's Cup. They lost again to the Swiss, 5–2.

The Anglers' El Dorado

Famous American Western writer Zane Grey gave New Zealand this name during the heyday of our game fishing. Zane Grey set up camp on Urupukapuka Island in the Bay of Islands close to the great marlin fishing grounds about Cape Brett. He also fished the Taupo region for giant trout, collecting his experiences in a book called *Tales from a Fisherman's Log* which has been frequently republished. Grey tells how his son caught 135 trout in 42 days, his brother 140 and Zane, himself, 87. All caught fish of eight and nine pounds weight, with son Romer topping them all with a fish of more than 15 pounds. The publicity encouraged fishermen from around the world to try their luck.

Anniversary Days

These public holidays generally celebrate the founding of New Zealand's first settlements. They are held on a provincial basis dating from 1852 to 1876, when the country was divided into separate provinces, each with its own elected government. The holidays generally take their timing from the establishment of a provincial capital. Dates are adjusted year by year in many places, from the actual birthday to match up with a convenient weekend, to make it a three-day affair. Generally, these are regional celebrations that reflect the character of the founding communities. Auckland celebrates with Northland on the Monday closest to January 29. The Auckland sailing regatta on that day is claimed to be the **Largest One-day Regatta in the World**. Auckland was actually founded on September 18, 1840, to be the new capital of New Zealand, an honour it lost to Wellington in 1865. Taranaki (known as the Province of New Plymouth from 1852 to 1858) has its actual birthday on March 31 but celebrates earlier in the month. November 1 is the actual anniversary date of the founding of Hawke's Bay as a province separated from Wellington Province in 1858. The Wellington anniversary is January 22, celebrating the arrival of the first shipload of immigrants of the New Zealand Company, aboard the *Aurora* at Petone, in 1842. In Nelson the province celebrates its anniversary close to the arrival date of its first immigrant ship *Fifeshire* on February 1, 1842. Marlborough's actual birthday is November 1. The Canterbury Anniversary is generally celebrated on a Friday in early November, with the public agricultural and pastoral **Show Day,** and the New Zealand Trotting Cup at Addington. The actual anniversary is December 16, marking the arrival of the *Charlotte Jane* and *Randolph,* first of the **First Four Ships,** at Lyttelton in 1850. Westland became a province separate from Canterbury following the gold boom, on December 1, 1873. It celebrates that official birthday at different times in various districts. This has to do with Westland's being a long-drawn-out province. Local communities within it tend to mark their anniversary day in conjunction with the nearest main centre across the Alps: Buller with Nelson and Greymouth with Canterbury, for example. The Otago provincial anniversary is shared with Southland on an actual date of March 23. The date commemorates the arrival, at Port Chalmers in 1848, of the first settlers of the Otago Association aboard the *John Wickliffe.* Celebration dates vary, however. Indeed Southland broke away from Otago and became a separate province in 1861, just before the gold boom, which proved an uncanny move financially.

Anzac Day

April 25 is commemorated with solemn ceremonies, often a Dawn Service, both in New Zealand and Australia. Anzac is the acronym of the Australia and New Zealand Army Corps which shared the disastrous landings against Turkish troops at Gallipoli that began on April 25, 1915. The ritual service includes the recitation of **Lest We Forget,** the sounding of the Last Post and the parading of veterans of wars in which New Zealanders have fought. Poppies worn in memoriam recall those that grew on the battlefields of France. Scouts and Guides also parade, most people wipe away a tear, and ex-service folk repair to the RSA to have a few drinks and reminisce. In recent years some of the past enemy have sent delegates. The national day of mourning for New Zealand's war dead has shrunk to a statutory morning in recent years, with a public holiday in the afternoon.

Aotearoa *see* Land of the Long White Cloud

'Arawata Bill'

William O'Leary (?1865–1947) took his nickname from the Arawata River near Haast in South Westland. The old prospector and explorer inspired Denis Glover's poem cycle, a tribute to the romance of the gold diggers, legends in the making. There is the addictive lure that drives the prospector:

> *Always the colour, in quartz or the river,*
> *Never the nuggets as large as a liver,*

And the heroic understatement of **Man Alone** in the bush:

> *Wata Bill stuck his shovel there*
> *And hung his hat on the handle,*
> *Cutting scrub for a shelter,*
> *Lighting wet wood with a candle.*

A River Rules My Life

High-country traditions, from a woman's point of view: this immensely popular book and a raft of sequels describe life on Mt Algidus station in the upper Rakaia Valley of Canterbury. When Mona Anderson married and went to live there, the only access was by fording the Wilberforce River, a source of the Rakaia. Her opening lines are memorable: 'The river was my Rubicon. I had heard stories about the terrible Wilberforce: so many people had drowned in it. I tried not to think about the time when I would have to cross it.' Mt Algidus is one of the high-country runs that ends at the snowline high on the Main Divide of the Southern Alps. The river of the title is typical of the high-country, a stony bed skeined with swift streams that rise unexpectedly in flash flood from melting snow or storm. To cross it the run-holders used drays pulled by horse teams; in one incident a sick cook is swum across the swollen river on a pony's back. An airstrip, finally, offers an alternative route in and out. Anderson's books give a vivid picture of life for women in such remote places as recently as the 1960s and an interesting perspective on a woman's role in high-country life. *A River Rules My Life*, by Mona Anderson (A.H. & A.W. Reed, Wellington, 1963, reprinted many times).

The Armed Constabulary

An armed police force set up in the aftermath of war with Maori in the North Island, the Armed Constabulary Field Force replaced the colonial defence force of Militia and Volunteers. Armed, mounted police of this field force initially manned garrisons in regions where **Te Kooti** and his followers harassed the countryside. From 1867, the Armed Constabulary gradually took over from the soldiers, their numbers rising to nine divisions of 60 to 100 men each, including two Maori divisions. The Armed Constabulary fought in the Bay of Plenty, against Titokowaru in Taranaki, and against Te Kooti in the Urewera borderlands. The European settlement at Taupo began with an Armed Constabulary garrison that has left its name on the hot springs complex there, still known as the A.C. Baths. The Armed Constabulary also served at Parihaka, surrounding the Maori prophet Te Whiti despite his determinedly passive resistance, in 1881. The Armed Constabulary was finally split into the New Zealand Police (traditionally unarmed but with increasing exceptions) and the Permanent Militia in 1886.

Armistice Day

At the 11th hour of the 11th day of the 11th month, there is declared a minute's silence to remember the war dead. The custom dates from the signing of the Armistice, to end the First World War, on November 11, 1918. While life generally proceeds unheeding of the occasion, radio and television stations cease transmission for that minute.

At Homes

From the Victorian period until after the Second World War, women with leisure time would make it known that they were 'at home' to receive visitors on particular afternoons. Each woman had her own afternoon and typically a group visited each other in turn. There was often much competition to provide the finest food and to keep secret the recipe of her speciality, even to the point of altering the list of ingredients slightly, if importuned to share. Here a newcomer or young bride might be introduced to her new community. Personal cards were printed containing the date and time when the bearer was 'at home' and accounts of such occasions were sometimes included in the social pages of the local newspaper. Cartes de visite were proffered on such occasions, the bearer calling first at a house and leaving her card by way of introduction.

Auckland–Wellington Rivalry

Parochialism is endemic in the New Zealand small-town psyche. The greatest rivalry, however, exists between Wellington and Auckland, dating from early competition for the capital of New Zealand. Auckland won first when Governor Hobson shifted the Capital from Okiato, Bay of Islands, in 1840 and founded the new town of Auckland, especially to be the capital. Infant Wellington was lucky to get a Lieutenant Governor. Pressure for a more central capital led to Wellington becoming the seat of government in 1865. Subsequently, one city developed as an administrative centre, a resented symbol of 'them', while the other languished as a trading centre until the boom years after the Second World War. Sporting rivalry is keen and popular, but there are more sinister examples – for one, Prime Minister Sidney Holland's insistence that Auckland have only a four-lane harbour bridge when locals predicted the need for eight lanes. The few Aucklanders in the 1991–93 National Cabinet, despite Auckland's pivotal political position, was seen as a wider national mistrust of Auckland. The comparatively enviable climate and outdoor lifestyle of Auckland *vis-à-vis* Wellington has not helped. People who live elsewhere may comfort themselves with Denis Glover's reported *bon mot* that 'if Wellington is the arsehole of New Zealand, Auckland is a place 400 miles up'.

'Aunt Daisy'

(Maud Ruby Basham, 1879–1963.) Rapid-fire delivery and a network audience made 'Aunt Daisy' a memorable voice in the radio days of the 1940s and 1950s. The theme tune 'Daisy Belle' followed by her oft-imitated 'Good *morning* everybody' set apace a half-hour daily gambol through a host of recipes, household hints, thoughts for the day and advertising chatter. Born and raised in Britain, Aunt Daisy became a pioneer in radio (along with **'Uncle Scrim'** Scrimgeour and 'Uncle Tom' Garland in Auckland) on the Friendly Road stations. When 1ZB became part of the State commercial broadcasting service in 1937, Aunt Daisy went to Wellington and broadcast for the network for more than 20 years. She had the wit and clarity of diction to enable her to rattle non-stop through her half-hour programme. Some people still tell possibly apocryphal tales in which Aunt Daisy rushed into some ambiguity through speaking so fast: 'And what a glorious morning it is – the sun is shining right up my back passage …'. Seriously respected as a radio guide and mentor, her many books of household hints and recipes are still to be found in garage sales. A.S. Fry recorded her life in *The Aunt Daisy Story* (A.H. & A.W. Reed, Wellington, 1957).

Axemen's Carnivals

Sport of the timberlands, competitive wood chopping and sawing is a sport that now involves both men and women. A living example of the way early settlers competed with each other at the basic skills of their work, a recreation that did not involve forming large teams in districts with a scattered population.

B.Y.O., B.Y.O.G.

Bring your own grog has spread from a social nicety to a way of dining out without being ripped off by restaurant wine lists. The idea originally allowed people to drink with meals on unlicensed premises but has now created a whole class of restaurants where liquor is permitted but not necessarily served from restaurant stock. Classier operations advertise for B.Y.O.W. custom, on the presumption that a couple with a bottle of wine between them is going to be more genteel than a bunch of visiting footballers who bring a supply of tinnies or a **Half-G** to drink.

Baby Farming

The practice of taking unwanted children into care for money, which led to the hanging of Minnie Dean (1840–95) for murder. She advertised for children to care for, looking after as many as 11 at a time at her home in Winton, Southland. When some went missing police investigations began and three bodies were found. Minnie Dean became the first woman to be hanged in New Zealand.

Bach, Baches

Originally the primitive holiday cottages of New Zealanders, though the expression has spread, only possibly in self-deprecating style, to the more opulent second homes of the 1980s. People in Otago and Southland use the expression **Crib** for such buildings. The expression 'bach' is a corruption of bachelor: many single men occupied farm whares or huts in pioneer times, and their basic living style therein was known as 'baching'. Holidays and weekends 'at the bach' are enshrined in many nostalgic passages of our literature. Katherine Mansfield drew a classic word picture of life at the bach in her story sequence beginning with *At the Bay*. In the days when New Zealand 'closed down' every weekend, and for six weeks of the summer holidays, this is where the better-off went. The buildings then were unpretentious, often ugly, though their very impermanence minimised the impact on their often wild and beautiful settings. Many baches are not much more than sheds, with recycled windows and one or two multi-purpose rooms. Tents on the lawn accommodate extended families or friends of the children. On the Coromandel Peninsula, particularly, old tramcars have been pressed into service as baches, while at Taylor's Mistake near Christchurch, squatters sealed off the mouths of sea caves to create holiday homes within. Favoured construction materials are fibrolite or **Corrugated Iron**, good bracing for a small building that often has to withstand the rigours of nature, unattended, through winter storms. The roof is often flat, easier for the lay builder to construct, and the outrageous paint colour may be left over from some other job or bought on special rather than chosen for its aesthetic appeal or suburban conformity. The simple buildings often defy construction and health codes, as befits a **Do-It-Yourself** building on a limited budget. Some baches are deliberately structured inside the legal definition of a removable farm shed to avoid local ordinances. Others squat on reserves surviving from the days before regulations and the public ownership of so much of New Zealand. In 1991 the Department of Conservation had some 2000 illegal tenants with family baches still surviving on the Crown estate. With such informal tenure the bach tended to be a relatively inexpensive building, even though the site may be in the million-dollar bracket. Originally the coal range, **Long Drop** and cane furniture were typical accoutrements. The bach was where old furniture and incomplete sets of crockery wound up. The eclectic style of the interiors could approach the semblance of a folk museum after a generation or two. The water supply came off the roof and the shower was fed by a bucket tied up a handy tree. There was

little to do in the way of housework though some flustered mums spent unhappy times trying to maintain a glimmer of suburban order. For the bach is basically a permanent camping site. As ostentation has become more acceptable in the social milieu of more recent times, many holidaymakers have chosen instead to replicate the suburban home on its garden plot while councils have matched their aspirations by insisting on sealed roads, kerbs and channeling and underground power. Baches may still be recognised in older districts or among more modern housing – there are even the recognisable remains of such beach homes among the more recent suburbs of North Shore City, once a ferry and coach ride beyond Auckland. Paul Thompson wrote and photographed *The Bach* in colour, celebrating the idiosyncrasies of our native style (Government Printer, Wellington, 1985). Sadly, there are now signs the bach of the past is becoming beyond the expectations of the ordinary people who inspired the tradition. The property market has changed rapidly since the early 2000s, with a burgeoning Internet market for coastal properties. This has pushed some crude baches above the million-dollar mark on the strength of their site. Prices above $500,000 have become the norm for former baches within two hours of Auckland, with only a glimpse of the sea.

The Back Blocks

The 'back blocks' of land lay behind those front blocks of farmland which were handier to roads or railway lines in pioneer times. They are a relative of the back country, which lay in the hills behind the more accessible home farms. Traditional views of the back blocks are discussed under the **Back of Beyond** and **Up the Boo-ai**.

The Back of Beyond

Traditionally this is as far inland as a man might go, though many were accompanied by their women in pioneer days. Such isolation is known to Australians as 'The Back o' Bourke' or 'Beyond the Black Stump'. In New Zealand folk are more likely to be **'Up the Boo-ai'**.

The Backbone of the Country

Farmers were long regarded as the economic base of the country because their product brought in by far the largest part of New Zealand's overseas income. Thus they were favoured and encouraged by politicians, many of whom were farmers. Only the rise of timber and tourism as alternative sources of income challenged the farmers' influence; that and the fact that in the 1980s the burgeoning tertiary class began to question why farmers' incomes should be guaranteed and subsidised by urban taxpayers when they were less than efficient. While farming is still the backbone of the economy, it is not at the expense of everybody else.

Backyard Sheds

The author Barry Crump said 'a man needs a shed' when introducing me to one on his farmlet at Waihi, during the making of a film for television. The phrase struck me as summating all the features of a 'man's own place', on the farm or in suburbia. Here a man can keep handy things the wife wouldn't like inside. There is room for old sports gear and tools he might get around to cleaning up some day. A man's tools ought to be safe in a shed, where children aren't allowed to pry, nor others borrow them. In the days when motor registration plates were changed every year, the beams of the shed were a good place to hammer up the old ones. It was also a place for the odd risque calendar from the tyre company and a place to keep an old harness, a show ribbon or a bike. My grandfather kept his old business records, dating back to the 19th century, in his shed. My father-in-law used his when he fancied smoking a pipe after dinner. Labour MP the Hon. Trevor de Cleene spoke in a television profile of taking the occasional nap in his garden shed, listening to the rain on the roof and remembering days out hunting in the bush. A man's shed soon begins to reflect the character of his life and interests in a way the **Front Room** never does.

Ballantyne's Fire

In Christchurch 41 people died when the three-storey department store of J. Ballantyne and Co was gutted and ladders could not reach the upper floors fast enough. Despite its pre-eminent position in the central shopping district the store was originally rebuilt only one storey high.

Balls

Once a widespread feature of the social calendar, formal dances were held regularly during the winter. The occasions grew from the debutante or 'Coming Out' Ball at which girls became young women through the ceremony of public presentation to some dignitary. In country districts particularly, the ball season featured dances organised by various community groups. The hall was decorated with the bounty of the bush, such as tree fern leaves and strands of lycopodium. Catering was often on the **Ladies a Plate** principle. Long dresses for the women and dinner suits for the men were obligatory. The Bachelors' and Spinsters' Ball was reciprocated by the married community with a Benedicts' Ball. There are still pockets of old-time dancing that follow this form: the Whitebaiters' Ball in Haast, for example. From the early days the formal ball was a focus for special interest groups, particularly charities, as part of their fund-raising activities. Major corporates and industries, such as broadcasting, the fine arts and the entertainment industry, held an annual ball. The regular calendar of public balls has been diminished somewhat in recent years by the fashion for informal dining out and the demise of ballroom dancing as a social skill. The formal ball tends now to mark only the most serious moments in the community: the dedication of a new hall, a civic occasion or a reunion. School balls are still held but many have been banned because of alcohol abuse by students.

The Battle for Bellevue Spur

This muddy promontory, commanding Passchendaele, was the scene of a costly battle for New Zealand troops in France during the First World War. Fighting through mud and shell holes the New Zealanders had to take a hill defended by German troops in concrete bunkers. The action on October 12 was unsuccessful. It cost the lives of 600 New Zealand soldiers and 40 officers. Counting injuries, the casualties were 1500 men in the Second Brigade and 1200 in the Third Brigade.

The Battle for Cassino

New Zealand troops recall this Italian battle as a major episode of the Second World War. It cost them 1596 casualties, including 269 killed outright and 74 dying later of wounds. The New Zealand Army Corps, serving under the American Fifth Army, replaced US troops who had been attacking the monastery hill for 10 weeks, in January 1944. With them fought an Indian Division. The New Zealand troops fought twice for the town while the Indians attacked the monastery hill. Flights of American bombers and artillery supported them, in the process largely destroying the ancient abbey and monastery of Monte Cassino, which commanded the battlefields. After six weeks the New Zealanders and Indians were withdrawn, disappointed to be relieved by Americans, though they had taken most of the town. It finally took the combined weight of the Fifth and Eighth armies to overpower the area and clear the route to Rome. The battle has been the subject of several books.

The Battle of Crete

New Zealand troops began the Second World War on the back foot. Driven south through Greece, the Fourth and Fifth Brigades were withdrawn to Crete by the Navy on April 24–27, 1941. Under Major-General 'Tiny' Freyberg a force of British, Australian and New Zealand troops, 28,600 in all, was to hold Crete as a strategic naval base. The advancing Germans made an airborne attack, forcing the New Zealanders to withdraw over the central spine of the island where only some escaped. During the withdrawals from Greece and Crete 932 New Zealanders died, 1354 were wounded and 4036 taken prisoner (730 of them wounded before capture). The New Zealand casualties were second only to the losses during the Battle of the Somme in the First World War.

The Battle of Manners Street

On the night of April 3, 1943, American marines brawled with New Zealand soldiers outside a nightclub in Wellington. Legend has it that the attitudes of US Southerners towards Maori New Zealanders angered the locals. Other versions spring from the jealousies and rivalries between the services during the Second

World War. No one was killed though a great deal of damage was done to adjacent shop windows. Overall some 100,000 American servicemen passed through New Zealand while many young New Zealanders were serving overseas, creating some tensions over the girls they left behind. A common complaint made against the Americans ran 'they're over-paid, over-sexed and over here'.

The Battle of the River Plate

New Zealand sailors claim the scuttling of the German pocket battleship *Graf Spee* as their first great victory. A British cruiser HMS *Achilles* was manned by men of the New Zealand Division of the Royal Navy when she bailed up the *Graf Spee* in the neutral port of Montevideo, Uruguay, after a battle on December 13 1939. The Battle of the River Plate also involved *Exeter* and *Ajax*, further British cruisers. *Ajax* and *Achilles* trapped the damaged *Graf Spee* in Montevideo and caused her captain to scuttle the raider. The separate and distinct Royal New Zealand Navy was formed in 1941.

The Battle of the Waitemata

Armed Maori warriors of Ngati Paoa came to Auckland to challenge the Governor on April 17, 1851 and the citizens feared war. The incident began with the shoplifting of a shirt and an argument that escalated into a scuffle. A chief was hit on the head by a Maori policeman, an insult that led to the retaliatory war party. A dozen canoes with 250 armed men landed at Mechanics Bay, the chief Hoera demanding utu. Governor Sir George Grey readied his defence, including HMS *Fly*, the 58th Regiment, Artillery, Sappers and Miners, and the military settlers known as the **Fencibles** were called in from their fields. The Ngati Paoa were given two hours to leave, after which the

British established a defensive breastwork on Constitution Hill in case of further threat. Historical painter Kennett Watkins recreated the scene in his lithograph *The Invasion of the Ngatipaoa*.

The Bay of Plenty *see* Poverty Bay

Bay Whaling *see* Shore Whaling

Bay Villas

Wooden houses with bay windows in front and a verandah. Rooms lay left and right of a central hall. The popular housing type proliferated from the 1890s until the First World War. See *The New Zealand Villa,* by Di Stewart (Viking, Auckland, 1992). Succeeded by the **Californian Bungalow.**

The Beehive

The buzzing of debate and bureaucracy takes symbolic form in the beehive-shaped building that houses New Zealand's Cabinet offices and the Prime Minister's Department. There are 14 floors, two underground, and a floor area of over 25,000 sq m. The building replaced the old Government House, adjacent to the main Parliament Buildings, which had itself housed Ministers, Parliament and Governors-General before its demolition in 1969. The Beehive, designed by Sir Basil Spence who was responsible for Britain's modernistic new Coventry Cathedral, was an alternative to extending the Parliament Building that was built in 1912–18 in the classic Renaissance style. Diana and Jeremy Pope in their *Mobil New Zealand Travel Guide to the North Island* claim that Spence sketched the building on a table napkin while lunching with the prime minister of the day, drawing his inspiration from the Beehive trademark on a box of matches. Further along the melange of government buildings is the General Assembly Library, in Gothic style, dating from 1898. The suggestion has been made that the Beehive be demolished in favour of a more functional building but in 2003 the structure (which doesn't house all the Parliamentarians) was refurbished. The buildings overlook the magnificent Old Government Building on Lambton Quay described as the **Largest Wooden Building** in the Southern Hemisphere.

Beetroot

A red root vegetable that many New Zealand caterers delight in adding to most savoury counter-food. Damp red stains of beetroot in sandwiches and bread rolls are the trademark of a certain school of New Zealand commercial cuisine. Often the beetroot is accompanied by a sickly-white salad dressing that further wets the bread. If not addicted to beetroot, use its leaking colour as a culinary warning to shop elsewhere.

'Big Norm'

Labour publicists in 1972 re-presented their overweight Member for Sydenham in his new image as 'Big Norm' Kirk and captured Parliament. There was even a popular song about him, with a descending basso-profundo chorus of 'Big Norm, Big Norm, Big Norm'. The potential irony of glorifying a 'big norm' in those conformist days obviously escaped the voters. Norman Kirk, with his new hairstyle and the physical presence of a big man, became the first Labour prime minister for 20 years, only to die in office of weight-related illness in 1974, aged just 51. See *Diary of the Kirk Years*, by Margaret Hayward (Reed, Wellington, 1981).

The Big Tree

This was once a popular nickname for the giant kauri tree Tane Mahuta in Waipoua Forest Sanctuary. The largest in New Zealand, Tane Mahuta or 'god of the forest' is more than 51 m high and its estimated age is more than 1200 years. Nearby Te Matua Ngahere, Father of the Forest, may be even older, perhaps as many as 2000 years. The Big Tree appeared on the one-shilling stamp marking the Centenary of New Zealand in 1940. Big Tree was also the name of a New Zealand brand of petrol distributed before the Second World War. See also the **Largest Kauri**.

The Billy Cart

Two traditions attend the humble cart once beloved of children and also a useful way of shifting small loads about the yard. The name described handcarts with two or four wheels. The former may have originally gained its name as a cart pulled by a billy goat, harnessed between shafts, as a large dog was in the similar dog cart. Given the unco-operative nature of most billy goats, a more popular origin might be found in their use to drag billycans of cream from the milking shed dairy to the **Cream Stand** at the gate for collection.

Billy Tea

The billy is a small tin can, with lid and wire handle, in which to make a cuppa in the open air, with a fire of twigs under the boiling water. Throw in real tea leaves for flavour. Pour it out into tin (or nowadays plastic) mugs. Desirably, the brew takes on the smoky flavour of the burning manuka twigs as it boils. A **Thermette** is an alternative kind of billy, useful where the risk of fire is greatest.

The Bird of a Single Flight

The white heron (*Egretta alba*) is a rare bird in New Zealand and Europeans have accepted the Maori tradition that it be seen only once in a lifetime. Its Maori name is kotuku, remembered in the phrases he kotuku rerenga tahi ('bird of a single flight'), or he kotuku taunga kotahi ('bird of the single alighting'). White herons breed in a colony on the Waitangiroto River near Okarito in South Westland, but from summer they disperse to many corners of New Zealand. Thus single birds may be seen on wetlands or estuaries from Parengarenga in the Far North to the coastal marshes of Southland and Fiordland. Birds occasionally visit urban lakes where they may stay for several weeks. In August, the birds assemble again near Okarito to breed. Although the white heron is restricted to about 100–120 birds in New Zealand, there are populations on other Pacific Islands, in Australia, tropical Asia and Japan.

'Black Peter', Edward Peters

Edward Peters found gold in Otago four years before Gabriel Read but was little rewarded. Described as either an Indian or a Eurasian by the 1940 *Dictionary of New Zealand Biography*, Peters came to New Zealand in 1853 from the goldfields of California. Working at Tuapeka in 1857, he saw gold in the river and prospected for several years for small returns. Locally nicknamed 'Black Peter', Peters shared his discoveries, paying for stores with gold and telling the provincial surveyor of his finds. It was Peters' finds that led to the discovery of **Gabriel's Gully** and the Tuapeka goldfields, and the subsequent gold rush. Peters then claimed a reward for finding gold in the Tuapeka,

Waitahuna and Tokomairiro rivers. Nearly 25 years later the government offered him £25, provided the public subscribed a similar amount.

Black Robins and 'Old Blue'

The story of the recovery of the black robin from remote Little Mangere Island in the Chathams group is in the finest traditions of the former Wildlife Service. This band of underfunded game rangers and largely self-taught ornithologists brought the black robin back from the edge of extinction through field experience and personal dedication. One of the rarest birds in the world, the black robin was reduced to one tiny island and a population of only seven birds when rescue work began in 1976. The birds were caught over two seasons and rangers clambered up and down the steep cliffs of Little Mangere to transfer them to a former habitat, Mangere Island, which had been specially replanted for them. Bird numbers fell to five but the black robins still produced eggs, notably the matriarch 'Old Blue'. Some of the first eggs were removed from black robin nests and transferred to the nests of Chatham Island tits, raising the breeding rate. In 1983 a population of black robins was placed on South East Island to extend the range. At one stage 'Old Blue' was the only breeding female left and is thus credited with saving her kind. One of the wildlife officers involved, Dick Veitch, records the project in his book with David Cemmick, *Black Robin Country: the Chatham Islands and its wildlife* (Hodder and Stoughton, Auckland, 1985).

Black-water Rafting *see* Down Under, Down Under

The Bledisloe Cup

The traditional rugby rivalry between Australia and New Zealand these days has been subsumed into a three-way contest also involving South Africa. The historic Bledisloe Cup is now contested as a by-product of the Tri-Nations series. If New Zealand or Australia wins two matches against the other, during the Tri-Nations contest, then the Bledisloe Cup is awarded. If they win only one each, the cup stays with the holder. The Bledisloe Cup itself was donated by an early Governor-General (1930–35), Viscount Bledisloe, and has been contested since

1931. Lord Bledisloe left a greater legacy when he and his wife purchased the Busby property at Waitangi in the Bay of Islands, site of the signing of The **Treaty of Waitangi** in 1840, and gave it to the nation.

The Bloodstained Tombstone

The headstone of a murdered woman, buried in Barbadoes Street Cemetery in Christchurch, developed a blood-like mark shortly after its placement on her grave. Despite frequent scrubbing the bloodstain remained. The grave was of Margaret Burke, servant of **'Ready Money' Robinson**, who was knifed by another servant, a black African called Simon Cadeno in 1871. Robinson, famed for his great Cheviot run, kept a town house on Park Terrace in Christchurch, and this is where Cadeno, tormented by all for his colour, took revenge by knifing the woman in front of Mrs Robinson and a visitor. The tombstone was placed on her grave by the Robinsons and used to attract morbid visitors who wondered at the bloodstain. When vandals broke the stone during the 1960s, the stained portion was taken into safe keeping by the city council.

'Bloody Jack'

Whalers and sealers knew the Ngai Tahu chief Tuhawaiki as 'Bloody Jack'. As paramount chief of southern New Zealand he led the reprisal raids against Te Rauparaha, after that northern chief sacked Kaiapohia Pa, at Kaiapoi in Canterbury. Fighting alongside the chief Taiaroa, he had such success that Te Rauparaha allowed Ngai Tahu to keep most of the South Island. Tuhawaiki's nickname, however, originated not from his war record but from frequent use of the sanguinary epithet while attempting to learn English. The 1940 *Dictionary of New Zealand Biography* records Tuhawaiki's dislike for the nickname. Tuhawaiki signed the Treaty of Waitangi and also the deed of sale for the Otago settlement.

Blue Smoke

Ruru Karaitiana wrote this hit song which swept the Western world in 1948. It became the first commercial recording made for a New Zealand label, Tanza.

Bohemians

Referred to until the First World War as the German settlement, the Bohemians came from the Staab district, a corner of the Austro-Hungarian Empire, now in the Czech Republic, in 1863. Organised by Captain Martin Krippner, the Bohemians were promised 40 acres of land but found themselves landed in dense bush at Puhoi north of Auckland and had to become timber-fellers first. The first settlers, 83 of them, arrived on the *War Spirit* in 1863 but Krippner took the younger men off to fight in the Waikato Wars and they chose to settle there afterwards on confiscated Maori land. Those who remained at Puhoi were joined by further compatriots in 1865 and 1873. The settlement of Puhoi retains its Bohemian character (and some accents) to this day, with a wayside Calvary just before entering the village. See also **Up the Boo-ai.**

Bookies

The freelance and illegal operators who organise betting on the (traditionally horse) races. Once a familiar figure in public bars, or anonymous at the end of a telephone, the bookie has been largely superseded since the 1950s by the nationwide network of **TAB** agencies which ensures the State benefits from the people's peccadilloes.

Booze Barns

During the 1960s the perverse logic of the Licensing Control Commission re-allocated liquor licences from many ageing corner pubs to new hotels in the suburbs, surrounded by acres of car parking. To enjoy a drink you had to drive. Huge public bars, detached from motel-like accommodation, provided the venue for mass drinking. Often structural steel beams spanned a maximum floor area, with spindly uncomfortable stools and too few seats. The idea of a quiet, sociable drink was stifled by rock bands and the milling throng. Such 'booze barns' have deservedly lost custom as more enlightened liquor laws permit drinking with meals in local restaurants and bars. Since 1999 liquor has also been available seven days a week from off-licences – supermarkets, wine resellers and bottle stores, another factor in changing drinking habits.

Boxing Day Picnic, or New Year's Picnic

The great 'day after the day before' custom of New Zealand. In an attempt to shake off the consequences of over-indulging the body at Christmas or on New Year's Eve, many New Zealanders head for the beach, lake or riverside to relax in the sun and sleep it off. The more energetic or guilty may add gross exercise to their picnic with sack races, tugs-of-war and egg-throwing competitions. Such relaxations still bring a rare sense of community to many popular family holiday camps. For the more formal, horse-race meetings provide a more structured alternative.

Bracken

Widespread in the wake of bush fires, the bracken fern is a frequent visual symbol of pioneering tradition. Originally, Maori burnt the bush to encourage its growth, as the roots of bracken, known as aruhe, produced a starch that could be beaten out and cooked into hard cakes or eaten as flour. Later, European farmers fostered the growth of bracken as they burnt the hills to establish grass. See **Burning Off**.

Bracken, Thomas *see* National Anthems

Brass Bands

Brass bands have long been popular in New Zealand. First associated with the militia (but lacking the woodwinds that distinguish a military band), they were organised by communities, social groups, special causes and factory staff. Inevitably, local and national championships followed and a New Zealand brass band has on occasion been selected to tour foreign venues. One of the world's most famous marches, the 'Invercargill March', was written for a local band.

The Bridge to Nowhere

The ideal of **One Man, One Farm** took insecure root when soldiers returning from the First World War demanded land of their own. Farms were often allocated to them in raw back-country districts and the returned servicemen took to the bush like their pioneer forefathers. Among the settlements doomed to fail was Mangapurua in the upper Wanganui region. Opened in

1917, the isolated valley was at first entered from the Wanganui River, then by track from Raetihi. Some of the 40 farmers and their families gave up quite soon but others stuck it out until the **Great Depression** of the 1930s. The concrete bridge across the Mangapurua Gorge was supposed to improve access when it opened in 1936 but when cars crossed it they had to turn again and come back, unable to follow the track beyond. Shortly afterwards the government closed the settlement and the bush has been reclaiming it now for more than 50 years. The image of the concrete bridge deep in the bush and leading nowhere has occurred in several yarns including the film *Bridge to Nowhere*, which had nothing to do with what actually happened there.

The Bridle Path

By this route, early Canterbury settlers crossed the Port Hills on foot from Lyttelton to the estuary of the Heathcote at Ferrymead. Large ships could not enter the Sumner estuary so the pioneers of Christchurch found themselves separated from their main port at Lyttelton by a range of hills. Much has been made of the Canterbury Pilgrims' first view from the Bridle Path. Their new home was then a swampy area on the edge of a vast tussock plain which ran inland for some 50 km to range upon range of mountains. Some descendants of the pioneers still make an annual pilgrimage over the Bridle Path, on the weekend closest to the arrival anniversary of the **First Four Ships** (December 16, 1850). The walk is on the steep side and takes from one to two hours one way.

The Brig *Elizabeth*

A trader's greed led to a bargain that wiped out a Maori settlement in Akaroa Harbour. In return for a promised full cargo of flax, Captain Stewart agreed to carry a Ngati Toa war party from their stronghold on Kapiti Island south to Akaroa. The brig left Kapiti on October 29, 1830, carrying 170 warriors. At Akaroa the raiders suddenly showed themselves and took the pa of Tahapuneke. The chief Tamaiharanui and a large number of Ngai Tahu were taken back to Kapiti where for six weeks they were held aboard the *Elizabeth* while the flax was loaded. The prisoners were then put ashore to be killed and eaten by the Kapiti people.

The Brig *Venus*

The actions of mutineers who took the brig *Venus* from Hobart in 1807 led to several murderous raids by northern Ngapuhi against Bay of Plenty tribes some 20 years later. The men of the *Venus* captured women closely related to the high chiefs Te Morenga and Hongi Hika, and sailed away with them. They did the same thing at Miranda in the Firth of Thames, then sold the women off into slavery to Bay of Plenty tribes. These high-born women were subsequently killed, so when Nga Puhi had sufficient guns they sailed south to avenge them. The chief Hongi spent 11 months on his revenge, reportedly burning 500 villages, killing many as well as taking hundreds of prisoners. The *Venus* sailed off and her subsequent history in South America is reconstructed by C.W. Vennell in *The Brown Frontier* (A.H. & A.W. Reed, Wellington, 1967).

The Britain of the South

A popular description for New Zealand in the mid-19th century. Certainly, in Christchurch, buildings aped the ambience of an English cathedral town, and the surviving public buildings show they did it rather well. Nevertheless, the comparison was bathetically stretched. Charles Hursthouse used the phrase, as he enthused and exhorted potential immigrants, in a two-volume work entitled *New Zealand or Zealandia The Britain of the South*, published by Edward Stanford in London in 1857.

Brunner, Thomas *see* The Longest Journey

Buller's Birds

A study of New Zealand's birds, first published in 1873, that has become probably the most expensive of New Zealand antiquarian books. Sir Walter Lawry Buller F.R.S. (1838–1906), born in New Zealand of missionary parents, was greatly honoured for his work. Much of the credit, however, should go to his less remembered artist, J.G. Keulemans. The original edition had

35 hand-coloured lithographs by Keulemans in quite a different style from the more famous images that survive in the valuable second edition of *A History of the Birds of New Zealand*. This latter book, published in 1888, has 48 stone-plate lithographs by Keulemans. These images continue to be used for their accuracy and period charm. Inferior copies can be seen most readily in the 1960–70s reprints from Whitcombe and Tombs (*Buller's Birds of New Zealand*, edited by Graham Turbott) but the originals far outshine them.

Bullet Holes in the Church Wall

Bullet holes dating from times when settlers took shelter in their church against Maori attacks are features of two New Zealand churches. Holes in the walls of Christ Church at Russell recall the events of March 11, 1845 when Hone Heke and Kawiti attacked and burned much of the early settlement of Kororareka. The East Pukekohe Presbyterian Church also has bullet holes, from an attack on September 14, 1863. The five-month-old church had already been surrounded by a ditch and palisade. Inside, some 20 defenders fired through loopholes in the kohekohe logs. For three hours they faced attack from 200 Maori before the first soldiers arrived to relieve them. The battle continued without loss to those in the church, though three soldiers and 40 Maori died. See James Cowan's *Hero Stories of New Zealand* (Harry H. Tombs, Wellington, 1935).

Bullockies

The men (and a handful of legendary women) who drove the teams of working bullocks that once did the job of heavy trucks and tractors. Teams of up to 14 bullocks (bulls without bollocks) were yoked in pairs, either side of a pole, to drag heavy loads. In this way logs were brought out of the forest and heavy goods transported along primitive roads. Teams were carefully balanced. The 'nearside leader' was on the left and the 'offside leader' to the right. The team was completed nearest the load by the 'polers' nearside and offside. The whole was steered by calling on the two leading bullocks to respectively 'whoa back' and 'come here' thus causing the column to inch around on this axis. Bullockies, generally, had a bad name for swearing, driving their animals with occasional whip cracks and a stream of abuse when things went wrong. On the other hand, controlling a team of bullocks demanded a fine appreciation of animal psychology and a sympathy with the leading animals. Rare demonstration teams still exist, keeping the bullockies' skills alive.

Bully Hayes

The name of Bully Hayes is part of the folklore of the South Pacific. A buccaneer and 'blackbirder', William Henry Hayes (1829–77) was also notorious for cheating, and kidnapping women, keeping just a step ahead of authorities at a time when law was minimal and his American citizenship was largely a way of wriggling out of trouble. After losing money in Australia he came to New Zealand and teamed up with a family of entertainers, the Buckinghams, who were highly successful with a hotel-theatre at Arrowtown, Central Otago. Hayes built his own rough hotel and theatre, the Prince of Wales, then married Rosie Buckingham, star of the opposition show. While many people enjoyed Hayes' charm, others saw the devious man inside. When someone claimed that Hayes had lost an ear in punishment after cheating at cards, the barber shore his long locks and proved the point. Ridicule followed in the form of a Buckingham entertainment *The Barbarous Barber, or The Lather and Shave*. Hayes left Arrowtown about 1863, lost his wife through drowning at Nelson, and returned to plague the islands of the South Seas. He was killed in a fight at the Marshall Islands in 1877. A. Grove Day and James A. Michener wrote about Hayes in their *Rascals in Paradise*, as did George Louis Becke, who was once shipwrecked with Hayes, in *Bully Hayes, Buccaneer and other stories* (Sydney, 1913).

Bungy Jumping

A New Zealand bright idea where tourists leap from a high point while attached to it by a piece of elastic rubber, which pulls them up inches from death. The 'sport' quickly spread overseas but a leap into a New Zealand canyon from a bridge has more to offer in terms of ambience than leaping off a crane; or try hanging from a helicopter 300 m above Queenstown, or leaping from the Sky Tower or the harbour bridge in Auckland.

The entrepreneurial A.J. Hackett is credited with commercialising the idea. It is certainly gentler on the limbs than the form practised by Melanesians of Pentecost Island, who leap from high towers while attached by fibrous ropes to prove their manhood.

The Burgess-Kelly Gang

The most notorious of the gangs to operate on the goldfields of New Zealand was known as the Burgess-Kelly gang. They were four armed robbers, criminals from Australia, named Burgess, Kelly, Levy and Sullivan. Some say Burgess and Kelly were at one time members of the **Garrett Gang**. Certainly they were involved in incidents about Tuapeka in Central Otago where Burgess and Kelly were arrested and sent to jail for three years. Released in 1865, they swore to take a life for every lash laid on them while imprisoned. Levy was said to have a gang in the Kawarau Gorge, near Cromwell, which robbed the passing miners and threw their bodies in the river. These three met up with Sullivan in the 1865 gold rush to Westland. There they robbed banks and miners, using firearms. The explorer George Dobson, working with his brother Arthur to find ways from Canterbury to Westland, was one victim – mistaken for a gold buyer. The gang was caught following the murder of five men on the slopes of Maungatapu. Their victims were storekeepers returning from the Wakamarina gold diggings. When arrested Sullivan confessed and got life imprisonment. His partners were hanged, their corpses placed on public display, and their death masks taken for posterity. See *Confessions of Richard Burgess: the Maungatapu murders and other grisly crimes*, edited by David Burton (Reed, Wellington, 1977).

The Buried Village

In a quiet valley leading down to Lake Tarawera, near Rotorua, are the excavated remains of old Wairoa, buried during the **Tarawera Eruption** on June 10, 1886. Up to two metres of volcanic debris fell on the village and crushed the two-storeyed hotel. Sixty-three people sheltered in the whare of Guide Sophia, three more in a fowlhouse. Several people died, though fatalities in the village might have been higher had the eruption occurred during the tourist season when visitors came to see the **Pink and White**

Terraces at Lake Tarawera. The Terraces too were buried in the eruption, which blanketed the countryside for many miles with ash and mud, killing 153 people. Refer to *Tarawera: the destruction of the Pink and White Terraces,* by Geoff Conly (Grantham House, Wellington, 1985). See also the **Phantom Canoe**.

The Burning of the *Boyd*

Remembered still through the huge romantic painting by Walter Wright in the Auckland Art Gallery, in which Maori in canoes surround a burning ship on Whangaroa Harbour. The *Boyd* was a convict transport, returning from Sydney in 1809 by way of the newly discovered Whangaroa Harbour, where she was to trade for kauri spars. The captain's treatment of a Maori chief during the passage, and his people on arrival, is usually blamed for what followed. The clash with Maori ended with all but four of the *Boyd*'s 70-odd sailors and passengers killed. The captain and shore crew were killed in the kauri forest; the rest aboard ship. Towed to shallow water, the *Boyd* was then stripped and burned. The fascinating story of the dispute, the survivors and the wars of revenge that followed is told in *The Burning of the Boyd,* by Wade Doak (Hodder & Stoughton, Auckland, 1984). Doak also tells of his dives and underwater archaeology on the vessel.

Burning Off

Burning off the bush as a traditional method of clearing the land goes back to Maori times. Then it was to make room for **Bracken** to grow, its roots a source of staple starch food. Some suggest fire was also used to clear the ground in Canterbury and Otago for the hunting of moa, recorded in Maori tradition as the **Fires of Tamatea** in the 14th century. Settler-explorers in Canterbury customarily set fire to the Plains to help clear the way ahead. Settlers in the bush dropped trees and set fire to them in summer and autumn before planting grass seed. Often the fires got away, burning the surrounding countryside for many kilometres, most spectacularly in the Forty Mile Bush (see **Scandies** and the **Raetihi Bushfire**). The practice of burning off is a quick way to clear unwanted vegetation and scrub from marginal land. During the 1920s, in places like the Coromandel, it was extended to clearing standing timber including the now-precious kauri.

Burning off remains a controversial management technique in the high country of the South Island, where fire clears the ground of unpalatable native plant species and encourages fresh growth for sheep. It has also been the cause of much erosion and is now carried out only by permit.

Bush Fighting

During the New Zealand Wars, an irregular unit was formed to fight Maori on their own terms, as forest guerrillas, rather than the formal British formations of the time. An advertisement for their formation in 1863 called for 'Active young men, having some experience of New Zealand Forests, [who] may now confer a benefit upon the Colony, and also ensure a comparatively free and exciting life for themselves by joining a corps of Forest Volunteers, now being enrolled in this province to act as the Taranaki Volunteers have in striking terror into the marauding natives, by operations not in the power of ordinary troops. By joining the Corps the routine of Militia life may be got rid of and a body of active and pleasant comrades ensured.' The Forest Rangers were controversial in that their rewards were likely to include grants of confiscated land. The technique of matching guerrilla warfare with similar tactics was a success, however. Among the Forest Rangers was Major Gustavus Ferdinand von Tempsky, Prussian-trained, who became a legendary figure known to Maori as Manurau –'the bird that flits everywhere'– for his skills in bush warfare. When not fighting he painted exquisite water-colours of the battles in the bush, and wrote about the wars. He was killed in a forest battle while commanding the **Armed Constabulary** in the second attack on Titokawaru at Te Ngutu o te Manu in Taranaki, 1868. *The Colonial New Zealand War*, by Tim Ryan and Bill Parham (Grantham House, Wellington, 2002) gives histories of the units involved in the armed conflicts; *Forest Ranger*, by Richard Stowers is an interesting self-published history. Familiarity with the forests was a factor, a century later, when Maori and European New Zealanders excelled as jungle soldiers in South East Asian battlefields.

Bush Job

Something improvised or patched together, rather than perfectly done. Summed up in the Kiwi expressions 'She's near enough' or **'She'll be right'**.

The Bush Telegraph

The way news or rumour travels through the countryside. In the absence of newspapers and talkback radio messages still got through the back-country, albeit embroidered to suit, carried verbally by travellers, salesmen, swaggers and others calling at isolated farms and settlements. The bush telegraph took a technological leap forward on those rare occasions when folk gathered for a country show or race meeting. For the rest it relied on rumour. The system assumes respectability in the name of the publication *Bush Telegraph*, a weekly country newspaper serving the Bush District of Wairarapa and published in Paihiatua since the 1960s.

Bush Tramways

Temporary rails laid through the bush gave access to mill sites and areas where trees were felled in early days. Many of these comprised wooden rails on wooden sleepers, with the 'trains' pulled by horses and bullocks. In Westland, during the gold rushes of the 1860s, tramways were used for heavy haulage. With a gauge of a metre or more, the wooden tramways were ballasted between the rails to form a road for horse and pedestrian. Lines ran from Hokitika and several other settlements as far as their river ports. A horse tram linked Greymouth with Kumara from 1877 to 1893; the three-hour trip involved a link across the Taramakau River, on a **River Cage** suspended from a cable. Some tramways were later rebuilt with steel rails giving a stable path for steam engines into the forest. In the centre of the North Island the Taupo Totara Timber Company had a private line that used full-scale locomotives such as the American Mallet locomotive which is now preserved at the Glenbrook Vintage Railway. Another famous timber line was the **Piha Tramway** on Auckland's West Coast. See also the **Dun Mountain Railway**, Nelson, New Zealand's first. The atmosphere of bush tram and railways is kept alive on the preserved Pukemiro line near

Huntly in the Waikato, where bush railway fans hold regular working days. A two-foot (0.6 m) gauge bush railway is also run by enthusiasts in the Waitakere Ranges of Auckland.

Bushman's Toilet Paper

The large (and soft) leaves of the rangiora (*Brachyglottis repanda*) were useful away from civilisation. This beautiful shrub has grey-green leaves with white, softly furred undersides. Fortunately it is fairly common along the margins of North Island forest and the northern South Island.

Butchers' Shops

The traditional butchery has languished with the coming of meat counters in foodmarkets. Old-time stores, with carcasses hung on hooks and butchered to order, were common at **Local Shopping 'Blocks'** into the early 1970s. Then, along with community dairies and small grocers, the business of meat marketing was taken over by the supermarkets. Local butchers often had their own abattoirs for killing meat or belonged to a chain of small shops. Meat was hung in freezers or coolstores and swung out on aerial tracks as required by customers. Butchers cut the meat to the customer's order, on great stump-like wooden chopping blocks.

Bare floors were spread with sawdust to absorb any blood. The butcher's traditional uniform, as today, comprised a dark blue and white-striped apron. Look for the few left in country places beyond the lure of the supermarket.

Buzzy Bee

An iconic children's wooden toy with wings that rotate, making a clacking sound, as the bee is towed along. The original was made by John Ramsey of Auckland in 1947. The Buzzy Bee can still be found in nearly every child's home. It got a marketing boost during a royal tour when an infant Prince William was seen in photographs playing with the red, blue and yellow toy. Since the mid-1990s, the patent owner has expanded its range to several hundred further items using the shape or label of the Buzzy Bee.

'Cabbage Tree' Ned Devine

A famous driver for Cobb & Co both in Australia and New Zealand. Coaching tales often revolve around the character and skills of the drivers and the accidents that befell them. Ned Devine (1833–1908) took his name from a cabbage tree hat he reputedly wore for 50 years. His skill was said to be such that he could turn a coach on a coin. In *Early Days in Central Otago*, Robert Gilkison writes that 'the coach driver was king of the road in the old coaching days. He was at one and the same time the obliging friend of the public and the autocratic monarch ruling all who travelled. To sit on the box beside him was a much-sought honour, and he felt deeply insulted if offered money for the privilege.' Gilkison records that Devine was once confronted by a large and self-important stranger demanding the seat beside him. 'No sir,' said Ned, 'It's promised to someone else.' The stranger countered with 'Do you know I am the Minister of Mines?' to which Ned replied 'No, I don't, but it's a damned fine billet. You keep it as long as you can.' See **Coaches**.

Cabbage Trees

A quintessential element of the New Zealand landscape. To the Maori the cabbage tree is known as ti, the cause of some confusion with **Tea Tree**. Cabbage trees are members of the agave family and take several forms in New Zealand. The best known is ti-kouka (*Cordyline australis*), which grows throughout the country, in swamps, by rivers and on open grass plains and hills. In Canterbury ancient clumps of the trees served from Maori times as navigational points across the otherwise uniform tussock plains. Cabbage trees provided starch for Maori, who baked and ground the roots and ate the young shoots. Some European settlers also made use of the tree as a sweetener, when sugar was in short supply. The Maori folklore, suggesting that an early flowering of the cabbage tree presages a hot dry summer, has been appropriated into general New Zealand belief. Since the late 1980s, cabbage trees have been dying in large numbers as a phytoplasma spreads a disease known as Sudden Decline through mature trees. In this way clumps of trees aged up to 300 years have been lost in a season. Often a profuse flowering is followed by the falling away of the leaves. Efforts are now being made to save the tree by planting out less vulnerable youngsters to replace those lost. A rich store of cabbage tree lore and pictures can be found in *Dancing Leaves: the story of New Zealand's cabbage tree, ti kouka,* by Philip Simpson (Canterbury University Press, Christchurch, 2000).

Californian Bungalows

Dating from the 1920s and 1930s these houses have lower studs than the older **Bay Villas**. Rooms are orientated to catch the sun, not face the street, and the rooms flow into each other instead of formally lining a hall. See *The Bungalow in New Zealand*, by Jeremy Ashford (Viking, Auckland, 1994).

'Call Me Kiwi' Keith Holyoake

The Rt. Hon. Sir Keith Jacka Holyoake was proud of his self-made image and invited his supporters to 'Call me Kiwi'. As National prime minister, briefly in 1957 and from 1960 to 1972, he liked to recall that he left school at 12 and still made it to the top. Rising thus through the **School of Hard Knocks** was still admired as a Kiwi virtue in those days and 'Call me Kiwi' made the most of it, albeit in a 'plummy' accent which he must have learned from short-wave radio for no other populist spoke quite like him. 'Call me Kiwi' was in touch with the political mood of the country, though, frequently adjusting course in the face of changing pressures, acting successfully as a good facilitating chairman might with his little nation. He ended his public career as arguably our first political appointment as Governor-General, serving from 1977 to 1980. Sir Keith was the first New Zealander made a Knight of the Garter, later Sir Edmund Hillary followed him into this most select Order of Chivalry. See also the **Holyoake Highway.**

Camping Grounds

The idea of heading to the beach or the bush with tent and camping gear dates from the nineteenth century when people lived closer to nature. Living in the outdoors, informally, brought back the pioneer spirit and made a three-week holiday affordable. Camping grounds today are more formal, with council standards to be met for water and sanitation, but they do provide prime sites in places where progress has made informal roadside camping impossible. Camping grounds provided by local authorities, automobile associations and private enterprise are usually booked out in the peak of the season, following Christmas Day. Many people return to the same site every year, often mixing with the same holiday neighbours and building up camp traditions such as a fishing competition, the scramble to a nearby peak or beach races. In the 2000s the number of camping grounds is falling as owners find it more profitable to sell their beachfront properties for subdivision.

Camp-oven Bread

Many bushmen and workers relied on camp ovens for their staple tucker. The cast-iron ovens are too heavy to carry in the bush but are invaluable in camp. A bread or scone mix is spread inside the warmed pan and sealed with the heavy lid. The whole is pushed into the embers of a fire, which are raked over the lid as well. Flames turn the contents to cinders, but hot embers bake: 35 minutes is a good time for the first check on the progress of a properly baked mixture.

Canterbury Pilgrims

The name self-ascribed to settlers of the Canterbury Association who arrived at Lyttelton on the **First Four Ships** in December 1850. They were organised as a Church of England settlement, which probably accounts for the flattering vision of themselves as pilgrims in a new land. See the **Bridle Path**, **First Four Ships** and **Wakefield Settlements**.

Cape Maria Van Diemen

Named by the Dutch explorer Abel Tasman in 1643 as he left the north of New Zealand. It is the only Dutch place name to survive on the mainland from this first visit by a European expedition. Maria Van Diemen was the wife of the then Governor-General of the Dutch East Indies, Wilhelm Van Diemen. Historians credit Wilhelm Van Diemen with master-minding the Dutch explorations of the period.

Cape Reinga *see* The Jump Off

Cape Runaway

Lieutenant James Cook lost his patience with armed Maori while the *Endeavour* lay off East Cape on October 31, 1769. Five canoes put off from the shore, including one with 40 armed men who came, he believed, 'with no friendly intention'. Cook, 'at this time being very busy and having no inclination to stay on deck and watch their motions', had shot fired over them causing the Maori to turn and, understandably, 'run away'.

Captain Cookers

This colloquial name for wild pig recalls the fact that Lieutenant James Cook introduced them to New Zealand. There are records of releases by him at Queen Charlotte Sound in the South Island and Cape Kidnappers in the North, though some have suggested these were Polynesian varieties brought from Tahiti, not domestic pigs from Europe. Sealers and whalers liberated more. Pigs thrive in the habitat of bush margins and fernlands, and by the 1840s they were widespread. Both Maori and European used dogs to hunt them and a trade in wild meat grew up. Domestic pigs soon revert to the feral state and extend the wild stock. Dogs are still used to 'bail up' pigs while the hunter moves in armed only with a knife. See **Pig Hunting**.

Carpenter Gothic

The colonial building style that used wood to emulate stone. The pioneer carpenters carefully cut blocks of wood to look like keystones over doors and windows and placed wooden blocks at the corners of their buildings to look like quoins. Dentil courses of wooden blocks appeared to support the roof, there was wooden and iron lace to decorate verandahs, carved barge boards and **Finials** on the ends of gables to keep away the witches. Difficult to maintain but beautiful when restored, the Victorian Gothic houses and public buildings of New Zealand are plentiful in older towns and are often characterised as 'historic places'. See *Colonial Style: pioneer buildings of New Zealand,* by Charles Fearnley (The Bush Press, Auckland, 1986) for some beautifully photographed examples and a detailed description of the tradition.

Children of the Poor

The title of socialist John A. Lee's novel of deprived childhood in early Dunedin, published in 1934 in London and New York. The outspoken and radical Lee was a popular politician in the first Labour government, but eventually fell out with the party for his criticisms of the ailing prime minister, which earned him the soubriquet the **Man Who Killed Mickey Savage.**

Children's Games

Popular playground games from 1840–1950 inspired a complete book by Brian Sutton-Smith, New Zealand-born Professor of Human Development and Folklore at the University of Pennsylvania. He recounts that in colonial times people were too busy to play much with children, and that school grounds were often unsuitable for any but the simplest of games, like tops, marbles, hop-scotch and skipping. Sutton-Smith notes that as our informal rural past was succeeded by an era of controlling children, play was succeeded increasingly by sport and organised activities. Playgrounds long had a tradition of boys' and girls' sides and mixing across these unseen barriers at playtime was forbidden. New Zealand has spawned several indigenous games, including knucklebones and stick games, which originated in Maori times. For a collection of memories based on a survey see *A History of Children's Play: the New Zealand playground 1840–1950,* by Brian Sutton-Smith (New Zealand Council of Educational Research, Wellington, 1982).

Chinatowns

Chinese goldminers, mainly from Kwangtung province in southern China, were encouraged by the Otago government to settle there when the European miners left for the Westland fields in 1866. The Chinese were recruited from the Victorian goldfields in Australia and by 1868 there were 1200 of them in Otago. Chinese miners often worked the poorer fields, even reworking the places where Europeans had been before. The neat stacks of washed stones piled in orderly **Tailings** are still a sign of goldfields worked by the methodical Chinese. Although the population of immigrant Chinese reached nearly 5000 in the

1870s, their communities were often set apart from the European towns. The Chinese miners contributed to the wider community but some feared their industry, and prejudice was obvious in satirical songs and disrespect for their culture. There were several significant Chinese settlements: at Cromwell (where a Chinatown survived into the 20th century only to be drowned by the rising waters of Lake Dunstan), at Lawrence on the Tuapeka field, and Arrowtown, the latter recently restored by the Department of Conservation as a tourist centre. Some Chinese made their fortune and returned home while others stayed in New Zealand as founders of the community here. Many of those who died on the goldfields were later dug up and returned home to China for reburial according to their own rites. See the **Coffin Ship**.

Chopper Boys

The brave and possibly foolish lads who ride helicopters in search of wild deer. During the 1970s they used the aircraft as shooting platforms, flying into remote valleys to clean out the deer with machine rifles, then airlifting the meat to the nearest refrigeration 'freezers'. Then around 1980, when the value of deer for breeding rose, the 'chopper boys' entered the deer recovery phase. This involved shooting a net over a live animal in the bush, then leaping from the hovering helicopter onto the animal's back and trussing it up for a quick journey back to the farm. The survivors of this period now service remote fishermen, tourists, industrial sites and search and rescue, or work abroad – high-flying graduates of a country where there are more helicopters per head of population than anywhere else in the world.

Chopping Down the Flagpole

Symbolic of the breakdown in trust between Maori and British, after the signing of the Treaty of Waitangi, was the chopping down of the pole that bore the British flag high above the former capital of Kororareka (Russell) in the Bay of Islands. The Nga Puhi chief Hone Heke erected the pole himself after the signing of the Treaty, but in July 1844 he cut it down. Following some diplomatic moves Hone Heke re-erected the flagpole, only to cut it down again on January 9, 1845. This time the British re-erected it, sheathing the pole with iron and protecting it further with blockhouses. Hone Heke and Kawiti then attacked the town itself on March 11, 1845, sparking the **War in the North**.

The City of Sails

In an effort to promote its tourism attractions, on the back of yachting successes, Auckland renamed itself as the City of Sails during the 1980s. With the 1987 stockmarket crash, cynics renamed it Auckland, the City of Sales.

The City of Volcanoes

A traditional reference to Auckland, which is built across an isthmus dotted with volcanoes. While the spectacular conical hills are an obvious sign of the volcanic field, there are also other clues in the drowned sea-level craters such as Onepoto, Orakei Basin and Lake Pupuke. The Auckland volcanic field became active 50,000 years ago and the most recent eruption formed the landmark island of Rangitoto just offshore, less than 700 years ago. In that time some 36 cones were formed. A good number have since been quarried away to make road metal. Efforts to preserve the remaining cones include acknowledgment of their use by Maori. Most carry the signs of house sites, ditches and banks from former Maori fortresses or **Pa Sites** built on them. Formerly the stone walls of gardens could also be traced at their feet, though these have now become overlaid, in most places, with houses. Maori tradition attributes the volcanoes to a war between fairy people of Hunua and Waitakere. The Waitakere tohunga caused the isthmus to erupt as a Hunua war party crossed the intervening plain. Factual detail can be found in *City of Volcanoes*, by E.J. Searle, revised by R.D. Mayhill (Longman Paul, Auckland, 1981).

The Clobbering Machine

The process whereby those who stand out from the crowd are cut back to size. In local communities this may be done by way of a practical joke or spreading tales of feet of clay. On the national front, press and television prosecute the foibles of the rich or famous. The reasons for this censorious vigour most probably lie in human nature. People are not supposed to get 'up themselves' because this gets 'up the noses' of their compatriots. See also **Tall Poppies**.

The Cloud Piercer

New Zealand's tallest peak has been renamed Aoraki/Mount Cook because of its significance to both cultures. Various translations of this name include the popular 'cloud piercer', but see **Te Wai Pounamu**. Rote-learning school children, in the days before metrification, used to note it would be easier if four of its 12,349 ft (3763.9 m) of height were blown away. In 1991 nature took a hand when 20 m slid away from the southern face to leave a mountain 3744 m high.

Coaches – Cobb & Co

The great American legend lived in New Zealand (and Australia) too, though the name was borrowed by local entrepreneurs. Cobb & Co coaches were on the goldfields of the South Island from the 1860s, and also in the North Island. Cobb & Co's Telegraph Line carried parcels and mail. The driving contract for Royal Mail was a lucrative element of successful coaching routes. Often these ran from pioneer railheads though there were major coaching routes inland from Dunedin to Central Otago and from Canterbury to Westland. Lightweight coaches with leather springs were used at first to cope with the rugged conditions. The heavier Concord coach, introduced from the United States, was capable of carrying up to 32 passengers, although male passengers riding outside sometimes had to step down while horses negotiated steeper pitches. Passengers vied to sit on the 'box seat' beside the driver. A journey from Dunedin to the Dunstan goldfield in 1862 took three days to cover 200 km. Cobb & Co pioneered the route from Christchurch to Hokitika in 1866, the journey taking 36 hours. The last coaches scheduled in New Zealand crossed Arthur's Pass, between the railheads in the Southern Alps in 1923, the service ending with the opening of the Otira Tunnel. See **'Cabbage Tree' Ned Devine**.

Coaches – Newmans

The Newman brothers Harry and Tom drove their first coach from Foxhill in Nelson to Murchison on the Buller in 1879. In 1883 the coach route extended to the Lyell goldfield. Newmans went on to become a national operator of tour buses, aircraft etc. See *High Noon for Coaches*, by J. Halkett Millar (A.H. & A.W. Reed, Wellington, 1953).

Coasters

The West Coast of New Zealand regards itself as another country and tales abound of how for the 50-odd years of **Six O'clock Closing**, Westland's bars were open when the locals needed them. The province was established separately from Canterbury in 1873, after the goldfields were opened up, but the fortunes of the Coast have waned as each generation has taken another of its diminishing resources without re-investing the profits. Now

60 per cent is in Crown ownership in a string of superb national parks that timbermen eye with resentment. The place is so small in terms of population that Westland is covered entirely by one Parliamentary electorate shared with parts of rural Nelson, yet its parochial centres stretch almost as far apart as the distance from Auckland to Wellington. There is a wealth of good books, mostly well out of print, that tell the tall tales of the Coast and Coasters, including the *West Coast Gold Rushes*, by Philip Ross May (Pegasus, Christchurch, 1967) and *The Wild West Coast*, by Leslie Hobbs (Whitcombe and Tombs, Christchurch, 1975).

Coasters, Coastal Shipping

Only in the last 50 years or so has it become easier to travel about New Zealand by road than by sea. Until the Second World War, coastal ships worked a chain of minor ports, often carrying passengers as well as freight. The tradition dates back to the earliest days in New Zealand, when shipping was the only link between the main centres. Coasters were small vessels, often **Scows**, with shallow draught for river work and small crews. Most carried their own powered winches and derricks for unloading cargoes at remote wharves. **Inter-island Ferry** services originally ran from Wellington to Lyttelton and Nelson, as well as Picton. Coastal passenger vessels linked Taranaki with Auckland via the Manukau into the 1940s; practically the last coastal link into Onehunga has been the cement ships. Before the Second World War, dozens of coasters linked the river ports of the north, the Thames Valley and the Bay of Plenty. Overnight passenger services from Auckland to Whangarei, Tauranga and New Plymouth via the Manukau were run by the Northern Steam Ship Company, until the advent of railways in the 1920s provided an efficient alternative. Many of the towns in this region, while apparently far from the sea, are built at the original head of navigation on the tidal rivers that once served them. Gradually silting rivers and dangerous river bars were major problems for this trade. Many coasters were lost on the bar, while entering or leaving port, along the West Coast in particular. Coastal shipping declined with the completion of better roads in the north and railway links in the south. Ports such as Blenheim and Oamaru languished as it became more economic to rail or truck goods to a more central port. In the 1960s 'containerisation', the pre-packing of goods into containers that could be hauled by road, rail or sea, killed most of the provincial ports. Containers are now taken by land to the few export ports equipped to handle them. Once-busy provincial ports have become havens for fishing vessels and leisure craft.

Cockies' Joy

Unrefined sugar in the form of golden syrup, named in this allusion for its popularity with small farmers, known as cockies, as a breakfast spread. Cockies' Joy, liberally applied to bread or poured over porridge with freshly separated cream, gives a strong dose of high-energy sugar after milking the cows. Golden syrup is also a popular ingredient in sweet cakes and boiled puddings. See also **Hokey Pokey**.

The Coffin Ship

Chinese gold-miners who died on the New Zealand goldfields were often buried here, then exhumed for return to their homeland for reburial. In 1902 the coffin ship *Ventnor* hit a reef off Taranaki, while carrying homeward the bones of 499 Chinese from Otago and Westland. The ship got off the reef but went down south of Hokianga, with the coffins aboard. Details in *New Zealand Shipwrecks*, originally compiled by C.W.N. Ingram (Hodder Moa Beckett, Auckland, 2007).

Colonial Goose

Don't be fooled by this traditional dish on the menu of a country hotel. Not the succulent meat of the gamebird Canada Goose, or even hand-reared domestic geese – it's mutton. Probably so named as an effort to break the boredom of mutton, mutton, mutton on the menu in sheep country. According to *Classic Kiwi Recipes* by country food expert Sheryl Brownlee, this is 'stuffed mutton, shaped to look like a bird when cooked and presented for carving'. It still tastes like sheep.

The Commercial Hotel

Many provincial hotels still trade as the Commercial. Such hotels sought their custom from the army of commercial travellers who worked the country with sample bags to secure orders for city and foreign firms. At the Commercial there was some understanding of the special needs of the travelling man, working away from home, besides a reasonable tariff. Places were set aside with tables and chairs to write up the day's orders. Some provided sample or commercial rooms for the display of goods. Into the 1950s, for example, the trade representatives of some British book publishers presented their titles in a display at the local commercial hotel. Then booksellers visited, placed their orders, and the books were indented from Britain to arrive some months later. Email, websites, faxes and rapid transport and marketing have somewhat diminished the mystique of the commercial traveller or company representative in intervening years.

Compo

Compensation for an accident or disability. Until 1967 New Zealand followed the free world, enabling the injured to sue their employer or the neglectful party who caused their injury for compensation. The National socialist government, in an initiative directed by Sir Robert Muldoon, then produced the Accident Compensation Act, giving State compensation payments in lieu of the right to sue. A few unionists opposed this, one on the grounds that it would stop the workers' chances of getting a capital pay-out sufficient to set up in business, but most of the world looked on with surprise and envy. Inevitably, costs escalated beyond the Commission's capability to pay 'compo', as even prisoners, injured while trying to escape, were compensated. A watered-down system with higher (tax) subscription now operates, arguably creating some anomalies and unfairness for those who might previously have been more equitably treated through litigation.

Compulsory Military Training, CMT

Part of the jingoistic past. A scheme begun in 1911, before the First World War, conscripted all males between 14 and 20 for military training. This aroused the protests of pacifists, particularly in the labour movement. It was a Labour government, however, that in 1949 ordered all 18-year-old males into uniform for basic training in the Army, Air Force or Navy, then posted them to part-time Territorial forces. Provincial army battalions kept alive the names and traditions of First and Second World War regiments. In 1961 the scheme was changed to a system of selective national service, with trainees chosen by a ballot based on their birthdays. Since 1972 territorial trainees have all been volunteers.

Conchies

The maligned conscientious objectors of the First and Second World Wars. Some had religious objections: political labour took a broader view, arguing about internationalism and the workers of the world uniting. In the First World War conscientious objectors were forced onto the field of battle to prove the right of might; in the Second World War those who did not join medical teams or non-combatant units ended up in prison, more than 800 of them. Two conscientious objectors wrote eloquent books about their experience, republished in the 1980s. Archibald Baxter (father of the poet James K.) wrote about the First World War in *We Will Not Cease* (Cape Catley Ltd, Marlborough, 1980). Ian Hamilton wrote *Till Human Voices Wake Us* (Auckland University Press, Auckland, 1984) about imprisonment in the Second World War.

The Conquest of Everest

A New Zealand beekeeper, the late Edmund Hillary was the first to conquer Mt Everest on May 29, 1953, accompanied by a Sherpa of the expedition, Tensing Norgay. The announcement of this achievement on the morning of Queen Elizabeth's Coronation raised the event to legendary status. For a fading British Empire here was promise of a new Elizabethan age with Hillary as the second Elizabeth's Walter Raleigh. At 8839.8 m (29,002 ft), Everest had been a continuing challenge since the 1920s with only 10 previous expeditions gaining permission to explore. The rationale for climbing the world's highest mountain was explained by a previous expedition leader, Eric Shipton, in the simple expression 'because it is there'. In 1953 Hillary was climbing with a British expedition led by Colonel John Hunt. Both were knighted. In subsequent years Hillary returned often to the Himalayas, inspiring and helping local Sherpas to build schools and hospitals, etc. He also explored in Antarctica, making a journey to the South Pole by tractor in 1958. Hillary served as

New Zealand High Commissioner to India in 1985–89. He also became New Zealand's second Knight of the Garter and his portrait is on New Zealand's five-dollar note. Peter Hillary, his adventurous son, first conquered Everest in 1990. When he died in 2008, Sir Edmund Hillary was accorded the rare distinction of a **State Funeral.**

Cooking a Pukeko

The pukeko or purple gallinule is one of the few native birds to remain on the list of those that can be shot for sport. Unlike the tender duck, the pukeko is a bird of sinews and muscle, very tasty but usually stringy and hard to eat if not well prepared. Bushmen traditionally put a stone in the pot when cooking pukeko. Their recipe recommends boiling both bird and stone together for up to four hours, then throwing away the pukeko and eating the stone. An alternative method involves boiling the pukeko with an old boot.

Cooks

Whether cooking for sheep-station hands, public-works camps, or the army, the cook was regarded as a character. To this day the cook is a key factor in the success of remote enterprise and, while women appear quite often in the modern complement, most of the old-time cooks were men. Their cooking styles and bad habits soon earned them nicknames, often related to their obsessive cleanliness or lack of it. Making a variety of food in places remote from stores limited the range of food for the workers and added to the abuse and commendation extended to the cook. Tales of gangs revolting at a monotonous diet of mutton, or short rations, are legion. Sometimes owners, such as One-Chop Robinson, got the blame for parsimony. More often it was tales of cooking with weevil-infested flour, attacks of flies and vengeful cooks accused of fouling the soup. Cooks, like other lonely men in the back country, were prone to alcoholic binges. Unfortunately the effect of these was more noticeable among the cooks and many a gang woke to no breakfast and a cook vanished or lost in a drunken daze. Some gangs took the precaution of including the cook in their team. Others relied on the itinerants who worked the back-country camps and farms, some claiming culinary expertise they could not demonstrate, to the disgust of men who considered good tucker part of their terms of employment. See **Shearers' Meals**.

Coromandel Green

A popular form of 'wacky baccy' or **Electric Puha** during the euphoric years of the smoking '70s. As the use of marijuana has become more widespread, the industry has become less informal and there are now criminal organisations supplying various forms of 'green' grown in most parts of the country.

Correspondence Schools

A package of lessons and supplementary material broadcast on national radio was the way many children received their education in isolated districts from 1922. Sick children, too, could keep up to date with their schoolwork while in isolation. In the summer of 1948–49 all children of primary and secondary school age were taught by correspondence during an epidemic of poliomyelitis which caused schools to close. (See **Polio Epidemics**.) Better roads and changing settlement patterns have not reduced the need for 'distance education'. The enrolment in 2007 was around 20,000. In 1993, a similar enrolment included around 500 in early childhood classes, 2500 in primary school and 1700-plus in secondary schools. More than 7000 other students took one or two subjects to supplement their regular classes where the local school could not provide a particular subject, while a 'late-start' programme helped more than 7300 adults gain school-level qualifications by correspondence. A technical correspondence school formerly supplemented the work of technical institutes in training apprentices: it has since become the Open Polytechnic of New Zealand.

Corrugated Iron

This traditional building material gives a distinctive character to much of New Zealand's architecture. The 'tin' roof has been a feature of houses here since it was first imported from Britain by pioneer settlers. The material is rigid and its corrugations shed water without leaking. Often used for facing temporary buildings it has proved so durable that some corrugated iron buildings have lived on longer than intended. Corrugated iron was developed in Britain during the 1830s. It is a comparatively light building material and stacks easily, so cargoes of it were regularly imported for pioneer buildings. New Zealand companies, notably Samuel Parker of Auckland from 1886, soon got into the business of manufacturing the distinctive corrugations into imported sheet steel and galvanising it with zinc as protection against the weather. Corrugated iron, like **Number Eight Wire**, became part of the Kiwi idiom, not only for roofs but also for fences (drag a stick along the face of the corrugations for a nostalgic sound from childhood), use it over a fire to barbecue so the fat runs away in the grooves or make a dog kennel or a treehouse for the children. Listen to the rain on the corrugated iron roof to get to sleep. Keep a few sheets handy around the yard to keep timber dry or retain a garden. The sculptor Jeff Thomson has used corrugated iron to create beasts and other life-sized objects with a strong New Zealand appeal. As a structural material corrugated iron excels. Sheets make rigid the framing of buildings, often providing the sides of shops and other structures built close together, as a protection from spreading fire. As a roofing material it may last 60 years or more. Use it for **Backyard Sheds** and **Long Drops**. Major structures such as theatres (with false fronts in wood) and factories have all been built in corrugated iron. The material gives a special character to many New Zealand landscapes. Enjoy *Corrugated Iron in New Zealand,* by Geoff Chapple, John Maynard, David Mitchell and Warren Viscoe (A.H & A.W. Reed, Wellington, 1983), an historical essay with vernacular photographs, and *Wrinkly Tin*, by Stuart Thomson (Steele Roberts, Wellington, 2005).

Count Felix von Luckner

The debonair Count became famous during the First World War for his escape from imprisonment on Motuihe Island in the Hauraki Gulf, in December 1917. Originally the commander of *Seeadler*, a German raider disguised as a sailing trader, he lost his ship in a tropical storm at the Society Islands and was arrested in Fiji while searching for another to take. Von Luckner encouraged other German sailors interned on Motuihe to help him equip the camp commandant's boat with supplies so they could escape and capture a larger vessel. They left in a storm and found a hiding place among the Mercury Islands, off Coromandel. There they captured the sailing scow *Moa* but her sister ship *Rangi* got away and a chase began. The cable steamer *Iris* caught up with *Moa* and von Luckner at the Kermadec Islands and the Germans were brought back to New Zealand. Von Luckner and his navigator were then interned on Ripapa Island at Lyttelton Harbour for six months. Back on Motutapu he tried again, twice, to escape and was finally released after the war, in May 1919.

Cow Cockies

The expression 'cocky' for a small farmer, particularly in dairying, is inherited from the Australian vernacular. There, small farmers were called 'cockatoos', for reasons still argued over but it obviously derives from those flocking birds of the countryside. The expression originated before the Australian gold rushes and probably came over to New Zealand with the miners from the Australian fields in the 1860s.

Cradle to the Grave Social Security

The description of State welfare in the 1930s to 1980s encompassed the predictable crises of life and provided a benefit to allay each one. The Labour government of 1935 introduced a social security tax of 1s 6d in the pound to fund the scheme, offering in return universal superannuation, old age pensions for the needy, benefits for the widowed and their children, a family benefit and a range of benefits for the sick, the unemployed and the unemployable. To this was added in ensuing years free doctor visits, medicine and hospitals and dental care for the young. With free medical care, cynics spoke of welfare benefits from Conception to the Resurrection. How quickly things have changed since the **Crash of '87**.

The Crash of '87

In 1987, just as the stockmarket was about to top the magic 5000 figure for the first time, New Zealand's shaky financial superstructure of paper money in paper companies came tumbling down. Runaway inflation faltered and property values fell. Interest rates, however, took their time to fall, only reaching a low-enough level to encourage investment again in mid-1993. By then a lot of rich people had got rich again, but the nature of the country for the 'have nots' still reflected a recession, with around 250,000 unemployed or on assisted work schemes, not to mention those who had given up and 'retired'.

Cream Stands

A feature of the rural landscape of New Zealand even beyond the cow country. These wooden shelters on legs once stood by the front gate of most farms, their decks level with the tray of 'cream trucks' which called daily to pick up the cream cans. Until the 1960s switch to whole-milk collection, by bulk tankers, farmers separated cream from milk in their own dairies and sold it to the butter factories. The skimmed milk was usually fed to pigs. The cream stands date from the days when butter factories sent out horse drays on daily collection rounds. They can still be seen, a handy shelter for **Rural Delivery** drivers to drop off supplies, or for children to wait in the shelter for the school bus.

Crib

This Otago and southern expression for a simple holiday cottage is of Scottish origin. The popular weekend 'crib' is known to the rest of New Zealand as a **'bach'**.

Cultural (Colonial) Cringe

This Australian expression encapsulates a similar problem that used to trouble sensitive New Zealanders. The principle is that things done or achieved overseas are necessarily better than those done here. During the early 20th century there was an argument for this, as the infant Dominion had too small a population to sustain some artistic enterprises and there was sense in seeking a larger market abroad for books and paintings. Katherine Mansfield (1888–1923) made her own life and that of those around her miserable with her desire to escape from New Zealand and lead the literary life abroad. Ironically her best work sings with pictures of this country. Artists such as Frances Hodgkins (1869–1947) likewise worked as expatriates.

E.H. McCormick records in his 1940 centennial survey of *New Zealand Literature*: 'Writers sought in the old world surroundings more sympathetic and stimulating than those of New Zealand; they migrated to London as Americans of the "lost generation" migrated to Paris.' Writers in the 1930s took a more bellicose stand on our emerging traditions while still seeking the recognition and rewards of publication overseas. The lack of national self-confidence was expressed in 1939 by the poet Allen Curnow with the lines:

> *Not I, some child, born in a marvellous year,*
> *Will learn the trick of standing upright here.*

Confidence has improved since then, particularly when comparative prosperity produced the funding for a professional and full-time arts industry. Local actors largely replaced the overseas touring shows, communities supported fine orchestras, new magazines provided sophisticated avenues for journalism. Cheap and quick air travel has, along with mass communications, allowed artists to live here while working internationally. Hopefully, many New Zealanders finally lost their cultural cringe when Keri Hulme won the prestigious Booker McConnell Prize for the best English novel of 1985, without apparent concession to any other tradition but her own. See **the bone people**.

Curling

Something like bowls on ice, played with large stones, shaped like round scones with a handle atop. A tradition in Central Otago where creeks and ponds ice up and stay that way with midwinter hoar frost. The tiny communities of the region may field several teams, pub playing pub, or contesting inter-township rivalry. In the harsher winters teams of curlers are called, at 24 hours' notice, to a bonspiel, with as many as 29 teams taking part. Curling originated about 1837, in Scotland, homeland of many Otago settlers. Competitions in Central Otago date back to 1873 and the Court of Curlers to 1886. New players are initiated into the Court following a formal dinner at the bonspiel. The ceremony and arcane titles of the Court are kept secret from those who have not been 'curled'.

Dagg, Fred *see* Fred Dagg

Dairies

A misnomer in part; for while they sold ice cream and milk in bottles, the major business was after-hours supply of household aids, bread, a few permitted food lines, sweets, soft drinks and tobacco. While some dairies still survive, providing a seven-day service to all hours, the modern equivalent is more food oriented following the abolition of restrictive trade practices through the 1980s. Prior to that dairies had locked corners where groceries could not be displayed when competing groceries were shut. Supermarkets spelt the end of thousands of such businesses during the 1960s and 1970s. Once-flourishing **Local Shopping 'Blocks'** now stand empty, or converted to small manufactories and warehouses, at the centre of the suburban communities they used to serve. Many petrol stations now fill the role of the dairy.

Dairy Factories

Local landmarks in cow country, most were set up within a daily dray ride of their farmer shareholders. Cream was separated from the milk and sent to factories in cream cans to make butter. (Skimmed milk was retained as feed for pigs.) The co-operative manufacture of butter developed in the 1880s to take advantage of the market for frozen butter in Britain. In recent years large numbers of dairy factories have closed as the industry rationalised its products and methods. Now, whole milk is collected by road tanker and taken to regional factories producing a range of dairy products including dried milk powder, casein, cheese and butter. The dairy factories with their distinctive front-loading doors and unloading platforms have been adapted as local manufacturing plants, craft markets, or simply abandoned.

'Dallies'

A slightly derogatory nickname for the Dalmatian settlers who came from the Adriatic coast around the turn of last century and made their living on the gumfields of North Auckland. From 1885, parties of 'Dallies' arrived on the gumfields, usually sending their earnings home, until by around 1900 there were nearly 5000 of them working there. In 1898, a gumdiggers' union persuaded the government to create reserves of the best gumlands for the use of British, Maori and New Zealanders, restricting the Dalmatians to less profitable Crown land. While some eventually returned home, others did so only to bring out a wife and many remained, adding to New Zealand culture many surnames ending in 'ich' and an inherited tradition of grape growing that has largely inspired the development of New Zealand's wine industry. See **'Dally Plonk'**.

'Dally Plonk'

Unflattering earlier name for cheap wine made by settlers from the Dalmatian coast. How times change! As New Zealanders moved from beer-drinking to wine-drinking they created a market for superb wines, many of these the product of the descendants of pioneer vintners.

Damper

A form of unleavened bread made from flour paste and baked in the campfire. Old-timers customarily made it when they 'damped down' their fires at night. A hole is scraped in the hot fire and the ball of damper placed on the ground. Fine ash over the dough protects it when the fire is scraped back over the top, then the whole is sealed from flaring up in the night with earth or wet leaves. In the morning the fire was quickly lit by opening it up to the air again and adding fuel. The damper, meanwhile, had cooked and made a tough but ready-to-eat breakfast loaf. A similar method, using a cast iron camp oven or other container, produced a better-tasting **Camp-oven Bread**, which was a staple food in bush and mustering camps.

Dawn Maiden

Romantic translation for the young woman said to be fathered every night by the Maori god Tane. She then rises in the east, bringing the first flush of dawn. The sun, set up by Tane, marches across the heavens until the day is swallowed again in the red fire of sunset, down into the world of darkness of Hine nui te Po.

Deer Recovery *see* Chopper Boys

The Desert Road

Crossing the volcanic plateau from Lake Taupo to Waiouru, this section of State Highway 1 skirts the active Tongariro volcanoes and takes its name from the bleak cinderlands of the Rangipo Desert. Little of substance grows in this windswept place but the views are expansive and magnificent.

Diggers

New Zealand and Australian soldiers of the First World War served together and shared the name. Originally, the word was a popular reference to gold-miners during the 19th-century **Gold Rushes** in both countries. In New Zealand there were gumdiggers searching for kauri gum, too. The connection has not been confirmed. Certainly the task of trench warfare involved some digging but that task was common to all forces. The name persisted through the Second World War and returned soldiers are sometimes referred to as 'old digs'.

Diggings

Colloquial English name for an alluvial goldfield, e.g. the Horseshoe Bend Diggings, the Kyeburn Diggings. Here miners dug for suitable deposits and washed the gold out of the rocks and sands. The waste was left behind as **Tailings**.

Dinosaur Forests

This expression, popularised by the British naturalist and television personality David Bellamy, refers to the ancient lineage of New Zealand's forests. Bellamy's claim relates to the evolution of many of our trees in the ancient continent of Gondwana in the time of the dinosaurs 200 million years ago.

Our fern-like plant *Dicroidium* has been found embedded in fossil deposits contemporaneous with the dinosaurs. About 140 million years ago New Zealand was 10 times as big as its present boundaries, and land bridges with other southern continents allowed some species, such as southern beech, to become common to other land masses, including South America. Ancestors of our podocarp rainforest trees developed then, as did the kauri. Subsequently New Zealand shrunk away from the Gondwana land masses, but its ancestral trees survived. This happened before the widespread rise of mammals, which may account for the survival of a few ancient creatures such as the native frog and **Tuatara** from those times. For popular accounts of New Zealand's physical evolution see *Prehistoric New Zealand*, by Graeme Stevens, Matt McGlone and Beverley McCulloch (Heinemann Reed, Auckland, 1988), and *In Search of Ancient New Zealand*, by Hamish Campbell and Gerard Hutching (Penguin, Auckland, 2007). See also **'Living Fossils'**.

The Discoverer of New Zealand *see* Kupe, Abel Tasman

Do-it-yourself

New Zealanders are handymen and women. Instead of hiring a contractor they will often build their own sheds, paint their own homes and do their own home improvements. Home car maintenance is also popular. What may have begun as a practical necessity in pioneer times has been kept alive through difficult times, a virtue born of necessity.

The Dog Tax Rebellion

War nearly broke out in Hokianga in 1898 over the imposition of a dog tax by-law. The town of Rawene was evacuated when a **Hau Hau** faction based in Waima threatened armed protest to demands for local taxes. Trouble escalated to the point where a total of four vessels, six police with a cannon, a colonel with 120 men and a squad of sailors arrived to uphold the law. Negotiations by the local Maori parliamentarian, Hone Heke Rankin, defused the situation, arms were handed in, arrests made and, in time, the fines commuted. The story is well-told with supporting documents in *Hokianga*, by Jack Lee (Hodder and Stoughton, Auckland, 1987).

Dog Trials

New Zealand's **Working Dogs** are a source of wonder and amusement to overseas visitors. The sight of a trained dog bailing up sheep, or dancing across their backs to another part of the mob, brings out the cameras and keeps a number of demonstration farms and sheep shows in business. Seizing any opportunity to show off the skills of their dogs, owners compete in local and national working trials. A television programme featuring dog-trialling has entertained peak-time audiences in New Zealand and spawned a British version. National sheepdog trials are held with events such as Short Head and Yard, Long Head, Straight Huntaway and Zig Zag Huntaway. *Working Dogs*, by Neil Rennie (Beckett Sterling, Auckland, 1990), shows how to train and work a sheep or cattle dog.

The Doll's House

Quintessential short story from Katherine Mansfield. Mansfield (1888–1923) was born Kathleen Mansfield Beauchamp, a daughter of the banker Sir Harold Beauchamp in Wellington, and educated finally at Queen's College, London. On returning home, she pined for London, eventually returning to live there and on the Continent. The death of her brother Leslie at Flanders in 1915 may have brought back a more idyllic memory of New Zealand, which she recalled in short stories still respected as early examples of that literary form. The eponymous doll's house has been constructed from details in the story and may be seen on display in the Katherine Mansfield birthplace exhibition in Wellington. *The Complete Stories of Katherine Mansfield*, republished by Golden Press, includes her collections *Bliss*, 1920, *The Garden Party*, 1922, *The Dove's Nest*, 1923, the posthumous *Something Childish* and a reprint of *In a German Pension*, 1911.

Douglas, Mr Explorer

The title commonly accorded to Charles Douglas (1840–1916), a Scot who explored much of South Westland from the 1880s to 1900. His maps and observations were recognised with the Gill Medal

of the Royal Geographical Society in 1897. Douglas discovered several mountain passes from Westland to the east, such as the Copland, and made first ascents on many alpine peaks. Once, in the Waiatoto region, Douglas climbed for 2000 ft (609 m) without boots. Consequently Mt Ragan was renamed Stocking Peak in the 1980s. Douglas's exploits, during which he was often accompanied by his dog Betsy Jane, are recorded in *Mr Explorer Douglas*, edited by John Pascoe (A.H. & A.W. Reed, Wellington, 1957).

Down Under, Down Under

Caving in New Zealand's limestone regions is a popular sport. The tomo (caves or holes) of the Waikato region are popular with wild-cave explorers, as well as the tourists who visit the Waitomo Caves to see the glow-worms. Black-water rafting involves drifting in the dark, down unlit underground passages. The north-west Nelson region and the Paparoa National Park in Westland have extensive cave systems. Besides the glow-worms, many caves contain the bones of long-extinct birds such as moa which tumbled in via pot-holes. The Nettlebed cave system located on Mt Arthur is the deepest at 889 m. Bulmer Cavern in Mt Owen is the longest at 50,125 m, or more than 50 km. Details can be found in *Delving Deeper: half a century of cave discovery in New Zealand* by Moira Lipyeat and Les Wright (Hazard Press, Christchurch 2003).

The Draper's Man

Travelling salesmen, often representing city stores, once travelled the country districts seeking orders for cloth and sewing materials. Two visits a year allowed the introduction of seasonal lines. Often the salesmen carried stock in cases with them, or showed samples to be supplied later from the city base. Much of this business is now conducted by mail order. The door-to-door system still persists with a few companies that work on a direct-selling basis, often through tea parties, where a group of potential customers is offered special-brand clothes or cosmetics.

The Drift North

Since the declining days of the gold rushes, more people have moved to the North Island than to the South. The northward drift of population has been a trend for the past century. Wellington and Auckland have proved attractive to migrants both from overseas and within New Zealand. Job opportunities and their respective positions as headquarters of State and private enterprise have encouraged this. Although New Zealanders are a restless lot, moving from place to place even within their regions, the drift north can be traced as a movement favouring the next province to the north, from Southland to Otago, Otago to Canterbury, and so on, to Auckland. By 2006, 32 per cent of New Zealanders lived in Auckland, by then a city with a population of over 1.3 million people. The initial drift from the countryside to the towns is apparent between 1911, when around 50 per cent of the population lived in towns, and 1961 when the urban population passed 75 per cent. Now, urban populations have stabilised at around 85–86 per cent of New Zealanders. On a worldwide scale of urbanisation compiled in 2000, New Zealand had the fourth-highest urban population proportion in the world – at 86 per cent it was well ahead of Japan at 79 per cent and the United States at 77 per cent. (Source: *New Zealand Official Yearbook 2002*, Department of Statistics, Wellington.)

Drovers, Drovers' Roads

Before trucking took over, stock from back-country farms was often driven to market or the freezing works by sheep or cattle drovers mounted on horseback. Some of the drovers' roads followed a broad trail, wide-fenced, where stock could graze as they went. More often they followed a natural water course, or skirted the coast. Famous cattle drives around the East Cape beaches and in South Westland are part of local lore and a surge in trucking costs has led to the occasional revival of a few such drives in recent years. Some of the most spectacular droving routes date from the gold-mining era of the 1860s when stock was driven over mountain passes, such as Brownings and Harpers, from Canterbury to Westland, to feed the miners.

Dry Towns

The consequence of the **Prohibition** movement was that some Parliamentary electorates in New Zealand voted against the sale of liquor in their area. Towns in these places were widely known as dry towns. One such, Oamaru, experienced more than 50 years of Prohibition before its largest 'private hotel' reopened under the control of a community-owned licensing trust in the early 1960s. The 'liquor vote' was taken triennially (at the same time as the Parliamentary election) with the choices being Continuance, Prohibition or State Control (a community licensing trust). Those options were discontinued after the 1987 General Election. The remaining dry areas voted for Restoration or No Licence. Only Eden, Grey Lynn and Roskill in Auckland, and Tawa in Porirua remained 'dry' following the 1993 General Election. Three 'local restoration' polls were held at the same time as the 1999 General Election, when the last three areas, Eden, Roskill and Tawa, ceased to be 'dry'.

Duffer Rushes

Such was the volatility of life on the goldfields that rumour could easily spark the cry 'Shift ho' and the miners would take off *en masse* to another site expecting more gold. Such **Gold Rushes** could involve as many as 1000 men racing across country to be first at the new prospect. A rush was said to be a 'duffer' when there turned out to be no gold. People accused of starting duffer rushes were those who stood to benefit, such as storekeepers and carriers, or those who may have 'salted a claim' to make some easy money. The most famous duffer rush occurred in Westland in 1866 when, fuelled by rumour alone, 1000 men pursued Albert William Hunt, the man who discovered Westland's first big field, in an incident described as **Hunt's Duffer**.

The Dun Mountain Railway

Claims are sometimes made for Nelson having the first railway in New Zealand. The claim is based on a horse-drawn tramway that opened on February 3, 1862, 14 months before steam trains operated on the Christchurch line to Ferrymead. The 21.5-km line ran from the Dun Mountain chrome ore mines, behind the city, down to Port Nelson. When the mountain line was closed, a city section of 2 kilometres was kept open, operating a passenger tram service until the rails wore out in 1901. The hills beyond the town were too steep for steam locomotives, defeating Nelson's claim to be first with a real railway, though it was empowered in legislation to be such. See further parochial unhappiness on the subject under **Nelson's Notional Railway**.

The Dundonald Coracle

A framework of koromiko tied together with rope and wire, now in Canterbury Museum, recalls the way that shipwrecked sailors paddled to the main (sub-antarctic) Auckland Island to await rescue in 1907. The four-masted barque *Dundonald* struck Disappointment Island on March 7, 1907 and the survivors struggled ashore from her top masts. After seven and a half months living off birds and seals, the castaways built three coracle frameworks and covered them with canvas. In these primitive craft 15 men managed to transfer themselves from Disappointment to Auckland Island. There they found a provision store for shipwrecked mariners. The men were found eight months after shipwreck by the government steamer *Hinemoa*, which called at the southern islands from time to time.

Dunnies *see* Long Drops

The Dunstan Trail

Old miners' route inland from Dunedin to the Dunstan goldfields about Clyde. It is still possible to follow a portion of the trail by four-wheel-drive vehicle, over the Lammermoors and the Rock and Pillar Range between the ghost towns of Deep Stream and Styx (Paerau) on the edge of the Maniototo Plain. The route then crosses Rough Ridge to Moa Creek and Alexandra. The trail was broad once, as heavily laden prospectors braved extremes of weather on their journey inland, picking the easiest course up the spurs onto the plateaux. Cobb & Co brought coaches to the trail in 1862, offering a three-day ride from West Taieri to the Dunstan. Competition reduced the time to a day, from 4.00 am until midnight, but by 1864 coaches chose the easier **Pigroot** into Central Otago. David McKee Wright recalled the romance of the Dunstan Trail in his *Station Ballads* of 1897:

> *There's a green grassy slope by the boundary fence,*
> *With the scrub bushes sheltering round,*
> *A hollow that shows where a building has been,*
> *And there broken black bottles are found.*
> *A water-race too, that's been dry for long years*
> *Coming out of a creek at the back –*
> *It's all that remains of a shanty that stood*
> *At the foot of the old Dunstan Track.*
> *Oh, the days when the track was a road, boys,*
> *The rollicking days of old,*
> *When the bullockies came with their load, boys,*
> *The days of the first of the gold!*

The *Earl of Pembroke*

Probably the most famous ship in New Zealand history, though few have ever heard of her by this name. A tubby little collier, with a carrying capacity of 368 tons and a maximum speed of eight knots, the *Earl of Pembroke* had, however, the qualities of a good sea boat. Built in 1764 and bought by the British Admiralty in 1768, she was refitted for exploration, with 70 men accommodated in her holds and two years' supplies aboard. The new quarterdeck accommodated 24 officers and gentlemen below. Against the maritime folklore that it is bad luck to rename a ship the Admiralty assigned her to Lieutenant James Cook for his first expedition to the South Seas in 1769 and gave her the new name *Endeavour*. Cook's later voyages were also made aboard converted **'Whitby Cats'** though his *Endeavour* was sold to an American who registered it in France as *La Liberté*. The ship ran aground at Newport, Rhode Island, in 1793 and her historic timbers were stripped away. See the **Wreck of the *Endeavour*.**

Early Ships at Nelson

The Nelson settlement was the product of land dealing and promotion by the New Zealand Company in England. Their preparatory expedition arrived in 1841 aboard the *Arrow*, *Will Watch* and *Whitby*. The first organised settlers arrived aboard the *Fifeshire* on February 1, 1842, followed by the *Mary Ann*, *Brougham*, *Lloyds* and *Lord Auckland*. The *Fifeshire* left her name on the Fifeshire Rock, as she wrecked there, trying to leave Nelson Haven on February 27. See **Wakefield Settlements**.

Earthquake Disasters

New Zealand's reputation as the **Shaky Isles** has been borne out in some spectacular earthquakes. The site of downtown

Wellington was uplifted from the harbour bed in 1855 when the coast rose 1.5 m. The Murchison earthquake of 1929 may appear from statistics of deaths (17) and destruction to have had only a localised impact, but the effect on the sparsely populated surrounding country was also immense. Hillsides slipped to form lakes in the remote back country of north-west Nelson and damage occurred as far away as Karamea on the West Coast, Takaka, Nelson and Christchurch. The Napier earthquake of 1931 drained some 13 sq km of the Ahuriri estuary. In Hawke's Bay 256 people were killed, Napier shook down and burned, brick buildings collapsed in Hastings and damage extended as far as Gisborne, Wairoa and Wanganui. The Inangahua earthquake of 1968 took three lives and caused widespread damage in the mountainous regions about it.

The Edinburgh of the South *see* The New Edinburgh

The Edmonds Cookery Book

The biggest-selling New Zealand book which, in various forms, has been a popular basis for home cooking for nearly 100 years. Always an inexpensive volume, it was originally the by-product of the Edmonds baking powder factory, promoting the use of its

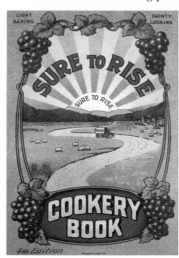

'Sure to Rise' product. The rising sun logo and the gracious gardens of T.J. Edmonds Ltd in Ferry Road, Christchurch, were related icons. Now the company has passed into other corporate hands and the factory gardens have gone. Yet the product lives on, supported by huge annual sales of the *Edmonds Cookery Book*. The first book of 50 pages was published in 1907. A 'deluxe' edition launched in 1955 was reprinted 31 times in the ensuing 27 years in printings of up to 200,000 a time. By 1990 total sales exceeded three million copies. In 1989 The Bush Press produced a companion volume, the *Edmonds Microwave Cookery Book,* an adaptation of the traditional recipes with new ones suited to the microwave oven. It quickly sold 250,000 copies, creating a New Zealand publishing record. Although the Edmonds name has since spawned a whole range of cookbooks, the simple ring-bound edition is still a best seller. See also **Yates Garden Guide**

Eight-ounce Glass

The standard beer (240 ml), which has survived as a measure of communication between customer and any good barman, despite a generation of metrification. The same goes for the five-ounce 'pony' (150 ml) favoured by 'girls'. For that matter have you asked for a 180-ml drink lately, or a seven-ounce? The Australian 'middy' or 'schooner' is likely to be as well understood as a 12-ounce or British pint or half pint. Younger barmen who can't cope tend to wave a glass in the air and ask instead 'This size okay?' A lot of fluid has flowed down the canal since metrification, but some traditions die hard.

Electric Puha

Marijuana, wacky baccy, etc. See also **Coromandel Green**. The expression light-heartedly links the nature of the drug *Cannabis sativa* with the common Maori vegetable **Puha**.

The *Elingamite* Treasure

Sunk on a voyage from Australia on November 9, 1902, the *Elingamite* carried a fortune in gold and silver coins destined for the Bank of New South Wales. The ship struck the western island in the Three Kings group, north-west of New Zealand, with the loss of 45 lives. Some of the £17,000 worth of coins was recovered in 1907 after several attempts, but three divers died before the successful expeditions of 1964–65, led by Wade Doak and Kelly Tarlton. They recovered 12,000 silver coins, but only 21 of some 6000 gold coins were ever found. According to Wade Doak, more than one and a half tons of pure silver also lies buried in the wreck. See *The Elingamite and its Treasure*, by Wade Doak (Hodder & Stoughton, Auckland, 1969).

The Endeavour see *The Earl of Pembroke*

The Erebus Disaster

A tourist flight to see the Antarctic ice from the air ended in disaster on November 28, 1979, when an Air New Zealand DC10 plunged into the side of Mt Erebus, in the Ross Dependency, during a 'white-out'. All 257 on board were killed. Mr Justice Peter Mahon, in summing up a 75-day enquiry, absolved the pilots and accused the company's administration of defending itself by presenting 'an orchestrated litany of lies'.

Erewhon

The locale of Samuel Butler's famed satire on Victorian England is identifiably in the mountains of the South Island of New Zealand. The land of 'Nowhere' is entered by way of a high pass that well describes the mountains where the young Butler once explored. Butler came to New Zealand in 1860, fresh from Cambridge, determined to double his money as a sheep farmer. Despite his ignorance of farming he took up the Mesopotamia run on the Upper Rangitata River in Canterbury and set about exploring for a mountain pass into Westland. First, he probed the headwaters of the Rangitata and found a way out via the Lawrence branch. Climbing through the snow he looked over Butler Col to see the Rakaia River to the north. Beyond its glaciers, however, there was only a glimpse of Westland. Later, by following up the Rakaia River, Butler and his companion discovered the Whitcombe Pass over the Southern Alps. He chose not to follow down the rugged bush-clad gorges on the Westland side, but used the locale for the distant 'Erewhon' of his later book. In just four and a half years Butler made his fortune, while also finding time to play Bach on a harpsichord in his mountain hut, and to pen a series of articles criticising the 'age of machines', which was published in the infant *Press* newspaper in Christchurch. Having returned to England, Butler described his mountain journeys to introduce the imaginary land of Erewhon, and the *Press* articles also became part of his satirical examination of the state of industrial England. The present sheep station 'Erewhon' is across the Rangitata from Butler's station, but lay on his early route up the Rangitata Valley and the Lawrence. *Erewhon* is still available in recent editions, being favoured in university courses as a critique of Victorian values. *A First Year in the Canterbury Settlement* is a collection of Butler's letters about life here, published most recently in 1964 by Blackwood and Janet Paul, of Auckland and Hamilton.

Extinct Birds

New Zealand has a sorry history of lost birds, and many of those that remain are among the most threatened in the world. The reason is that New Zealand was isolated from other land masses some 85 million years ago and life developed here before the evolution of mammals. Consequently, birds (and other creatures) evolved and survived without threat from such predators. The arrival of the first settlers, Maori accompanied by dogs and rats, had a huge impact on the native wildlife. Fires lit to clear forest destroyed a great deal of bird habitat. Maori hunters soon drove the giant moa birds to extinction. In all, 32 species of native bird were lost in Maori times, including the world's largest eagle, which preyed on moa, as well as two geese, a swan and a pelican. The arrival of European settlers in the 19th century accelerated the process drastically, with an ever-increasing loss of habitat through forest clearance and swamp drainage. The introduction of a further range of mammals led to a rapid decline in bird numbers. Rats, mustelids (ferrets, stoats and weasels), dogs and cats had an immediate effect on bird populations and still do; later, possums were introduced and have proved to be a threat to plant health and nesting birds. Other introduced pests affecting bird populations include egg-eating hedgehogs, while the very fabric of the forest habitat has been altered by introduced deer, goats, chamois, thar and pigs. Since European settlement, a further 11 species of birds have been declared extinct and several more hover on the brink. See also **Huia Feathers, Moa Hunters** and the **Last Moa**.

The Fairy People

Maori traditions of the fairy people, the children of the mist, etc., have spilled into European consciousness over the past 200 years. Maori tell of the turehu, the patupaiarehe and the korakorako, the original settlers of the land. The turehu were often red-haired and the patupaiarehe pale-skinned. If caught by the dawn, the patupaiarehe lost their magic and faded. Maori evidence of such fairy folk, living high in the mistlands, has been matched by Europeans who have sensed the nature of the forest and heard distant voices in uninhabited places, through the sighing of trees, echoes and the tumbling of water. The turehu of Mt Moehau, in the Coromandel Ranges, were fused into European myths about a wild and hairy figure, the Moehau Giant, which several expeditions searched for in the 1960s. At one stage an Australian expedition of 40 was planned to find the monster. Various suggestions were made, for example that the creature might have been an ape escaped from a circus. Local business folk did little to dispel the myth of a strange creature or creatures living on the rugged peninsula. According to Robyn [Jenkins] Gosset, author of *New Zealand Mysteries*, the legend was 'killed off in April 1970' when a local man described to her how the story had begun as a joke. (*New Zealand Mysteries* by Robyn Gosset, The Bush Press, Auckland, 1996.) Despite our differing cultural backgrounds, many New Zealanders have had their imaginations stirred by the nature of our more remote places. It is quite easy, for example, to hear distant voices from time to time in the murmuring acoustics of the bush.

'Far as a Man May Go'

The saying, attributed to Captain James Cook of his voyages of discovery in the South Seas, has traditionally been applied to the seas about New Zealand. In fact Cook made the observation while aboard the *Resolution* on his second voyage, when the ship pressed into Antarctic seas and approached a land of ice. 'I will not say that it was impossible to get in among this ice, but I will assert that the bare attempting of it would be a very dangerous enterprise ...' he wrote. 'I whose ambition leads me not only further than any other man has been before me, but as far as I think it possible for man to go, was not sorry for this interruption.'

'Farmer Bill'

William Ferguson Massey (1856–1925), conservative Reform prime minister from 1912 until his death, earned his soubriquet from his advocacy of freehold rather than leasehold farms. Faced with industrial breakdown on the wharves during the primary export season of 1913, he had hundreds of farmers sworn in as special constables. See **Massey's Cossacks.**

The Father of Auckland

Shortly before Governor Hobson chose Auckland as the site for the new capital of Auckland, in 1840, two Scotsmen established a base on nearby Motukorea Island. Brown gave his name to the island and John Logan Campbell (1817–1912) became the 'father of Auckland'. A medical doctor, Logan Campbell founded a trading empire in the infant capital, including a liquor business and hotel chain. Using his fortune, Logan Campbell became the benefactor of Auckland and a much loved figure. He founded the co-operative Auckland Savings Bank, now owned by an Australian bank, and in 1855 became Superintendent of the Province of Auckland, a political post at the head of the regional system of government of that time. In 1901 he gave the city Campbell Park, the open land encompassing **One Tree Hill**, and was buried at the summit when he died in 1912, aged 95. Logan Campbell's experience as one of the first white settlers of Auckland is told in the readable reminiscence *Poenamu* which has been reprinted many times, as recently as the 1970s (by both Golden Press and Wilson & Horton).

The Featherston Riot

The Wairarapa town of Featherston was the site of a prisoner-of-war camp where Japanese servicemen were held during the Second World War. Some 800 prisoners were held in four compounds, once used as a New Zealand Army training camp. A mutiny by prisoners in Compound 2, on February 25, 1943, became violent. As Japanese with improvised weapons attacked, the New Zealand guards briefly opened fire. Forty Japanese died instantly and another eight died later of wounds. The wounded numbered 61 Japanese and seven New Zealanders, one of whom later died of his injuries. Students now study a play based on the incident, *Shuriken*, by Vincent O'Sullivan (Victoria University Press, Wellington, 1985).

Fencibles

During the **New Zealand Wars** of the 1860s military veterans of the British Empire were allocated land on the southern borders of Auckland in return for their willingness to defend the infant capital if required. Farmer settlements were built around Howick, Panmure, Otahuhu and Onehunga. The distinctive little fencible cottages and some of the defensive positions may still be found preserved in Auckland, including a cottage at Howick, a blockhouse at Onehunga and buildings in the historic village at MOTAT, Auckland's Museum of Transport and Technology.

The Fenian Riots

The pains of the Irish fought out on the West Coast goldfields at a time when a quarter of the population came from the Emerald Isle. When news arrived of the 'Manchester martyrs', Irishmen executed in Britain, Irish miners held a mock funeral at Hokitika on March 8, 1868. The ringleaders were arrested and troops brought in to supplement the volunteer militia. Things got worse when a Fenian took a shot at the visiting Duke of Edinburgh in Sydney. Then British 'loyalists' attacked the Fenians in the Battle of Addison's Flat (near Westport). David McGill reconstructs the time and the events in *The Lion and the Wolfhound* (Grantham House, Wellington, 1990).

Ferries

In early times river-crossings became major transport stops: a hotel, stables, store and ferry. Some can still be traced in the names of surviving villages, such as Lake Ferry, Wairarapa, though most have been

spanned by bridges. The ferry was usually a punt-like vessel that could be poled or pulled across the river, while kept on course by a cable. Ferries in Northland, from Port Opua in the Bay of Islands and Rawene in the Hokianga, are rather more substantial, depending nowadays on engine power to carry vehicles across the harbour arms. Traffic jams on the Auckland harbour bridge have led to the restoration of a number of ferry services across the Waitemata.

Field Days

Originally the description for a farmers' get-together in the field, usually to see 'how the other bloke does it', or to learn something from an expert. The National 'Fieldays' at Mystery Creek, near Hamilton, take the idea to the extreme. In early winter around 30,000 people a day slosh about in the mud to see the latest in farm technology and **Do-it-yourself** ingenuity. Scientists from Ruakura Research Centre share the stage with backyard inventors and manufacturers in a show-and-tell performance to capture the interest of farmers. It is the biggest gathering of farmers in New Zealand and probably one of the more useful. In 1993, the 25th Anniversary Fieldays were extended from three to four days to cater for the crowds. Nearly 140,000 visited and more than $100 million worth of business was done.

Finials and Fancywork

Finishing detail of colonial architecture. These turned wooden spires were added to the gable end of many wooden houses, included here as surviving folklore from Britain, where they were said to stop witches roosting. The acorn shapes on fence posts, stair newels and blind cords also have a superstitious origin. According to architect-historian Charles Fearnley, the acorn has 'two different and significant meanings'. To some it was a fertility symbol ('Tall oaks from little acorns grow') and the other meaning, more often connected with buildings, is that it is a charm against lightning. The life-sized wooden acorns on the blind cords protected each window of the house from lightning. Sourced from *Colonial Style: pioneer buildings of New Zealand*, by Charles Fearnley (The Bush Press, Auckland, 1986).

Fire in the Fern

A reference to the spread of **Hau Hau**ism among Maori during the late 1860s giving rise to further warfare and the hunt for **Te Kooti**. The simile for conflagration is apt. Used by William Pember Reeves in his pioneer history *The Long White Cloud* (published 1898).

The Fires of Tamatea

A South Island Maori tradition of the 14th century still expressed in the farming practice of **Burning Off** the hills. The fires of Tamatea are said by some to have swept the **Moa** birds from the bush and created the great grass plains of the South Island. Old burnt totara logs can still be found in the Otago hills, where some forest survives in damp gullies among the tussock tops.

The First Capital *see* Okiato, Old Russell

The First Christmas

The chaplain to the convict settlement of New South Wales, the Rev. Samuel Marsden, was the first to hold a Christian service for Maori in New Zealand, on December 25, 1814. Aboard Marsden's brig *Active* was the chief Ruatara, returning from Sydney, and Marsden held the service on the beach below Ruatara's pa at Rangihoua in the Bay of Islands. Hundreds of Maori gathered, uncomprehending, as Marsden preached from St Luke ii, 10: 'I bring you glad tidings of great joy.' He then sailed on to Paihia to purchase a hundred acres for a mission station.

The First Echelon

The first New Zealand soldiers to go abroad in the Second World

War were mainly volunteers. They landed in Egypt in February 1940 and fought through Greece, Crete and North Africa. After four years in uniform the First, Second and Third Echelons came home on furlough, only to be asked to return to war again. Many of the men argued that they should not have to, until all fit single men had served abroad. Censorship did not halt the debate, politicians were wary of the situation and in time the number required to return was whittled back and those who refused to return were officially forgiven by the end of the war.

The First European Settlement in New Zealand

Deep among the enclosing islands of Dusky Sound is tiny Luncheon Cove, site of the first known European house in New Zealand. Here, in 1792, Captain Raven of the *Britannia* set ashore 11 men to go sealing. They built a large house with flax thatch, and a drain running past that can still be traced in the bush. In small boats they would sail from reef to reef killing seals for their skins and oil. The sealing crew also built a small ship, a 65 tonner some 16.15 m (53 ft) long, in case the *Britannia* never returned. Ten months later, when *Britannia* did come back, the ship was left on the stocks at Luncheon Cove. She was later finished by the crew of a rotting East Indiaman called the *Endeavour* and sailed away. See the **Wreck of the *Endeavour*.**

The First Four Ships, Canterbury

In Canterbury value is still placed on descent from the settlers who arrived in the First Four Ships. These vessels arrived at Lyttelton in December 1850, bringing the **Canterbury Pilgrims**, members of an Anglican settlement promoted by the Canterbury Association and the New Zealand Company. Christchurch got its reputation for being more English than England from this endeavour to transplant the ideals of Anglicanism and English society to these shores. The first ship into Lyttelton was the *Charlotte Jane* on December 16, followed the same day by the *Randolph* and the *Sir George Seymour* on the morrow. The *Cressy*, with a damaged mast, arrived on December 27. An immigration barracks awaited them at Lyttelton, but a road over the Port Hills was not complete so the pilgrims crossed over to the swampy site of Christchurch by way of the **Bridle Path** on foot.

The First Four Ships, Otago

The Otago Association had its first four ships of immigrants, too. This New Zealand Company settlement was of Free Scots Presbyterians in Dunedin, 'the **New Edinburgh** of the South'. First to arrive in 1848 were the *John Wickliffe* and the *Phillip Laing*, bringing a total of 344 settlers, only 15 of whom had bought land. The *Bernicia* and the *Blundell* brought a further 200 settlers later that year. Dunedin was slow to flourish, but became the most prosperous place in the country after gold was discovered inland in the 1860s. See **Wakefield Settlements**.

The First Man to Fly

Claims are still sometimes made that New Zealander Richard Pearse (1877–1953) possibly flew before the Wright brothers, making his the first-ever powered flight. First Pearse built his own twin-cylinder engine, then put together an aircraft from scrap materials found about his father's farm at Waitohi, South Canterbury. Then, in 1902 and 1903 he flew his aeroplane, in short hops, across the farm paddocks. The length and nature of these 'hops' have been the subject of arguments about whether Pearse really flew before the Wright brothers. Pearse built two further aircraft. The third can be seen at the Museum of Transport and Technology in Auckland along with a four-cylinder engine built by Pearse in 1909. After reviewing the evidence of witnesses, C. Geoffrey Rodliffe asserts that, 'The question at issue is not whether or not Richard Pearse flew, but when he first did so – during the Easter holidays in March 1902, or just before Easter at the end of March in 1903.' The Wright brothers' first flight was in December 1903. Refer to *Richard Pearse: Pioneer Aviator*, by C. Geoffrey Rodliffe published by MOTAT (Auckland, 1978).

The First Place to See the Light of Day

Said of Mt Hikurangi, East Cape. This claim is based on its elevation of 1839 m above the easternmost part of New Zealand, and being the first to receive the sun's rays as they cross 180 degrees of longitude east of Greenwich. This puts New Zealand 12 hours ahead of Britain. The claim does not provide for the wobble in the International Date Line, however, which allows Tonga, eastern Fiji and the Chatham Islands, all farther east, to be in the same time zone as New Zealand. In strictly longitudinal terms Tonga should be nearly 24 hours behind New Zealand on the other side of a 180-degree dateline. The deviation in the dateline lets Tongans and Chatham Islanders get up with New Zealanders 24 hours earlier than geography would otherwise allow. So they must then be the first to see the light of any new day even if, in strictly geographic terms, theirs is but the dawn of yesterday. Geographically, Hikurangi is the ancestral mountain of the Ngati Porou tribe, handed back into their control by the government to mark the dawning of the first day of the 1990 sesquicentennial celebrations.

The First Sighting of New Zealand by Cook's Expedition

The credit for first sighting New Zealand on the voyage of the *Endeavour* in 1769 was given by Lieutenant James Cook to a ship's boy, Nicholas Young. Cook offered the reward of a gallon of rum to the first to see land – two gallons if they found it at night. Nicholas, recorded by a shipmate to be aged about 12 years, was employed as a 'surgeon's boy'. Cook named the southern tip of **Poverty Bay** Young Nick's Head, though it is more likely the boy saw first the mountains behind.

First Up, Best Dressed

In Depression days children often walked to school in bare feet. In large families the first out of bed often got the best of the available clothes.

Fish and Chips

'Shark and taties' or lemonfish deep-fried in batter accompanied by French fries, as we call chips these days. The basis of the fast-food business before its Americanisation by hamburgers following the Second World War and subsequently McDonalds, KFC and others. Generally, fish and chips come insulated by layers of newsprint. Small fish and chip shops may be found trading late in the vicinity of hotels and at highway junctions. Still a popular takeaway, appearing also in refined form, using snapper or terakihi, etc., in formal restaurants.

The Fish of Maui *see* Te Ika a Maui.

Fly Camps

An overnight bivvy or bivouac camp, high in the mountains or far from base. Set up usually with a tent fly spread over the sleeping area or making a shelter against an overhanging rock. The fly camp is a refuge from the elements when advancing to climb a peak early in the day or wanting to be there on the tops when the game animals are moving. Modern lightweight tents are as light and easy to carry as the old japara tent fly of yesteryear, but the name sticks for that advance camp.

Fool's Gold

A scatter of shining dust in the washings of a gold pan fooled many a **New Chum** that he was on the way to riches. In fact the material was mica dust or iron pyrites, which was shortly washed or blown away. Heavier gold dust settled to the bottom of the pan.

Football Jerseys

Rugged cotton-interlock jerseys, at first in colour bands and now often in colour panels, symbolising the team colours of their wearers. New Zealand-made football jerseys are now sold overseas and have become a fashion garment, popular with tourists who may return home with what looks like an All Black jersey. Yachting and cricket gear has assumed similar panache.

45 Degrees South

Not just a well-named Dunedin whisky but also a geographic latitude midway between the Equator and the South Pole. It is marked by the roadside of State Highway One near Hilderthorpe, just north of Oamaru in North Otago. No particular magic attends, but the knowledge can help to give a sense of place and progress to a journey across the flat plain, in either direction.

The Forty-Hour Week

The fundamental right of the worker was long believed to be a living wage for a 40-hour week. Its proponents called for 'eight hours of work, eight hours play, eight hours sleep and eight bob a day'. Samuel Duncan Parnell (1810–90) introduced the idea to New Zealand as early as 1840 when he arranged for his builders to work 40-hour weeks in infant Wellington, yet the 40-hour week became general only from 1935, when it was introduced to union awards by the first Labour government. In many sectors the hours were shrunk further over the years, notably to an expected 37.5 hours a week in government and local-body service, a sector that came to employ more than 40 per cent of 'workers' in the years before '**Rogernomics**'. Parallel to the 40-hour week was a punitive tax regime which imposed a penalty tax on those who earned more by way of secondary employment. The tighter job market and increased competitiveness since 1987 has meant fewer people enjoy the luxury of a five-day, 40-hour week.

Fossil Forests

Trees preserved in swamps or volcanic material provide a fossil or sub-fossil record of New Zealand's ancient forests. Sometimes these have turned to stone, as in Curio Bay, Southland. At Takapuna Beach in Auckland the ghost outlines of burnt kauri trunks may be seen in a volcanic reef. The remnants of kauri trees, buried in swamps for 30,000 to 50,000 years, can be recovered for use in furniture. See **Swamp Kauri**.

The Founding of Britannia

The New Zealand Company founded its first Wellington settlement, called Britannia, on the banks of the Hutt River at Petone in January 1840. The river flooded and the disgusted settlers moved to Thorndon, now in central Wellington. See **Wellington's First Five Ships**, **Wakefield Settlements**.

Four by two, 4" x 2"

It is said that the innovative New Zealander can build anything from a piece of **Number Eight Wire** and a piece of 4" x 2". The 4" x 2" is builders' framing timber, its name surviving from the days of Imperial measurements. The size, 10 cm x 5 cm in metric measure, is still the standard for construction framing. There must be few places in this land of **Wooden Houses** where there are not a few short lengths lying about in a **Backyard Shed** or stored under the house awaiting a **Do-it-yourself** project.

Fred Dagg

A New Zealand country character created by humorist John Clarke, who subsequently went on to Australia where Dagg became an archetypal Australian. In 1973–77, Fred Dagg personified the **Practical Kiwi Joker** and the **Good Keen Man,** in a number of television skits on current affairs shows, before discovering that pastures were more fertile across the Tasman. Fred and his family of 'Trevs' also made a film and recorded an album that included the still-popular hit song about **Gumboots** before 'shooting through'.

Freedom of Religion

New Zealand is a secular state, though school boards have the option of allowing religious instruction of a non-sectarian, non-compulsory kind. Many Catholics choose to send their children to Church schools. State subsidies now go to churches of many denominations on the grounds that they are providing basic education as well.

Freezing Works *see* Frozen Meat

French Akaroa

French surnames and place names give character to the Banks Peninsula district of Akaroa. The settlement sprang from French ambitions in the Pacific, a factor influencing British annexation of New Zealand in 1840. As preparations were made for the **Treaty of Waitangi,** settlers of the Nanto-Bordelaise Company prepared to settle at Akaroa on Banks Peninsula. When a French Government escort vessel, *L'Aube*, arrived at the Bay of Islands in July 1840, the new Governor William Hobson despatched HMS *Britomart* under Captain Stanley to 'take possession' of the South Island again. When the French settlers aboard *Compte de Paris* landed at Akaroa on August 19, 1840, the British flag had been flying there for just nine days.

French Pass

An 'only just' for the commander of the French exploring expedition of 1826–27. Dumont d'Urville carefully premeditated the chances of sailing his ship *Astrolabe* through the channel between the Marlborough Sounds mainland and the island that now bears his name. He nearly lost his ship, for the calm conditions he sought were accompanied by a loss of wind and the *Astrolabe* carried over a reef in the tide race. Once through, d'Urville named the narrow passage for France but modestly accepted his officers' request that he name the adjacent island d'Urville because he 'did not think it right to refuse this mark of esteem from such brave men'. D'Urville's record of New Zealand is translated in Olive Wright's *New Zealand 1826–27* (Wingfield Press, Wellington, 1950).

Friendly Road *see* 'Aunt Daisy' and 'Uncle Scrim'

The Front Room

Having a front room was a mark of civilisation in the bush and there are still many homes in New Zealand where the front room is considered special. In the days of the gracious villas and their verandahed cottage equivalents, the front room lay to the left or right of the front door, regardless of whether or not the house faced the sun. Many a north-facing house condemned its occupants to living on the shaded south side because the front room, shrouded in heavy curtains, was reserved for best. Here the women of the house entertained formally, holding **'At Homes'** on a regular basis, even announcing the fact in local newspapers or by card of invitation. It was a place used by the family mainly on Sunday. The front room usually contained a formal lounge suite, with high-backed chairs and tables for taking tea. There were rugs or animal skins on the floor. The thick velvet curtains hung by brass rings from wooden rails above the windows, with white lace or muslin screening between. Paintings of ancestors or places of origin adorned the wall, along with gilt mirrors. Some bravely included local scenes, painted in dark oils, of southern fiords or the bush. This was a place to keep the family Bible and perhaps a

piano. A photograph or two recorded a wedding, or someone who died in the wars. Families lived at close quarters, sharing bedrooms and dining-room, rather than use the front room every day. Although the decor may have changed with the years there are still many New Zealand homes where the formality of a front room is maintained, used for receiving guests on a more formal basis than in the kitchen or family room.

Frozen Meat

The invention of refrigeration saved the New Zealand farming industry from economic depression in the 1880s. Formerly dependent on the sale of wool and hides, farmers welcomed refrigerated vessels that made it possible to export meat as well. The first shipment left Port Chalmers for Britain aboard the *Dunedin* on February 14, 1888. The shipment was arranged by Thomas Brydone of the New Zealand and Australia Land Company, who had nearly 5000 sheep slaughtered at its North Otago property at Totara. The Totara farmstead is now a national historic place. Freezing works soon became a feature of country districts and provincial centres, and a major industry. Changing standards and demands during the 1980s led to a rationalisation of meatworks. Large factories continue to close while new specialist slaughterhouses have begun butchering meat to the requirements of more selective foreign markets. The best meat still goes abroad.

Gabriel's Gully and Gabriel Read

On a branch of the Tuapeka River, near Lawrence, Gabriel Read discovered gold on May 23, 1861. 'At a place where a kind of road crossed on a shallow bar I shovelled away about two and a half feet of gravel, arrived at a beautiful soft slate and saw the gold shining like the stars in Orion on a dark frosty night.' Read, a Tasmanian veteran of the Californian and Victorian goldfields, began his search on behalf of the Otago Provincial Council. He followed the evidence of **'Black Peter'** or Edward Peters who had been living off small returns of gold, and thus sparked a gold rush that brought diggers from throughout New Zealand and from the North American and Australian fields. Read's gold changed the fortunes of the depressed Dunedin settlement and made it the commercial centre of New Zealand. The goldfields produced upwards of a million ounces of gold in the first two years. Read received two grants of £500 as his reward. He sought little personal fortune from his discoveries, instead helping the diggers to organise themselves along the lines he had learned in California and Australia. After finding the rich Waitahuna field, also in the Lawrence area, Read sought release from his post with the government and made his home in Hobart.

Gallipoli

The landings by the combined Australian and New Zealand Army Corps at Gallipoli in the Dardanelles came to traumatise both nations. The horrific losses as the Anzacs stormed ashore into the waiting guns of the Turks on April 25, 1915, are marked annually in both Australia and New Zealand by a national day of mourning that now commemorates all war dead. Some 2721 New Zealanders were killed at Gallipoli and 4752 wounded.

Gambling

New Zealanders have a reputation for frequent gambling. Horse racing, lotteries and casinos are the high-profile fields, with housie and gaming machines competing with prize competitions for people's interest. The State has been the major entrepreneur, at first banning some forms of gambling then gradually introducing games and taking the operator's profit for charitable and artistic purposes. This is supposed to make gambling fair, more respectable and controlled. That there is big money in gambling is revealed in the accounts of the **TAB** (horses, greyhound racing and some sporting events) with a turnover of more than a billion dollars in 2000–01. The Lotteries Commission runs games of chance including the Lotto range, Instant Kiwi 'scratch cards' and Daily Keno. Its customers consist of 1.2 million New Zealanders a week. Notable New Zealand lotteries of the past have been the Art Unions, which became the Golden Kiwi in 1961. There are six licensed casinos, two of them in Queenstown. The installation of limited pay-out coin games in hotel bars continues to amuse and frustrate Australian tourists who also find it hard to understand the workings of our 'poker' machines, which have to give a third of all profits to the community. A 1991 estimate of the pub/club 'pokies', before the creation of casinos, gave a turnover of $635 million – more than for Lotto and Instant Kiwi combined. In 2000, club/pub pokies turned over nearly $3.75 billion. The gross amount wagered in 2004 was around $8.6 billion, but that includes a factor for reinvested winnings. The actual expenditure was $2.39 billion. (Statistical detail from *New Zealand Official Yearbooks 2002/2006*, Statistics New Zealand, Wellington.)

Garage Sales

Clearing out unwanted household goods, often before shifting house, for some quick cash and Saturday fun. Take the car out of the garage and set out the surplus – there are those buyers who are so addicted they will pick up anything for a bargain. Some folk promote regular but 'moveable' garage sales as a tax-free lurk. Smaller lots shift fast at a Boot Sale, selling from the back of a car at the local flea market, but beware the pre-dawn rush of dealers swiftly leaving you with dross. Offer toys the kids no longer want, tired paperbacks, pots, pans, china and ghastly gifts. Tools and hardware items go well; so do building scraps and bits left-over that a handyman might find a need for sometime, if the new owner has a bigger garage.

The Garrett Gang

A convict veteran of Norfolk Island, Henry Garrett arrived on the Otago goldfields to make his fortune from the miners in 1861. With a gang of seven others he laid a trap on the bush road over Maungatua, the route taken by gold-miners returning to Dunedin from **Gabriel's Gully**. Two men met each traveller and told them of a short cut through the bush. Here, away from the road, they were tied to a tree and robbed. By the end of the day 15 men were tied to trees, though a boy with 200 ounces of gold got through because his dray could not negotiate the track to the trap. Garrett escaped to Sydney but was brought back and imprisoned in Dunedin. From *Gold Rush Country of New Zealand*, by Gordon Ell (The Bush Press, Auckland, 1987). See **Burgess-Kelly Gang**.

General Freyberg, VC

A Morrinsville dentist who later became a commanding general in the Second World War first distinguished himself at **Gallipoli** in 1915. Lieutenant Bernard Freyberg swam ashore under cover of darkness on the eve of the Anzac landings to create a diversion from the main point of planned attack. A New Zealand champion swimmer, Freyberg towed ashore a raft of flares and set them off along a beach in the face of the enemy. Then, in the freezing waters of the Dardanelles he had to find his way back to his blacked-out ship. Freyberg was awarded the Distinguished Service Order for this act of daring, the first of three he received during the First World War. Later, in France, he was awarded the Victoria Cross for personal valour in the battle for Beaucourt. After the war Freyberg remained with the British Army, as a professional soldier, until retired on fitness grounds in 1937 (he was wounded nine times during the First World War). When New Zealand entered the Second World War, Major-General Freyberg was put in command of the 2nd New Zealand Expeditionary Force, leading it through North Africa,

Greece, Crete and Italy. After the war, as Lieutenant-General Sir Bernard Freyberg, he was Governor-General of New Zealand for six years. Later he was made a Baron and Lieutenant-Governor of Windsor Castle.

General Grant's Gold

The treasure of the *General Grant* has drawn several expeditions south to the stormy waters of the Auckland Islands, where the ship struck on May 6, 1886. The *General Grant* was supposed to have been driven into a cave in the sea cliffs, adding to the romance and danger of the search for her gold. Although 15 survived the wreck, no one has yet been able to pick up her gold bullion from the Victorian fields. The castaways settled on Disappointment Island and spent 18 months living on seals and birds before rescue. In that time four more men were lost; three on an abortive journey without compass in search of help, one of illness. Expeditions to locate the gold have been undertaken as recently as the 1970s.

Gentle Annie and Roaring Meg

Two popular place names surrounded by yarns that are usually unsubstantiated. Any Gentle Annie usually means a big, steep climb. A Roaring Meg is often a rumbustious stream hard to cross. Local folklore can usually dig up a barmaid with similar qualities who worked nearby. A popular washing machine once appropriated Gentle Annie's reputation. For similarly recurrent popular place names, see **Goat** and **Rabbit Islands**.

Gentlemen Farmers

Landowners who don't get their hands dirty on the farm. Some of the prosperous run-holders of the South Island earned the title during the wool boom of the 1950s, but the English traditions were basically lost in pioneer times when practicality demanded that everyone worked on the sheep runs. Absentee owners are sometimes described as gentlemen farmers when they appear with their managers at rural occasions. New Zealand has a growing tradition of part-time 'farmers' commuting each day, to and from **Ten-acre Blocks**. City investors are known as **Queen Street Farmers** and similar terms of deprecation.

George Fairweather Moonlight

The lyrical names of this man suited his mysterious journeys in search of gold. Yet it has been suggested these were nicknames given to a foundling child left at the door of a Scottish workhouse on a moonlit night of fair weather. Moonlight was a 'forty-niner' from the Californian rushes who arrived in Otago via the Victorian fields in 1861. There his name first appears on the map at Moonlight, near MacRaes Flat. Then, further inland his name appears on a tributary of the Shotover, Moonlight Creek, flowing from Lake Luna near Moke Creek, where the prospector discovered a major goldfield. Moonlight joined the rush to the Wakamarina River in Marlborough in 1864 before exploring further inland and discovering new fields in the Buller valleys, the Matakitaki (where his name appears at Moonlight Point), the Mangles and the Maruia. In 1866, George Moonlight gave his name to new diggings on the inland slopes of the Paparoa Ranges, where Moonlight Creek is still on the map. Moonlight later became a storekeeper and hotelier in the Murchison district, but he died in search of gold. In 1884 he went missing on a prospecting trip in the Station Creek area of the Maruia and his body was not found for several months.

George Wilder

New Zealand's best-known prison escaper became a folk hero in the 1960s. People helped him stay on the run: the Howard Morrison Quartet produced a song about him. George Wilder first escaped in May 1962 while serving a four-year sentence and was at large for 64 days. This led to 39 more charges and his sentence increased to seven years. He escaped from Mt Eden Prison in 1963 and was at large for 172 days before recapture at a possum-hunter's hut off the **Napier-Taupo Road**. With his sentence now increased to 13 years, Wilder escaped again in February 1965, with others, but the ensuing hostage drama cost some public sympathy: he got five more years in jail. Wilder's escapades included doubling back when being hunted and joining his own search party, and leaping down a sheer 10-m bank to escape. Liberal calls for his rehabilitation led to Wilder's release on parole in 1969 after serving eight years of an 18-year sentence. A breach of parole led to another chase that ended in a raid on a Rotorua camping ground by the armed offenders' squad. Wilder was sentenced to another three years and the remainder of his previous sentence, but was released early. Another famous escaper, Joseph Pawelka, a butcher of Kimbolton near Palmerston North, kept search parties busy in 1910–11: during the hunt an armed civilian searcher was shot dead when he was mistaken for the escaper. Pawelka disappeared in 1911 and there is still speculation as to what might have become of him.

Geothermal Power

Harnessing the energy of volcanic steam has led to New Zealand technology being used in several geothermal areas around the world to make electricity. The first scheme at Wairakei, near Taupo, produced 153 megawatts and took the puff out of a celebrated geothermal wonderland including several famous geysers. Later efforts at Ohaaki, south of Rotorua, tapped 106 megawatts from deeper steamfields with less obvious effect on surface phenomena, though the ground around a meeting house began to subside. The geothermal power schemes generate six per cent of New Zealand's electricity, and more are planned.

Giant Lizards

Maori tales of giant lizards called kawekaweau fired the imaginations of bushmen in the 19th century. These creatures were said to be more than half a metre long but their existence was attributed to legends or folk memories of creatures experienced in other homelands of the Maori. More recent research, reported by herpetologist Tony Whitaker in the *Forest and Bird* journal, has involved comparing a giant lizard in a French museum with New Zealand's small geckos and noting how closely related they appear. Unfortunately, no one knows where the French collected the specimen.

Giants of the Three Kings

The *Journal* of Abel Tasman's search for the Great South Land in 1642–43 reveals a fascination with giants. Going ashore in Tasmania, the Dutch declared that only giants could have made the steps cut into some tree trunks. Off the **Three Kings Islands** of New Zealand they again decided that distant Maori, striding the clifftops, were truly giants and drew them as such in their *Journal*. Modern writers have pointed out that Europeans of those days probably had an average height of about 1.52 m (five feet), which could make a Maori male (said by Cook's naturalist Joseph Banks to be the size of the larger Europeans) an impressively tall person.

The Girls' War

Inter-tribal fighting in the Bay of Islands before the Treaty of Waitangi was sparked when two women of opposing tribes were said to have fallen out over a whaling captain in February 1830. The fighting spread among other women at Kororareka, or the **Hell Hole of the Pacific** as Russell was once known. Ultimately the male warriors joined in. A hundred were killed along the beach at Russell in the first day and 40 the next. Missionaries from Paihia interceded and the Rev. Samuel Marsden finally negotiated a peace. The tribal politics and personalities are well described by Jack Lee in *I have named it the Bay of Islands* (Hodder & Stoughton, Auckland, 1983).

Goat and Rabbit Islands

New Zealanders are prone to giving trite and unimaginative names to their landmarks. Maori on the other hand used much poetry and polysyllables, which has meant many of their names have slipped from common knowledge over the years. The lack of originality in the naming of Goat Island is actually replicated within a few kilometres off the Rodney coast, at the Marine Laboratory near Leigh and in Kawau Bay just to the south. Rabbit Island crops up next to Goat (formerly Takangaroa) in the Mayne Islands near Kawau and again off Opoutere Beach in Coromandel, formerly in Lake Wanaka (now Crescent Island), and again off Nelson. For that matter Rabbit's neighbour off Coromandel is called Slipper, as is another similarly shaped island off the Rodney coast not too far from the Rabbit Island there. An initiative from the New Zealand Geographic Board to reinvest some of the original Maori names not only brings back some of the past: it could also make navigation easier.

'God Defend New Zealand' *see* National Anthems

God Save the Queen *see* National Anthems

God's Own Country

'The finest place on earth.' God's Own Country was a favourite description of New Zealand, frequently lauded by the Liberal government of **King Dick,** Richard John Seddon. Egalitarianism and social welfare made New Zealand a promising place to live in the 1890s. Thomas Bracken, lyricist of 'God Defend New Zealand', produced an epic poem on the subject, beginning:

> *Give me God's own country! there to live and there to die*
> *God's own country! fairest region 'neath the southern sky.*

A later wit reduced the name to Godzone.

Gold and Greenstone Trails

The passes across the Southern Alps were originally used by Maori to reach the West Coast rivers where precious **Greenstone** was found. European explorers and gold-miners used their traditions to find trails from the settlements of Canterbury and Otago. Some old gold trails, such as Haast and Arthur's Pass, now carry major routes across the Alps. Others are all but forgotten except by trampers and mountaineers. Those routes include Browning Pass in the upper Rakaia and Harper Pass, linking the Hurunui in Canterbury with the Taramakau in Westland. It is hard to envisage today how miners on horseback and **Drovers**, with stock to feed them, ever made their way over the unbridged rivers and through the rocky defiles of the Alps.

Golden Kiwi *see* Gambling

Golden Shears

The national championship for competitive sheep **Shearing**. Such competition is innate in a trade that rewards practitioners on a piece rate basis, and where workers have a hierarchy, based on their rate of throughput. Competitions originated about the turn of the 20th century and can often be watched at the local **Agricultural and Pastoral Show**. The international Golden Shears have been held annually in Masterton since 1961.

Goldfields Balladeer *see* The Inimitable Thatcher

Goldie's Maori

Detailed portraits in oil of Maori leaders painted by Charles Frederick Goldie (1870–1947) command high prices today. Born in Auckland, Goldie spent four years studying painting in Paris before returning to Auckland to teach and paint. His co-operation with former master Louis John Steele produced the familiar epic painting of 'the arrival of the Maori' with skeletal figures pointing landward in pop-eyed anguish. His most successful work, sometimes repeated years later, depicted the facial moko or tattoo of many surviving 19th-century Maori. Another illustrator of Maori elders and their moko was Bohemian-born Gottfried Lindauer (1839–1926). See **Maori Woman and Child.** Both are widely represented in galleries, and particularly by large collections in the Auckland Art Gallery and the Auckland War Memorial Museum.

Gold Rushes

News of a gold find could run like wildfire through a goldfield in the early days. Men who were not doing well – and that was the majority – would light on the prospect of a new find and follow the leaders to the next prospect. Overnight tent towns of 1000–2000 would spring up, only to be abandoned, perhaps only days later, for a better prospect. Westland has many examples of ghost towns that once boasted theatres, pubs and newspapers, that flourished for at best a year or two before sinking back into the bush. Rushes occurred in every gold-bearing district, however; the first was in Coromandel where the Rings found gold in 1852. The tradition dates back to the discovery of gold in North America. The practices of the 'Forty-niners' of the Californian Rushes of 1849 spread with them to the goldfields of Australia, and then New Zealand and on, to the Yukon fields of Alaska. In San Francisco the harbour became jammed with ships whose sailors had deserted in response to the cry 'Rush ho'. At Collingwood in Nelson Province a gold rush in 1857 brought men not only from all over New Zealand but also veterans who had been on the Victorian and Californian fields. The rush to the Tuapeka fields was sparked by **Gabriel Read** reporting

gold to the Otago government in 1861. Within a week 1000 men were on the diggings, walking over rough tracks from Dunedin carrying tent, equipment and supplies weighing perhaps 35 kg. Runholders with food for sale and ferrymen often profited more than the individual miners. Ships from around New Zealand and overseas brought more miners as the discoveries spread through inland Otago. The population of the Province doubled in two years, quadrupled in four. Many miners left reasonably paying ground for chances of new riches as the rushes continued through the Tuapeka valleys, about Lawrence, into the Dunstan, the Arrow, Shotover, St Bathans and Naseby districts. Then 2000 miners in a fortnight left for the Marlborough fields when gold was discovered in the Wakamarina Valley in 1864. The rushes then moved to Westland, beginning with the great Hokitika Rush of 1865. Population rose rapidly on the Coast to around 30,000 people. Sometimes the government gold commissioners tried to bring order to the rushes, issuing licences and 'opening' the field officially. But the fastest to the field still got the best spots. Sometimes rumour got ahead of reality, resulting in a **Duffer Rush**, to a place with no gold. Miners reaching a field would 'peg out' a claim, driving in posts at the four corners of a square, with each man entitled to a plot 24 ft by 24 ft (about 50 sq m). Once the immediate gold was won miners needed to join associations or companies to work more difficult land. Capital and organisation was needed to bring in water by race systems, sometimes from many kilometres away, and to fund machinery such as hydraulic lifts, poppet heads and sluicing monitors. For individual miners it was often easier to follow the rushes to new fields. There was even a gold rush in the Karangahake Gorge, a centre of quartz mining near Thames, when alluvial gold washed down from the reefs was discovered in 1875. The last gold rush was at Kumara in Westland in 1876.

'Gone up North for a While'

In the days before the contraceptive pill or abortion on personal grounds, hundreds of unfortunate young women left their home locality, before their pregnancy advanced enough to be noticed, and had their child elsewhere. Of the missing women it was sometimes explained that they had 'gone up north for a while'. Often this was true; the Motherhood of Man movement had a large maternity hospital in Auckland as did the Salvation Army and the Sisters of Mercy. Also, in the greater anonymity of a bigger city a young woman might board with relatives until confinement, without attaching the disgrace of unmarried motherhood in a closed southern community.

'Good Governor Grey'

Controversial, intelligent and independent, Sir George Grey (1812–98) took more than a vice-regal interest in the young colony of New Zealand. In his first term as Governor he learned Maori and recorded traditional myths and legends from the northern and central regions. He also made the State the only body able to buy land from Maori and established provincial councils to represent the settlements in New Zealand. Formerly a military officer and explorer in Western Australia, Grey was earlier Governor of South Australia (1841–45), studying native language and custom there in order to govern sympathetically two races. Grey arrived in New Zealand at a critical point during the war in the North in 1845, joining the troops himself. Again his interest in indigenous cultures and languages was influential. Grey's respect for Maori land and custom won him much support during his first term as Governor up to 1853. Then, after a seven-year term as Governor of the Cape Colony, Sir George Grey returned to New Zealand as Governor in 1861. This time he had to deal with the wars in Taranaki and Waikato. After his replacement in 1868, Grey spent time in Britain lecturing on colonial affairs and liberalism, and campaigned as an independent for Parliament. Then, in 1871 he returned to New Zealand, retiring to

Mansion House on Kawau, where he spent his time in study and transforming the island with exotic species. He was then Superintendent of Auckland (Province) in 1875–76, during which time the provincial governments were abolished. His liberal views formed the basis of a like-minded group who made him Premier of New Zealand (1877–79) and he remained a Member of Parliament until 1890. As a private member, Grey managed to introduce the principle of 'one man, one vote' in an amendment to a representation bill of 1889. Grey's collections of books and ethnographic materials enrich libraries in New Zealand and South Africa. The source of his wealth has never been traced but he died poor in London in 1898 where he had recently been reconciled with his wife after 40 years apart. Grey's *Polynesian Mythology* is often reprinted and has been the major written source of traditional Maori legends since its first edition, then in Maori, in 1854.

The Grace Darling of New Zealand

The original Grace Darling was the daughter of a lighthouse keeper in Britain who rowed with her father to save sailors from a sinking ship. Her New Zealand counterpart was Huria Matenga, a Maori chieftainess of the Nelson coast who, with her husband and one other, saved all but one of the complement of the brigantine *Delaware* when it wrecked on the coast near their home at Whakapuaka. The 241-ton sailing ship was sailing from Nelson for Napier when she struck on rocks offshore on September 4, 1863. The mate endeavoured to swim ashore with a line but was badly injured in the attempt and hauled back on board assumed dead. Then Huria and Hemi Matenga, along with Hohapeta Kahupuku, swam off into the boiling surf to capture a line. Huria reached the rope first and the swimmers returned ashore to secure it on the rocks. Progressively they helped ashore 10 men, supporting them through the breaking waves and rocks. Only when the line was gone did the mate recover consciousness, climbing into the rigging from whence he finally dropped into the sea and drowned. There is an attractive portrait of Matenga (Julia Martin) by Gottfried Lindauer in the collection of the Nelson Art Gallery that helps to keep the story alive.

The Graham Murders

Stanley Graham took the lives of seven men in October 1941. Graham, who farmed in the Kowhitirangi district near Hokitika, was convinced that neighbours were poisoning his cows. When the police turned up to investigate things got out of hand and he shot them. After killing three and fatally wounding a fourth policeman, Graham took to the bush, living off the land while around a hundred police and Home Guard soldiers pursued him. It took 13 days and three more deaths before Graham was fatally wounded. In *New Zealand Sensations* (A.H. & A.W. Reed, Wellington, 1962), Rex Monigatti records that the German wartime propagandist Lord Haw Haw poked fun at the authorities, claiming a cable was sent to Graham saying 'You hold the South Island. Hitler sending another man to hold the North.' In the early 1980s the Graham manhunt was made into the movie *Bad Blood*.

The Great Depression or The Slump

The most traumatic civil event of 20th-century New Zealand. After the prosperous 1920s New Zealand was plunged into a well of unemployment and social misery by the international breakdown that followed the Wall Street Crash of 1929. An economy dependent on primary produce sold overseas was particularly vulnerable. Many farmers, settled after the First World War and still owing money, were forced to abandon their properties. Soon there were an estimated 100,000 unemployed in a population of 1.5 million and at a time when comparatively few women worked. The pitifully small dole had to be worked for, often on make-work projects where manpower substituted for machines just to fill in the day. Although in time unemployed were put to worthwhile public works, such as constructing the Lewis Pass road with pick and shovel and wheelbarrow, 'the dole' also produced the degrading sight of groups of men taking the place of horses to pull harrows, and jobs where one group dug holes to be filled in by the next. The hopelessness of the 'common man' led to the election of New Zealand's first Labour (socialist) government in 1935 and new schemes of social security and State-directed reconstruction. New Zealand writers of the 1930s and 1940s were among the traumatised and their books and poems and journalism reflect the all-pervading gloom. There are two more recent social histories by Tony Simpson; *The Sugarbag Years* contains many recollections, while *The Slump* takes a readable approach to the origins and effect of the Depression (both published by Penguin Books). The generations that lived through the Slump were then plunged into the Second World War; many of those who survived appeared happy to live in conformity after the war, secured by State subsidies and handouts, which they understandably believed they had earned. Ironically, many lived to see the institutions and welfare they had worked so hard for pulled to bits, by their middle-aged children, following the 1987 stock-market crash. The more prosperous survivors of the Depression were even lumbered with a tax surcharge for having too much – some ending their days with the label 'Old Greedies'.

The Great Fleet

An expression for the 12 voyaging canoes, long believed to have brought the Maori people to New Zealand, in one **Great Migration** in AD 1350. Maori genealogical research has now suggested that the canoes did not sail together and that indeed the existing tribes of New Zealand descend from some 85 'canoes'. Some of these waka are themselves mainly symbolic of a people belonging together as a tribal group and some of the canoe migrations may well originate within New Zealand. Refer to the **Great Migration** and **Moriori, Maruiwi**.

The Great Migration

Generations of New Zealanders, many Maori included, were brought up accepting the myth of the great migration and other tales about the early settlement of New Zealand. These traditions told that Aotearoa was discovered in AD 950 by **Kupe**, rediscovered by his descendant **Toi** in AD 1150 and settled by way of a great migration from **Hawaiki** in AD 1350. The story was recorded by such 19th-century scholars as Stephenson Percy Smith and accepted by most until the 1970s. Then, ethnologist D.R. Simmons examined the Maori traditions again and found the dates of various tribes did not match up. By counting back the generations of tribal whakapapa, Simmons argued that the canoes could not have come together but were spread over some 300 years of journeying. Besides which, the legend of 12 canoes sailing in a **Great Fleet** to populate New Zealand did not sit easily with the stories of some 85 canoes recorded among the tribes. There were also several different accounts of Kupe's voyaging, and tales of more than one Toi. Modern analysis tends to concentrate on traditional tales of individual tribes related to archaeological evidence. Settlement of New Zealand by Maori is now estimated to have been around 800 years ago. The canoe traditions are those of individual tribes settling new land, in some cases from within New Zealand. Associations of different canoes may reflect closer relationships. See also **Moriori, Maruiwi**. The canoe myths are detailed in *The Great New Zealand Myth,* by D.R. Simmons (A.H. & A.W. Reed, Wellington, 1976). For a modern summary of migration theories see *The Quest for Origins*, by K.R. Howe (Penguin, Auckland, 2003).

A Great Place to Bring Up Kids

New Zealand's open-air environment and a raft of social measures gave this country the reputation of being a 'Great Place to Bring Up Kids'. The Post-War 'baby boom' generations in particular enjoyed their **Overseas Experience** then came home to have their families. Homes were readily available then, on **Quarter-acre Sections** with room for the children to play. The medical costs of pregnancy, birth and childhood disease were all provided free by the Welfare State. The **Plunket Society** provided free care to 'help the Mothers and save the babies'. Education was free right through from kindergarten to excellent universities. Along the way there was **Free Milk in Schools**, possibly the by-product of a subsidised or State-controlled industry with spare product to dispose of. Much of this came to an end in the late 1980s. Medical costs became means-tested, parents increasingly paid for extras in their children's education, and education at the tertiary level became a major expense for parents and students themselves. The consequent effects on public health and social welfare have become apparent. Now New Zealand, with its comparatively clean environment and high standards of care, remains a great place to bring up kids – if you can afford to pay.

The Great South Land *see* Staten Landt and Abel Tasman

The Greatest Walk in the World

In deep Fiordland, the Milford Track has been billed as the Greatest Walk in the World since 1908. According to Rosalind Harker in her book *On the Milford Track* (The Bush Press, Auckland, 1984) an article by Blanche Baughan of Christchurch called 'A Notable Walk' was renamed by the editor of the *Spectator* of London as 'The Greatest Walk in the World'. The article was subsequently reprinted as a booklet by Whitcombe and Tombs. The Milford Track runs for 53 km (33 miles) from Lake Te Anau to Milford Sound over the Mackinnon Pass. Much of it is flat walking through glaciated valleys, but there is a steep up-and-down to the 1073 m pass. Many tourists travel light and stay in catered huts. The journey takes four days, first up the lake then to Glade Hut, next to Pompolona, then over the pass to Quintin and then out to Milford Sound. The Milford Track was pioneered by Quintin Mackinnon (1851–92) who crossed it from the east in 1888, meeting up with the track that Donald Sutherland had cut to the falls on the west side. The tourist walks began soon after exploration with a series of huts opened in 1889. The walk is the second-most popular, after the Abel Tasman Coastal Walk, of a series of Great Walks in New Zealand's national parks. (See **Tramping**.)

Greenstone

The family of jades or nephrites valued and used by Maori as a source of tools, weapons and ornament. Known collectively as pounamu, the stone is found in central and southern Westland and inland of the Southern Lakes. Legends describe some forms as the descendants of Poutini, a fish turned into stone. Inanga is such a variety, named for the colour of the whitebait, and found in the Arahura Valley up country from Greymouth. Kahurangi is a cloudy coloured stone while kawakawa is the dark variety found in the Taramakau valley. Tangiwai from Milford Sound and Poison Bay appears, when held against the light, to have captured tears in its dark depths; it is not true greenstone but a rock called bowenite and is used only for ornaments. See *Greenstone Trails*, by Barry Brailsford (A.H. & A.W. Reed, Wellington, 1984), and *Mana Pounamu: New Zealand Jade*, by Russell J. Beck with Maika Mason (Reed, Auckland, 2002).

The Grey 'Barber'

A katabatic wind that falls from the mountains of the Grey River Valley and funnels through the Gap at Greymouth in a fine white mist. It is cuttingly cold, thus 'The Barber'.

Grid-ironing *see* Run-holders

Grubstake

The miners' working capital. Going to the goldfields involved a minimum of equipment – gold pan, pick, shovel, sleeping roll and tent, but a man still needed his 'tucker' or 'grub'. A packhorse made things easier and such animals were expensive when in heavy demand from the **Diggers**. Later, if gold was found, there could be bills for piping and sluices. Prospectors turned to the storekeepers for an advance on their earnings, a 'grubstake' to get them started. The practice of buying and paying debts from gold recoveries was widespread in remote places, where gold was easier to come by than bank notes.

Gumboots

The traditional wear of farmers in damp districts. Britons call them Wellingtons after the Duke who wore them as field uniform. New Zealand gumboots come in several forms, from a full calf-length down to a more flexible boot size, including a late-lamented lace-up form that was particularly popular and comfortable for walking. With the free market changes of recent years good gumboots became hard to get, as boots of Asian manufacture captured the market. The virtues of gumboots have been lauded by comedian John Clarke (**Fred Dagg**), whose popular chant chorused, 'If it weren't for your gumboots, where would you be?' With their passion for competition, Kiwi folk have even developed a spectator sport called gumboot throwing, which sometimes figures as an attraction at country gatherings.

HART Halt All Racist Tours *see* Stop the Tour.

Haka

A Maori dance form emulated by sports teams, schoolboys and others wanting to make a nationalistic impression. Once, most teams mouthed meaningless mumbo-jumbo before their matches; now increased cultural sensitivity demands proper words, proper gestures and proper Maori. The All Blacks give a rendition of Te Rauparaha's haka 'Ka Mate, Ka Mate' before their games, though the jump at the end should not be part of it, according to Timoti Karetu, whose *Haka! The Dance of a Noble People* (Reed, Auckland, 1993) defines the art form. He quotes an Arawa haka that expresses the combination of gesture and energy in the haka thus:

> *Ringa pakia*
> *Uma tiraha*
> *Turi whatia*
> *Hora whai ake*
> *Waewae takahia kia kino*
> *Slap the hands against the thigh*
> *Puff out the chest*
> *Bend the knees*
> *Let the hips follow*
> *Stamp the feet as hard as you can.*

The Half-Gallon Jar, The Half-G

In the days of glass and Imperial pints, bulk beer was taken home by the half-G. Beer cost less pumped directly into the flagon than it did in bottles, and was more portable. The taste, however, lacked the subtlety of the bottled variety which was more usually drunk in the private bar or in more refined homes. A half-G was the basis of many a party ('**Ladies a Plate**') and was often served out of the back of a truck or car, illegally, outside dance halls in the days of **Six O'clock Closing.** The modern metric equivalent, in plastic, has added only the virtue of bouncing if it is fumbled.

The Half-Gallon, Quarter Acre, Pavlova Paradise

Social critic and tele-don Austin Mitchell so dubbed our country in this drubbing of life in the Welfare State 1960s-style. The book title picks up on some of our favourite icons, the half-gallon flagon of beer, the average suburban 'section' size and Godzone's best tucker. (Published by Whitcombe and Tombs in 1972.) Dr Mitchell, by now a British Labour MP, returned to New Zealand to write a less effective sequel, *Pavlova Paradise Revisited* (Penguin, Auckland, 2002), by which time the locals' outlook had probably moved further on than he had.

The Hamilton Jet *see* Jet Boat

Hang on a Minute Mate

Barry Crump expressed the subtleties of this fundamental piece of Kiwi communication when he used it as the motif in his novel of the same name. The expression carries with it significant undertones to the sensitive New Zealand ear, especially when preceded by the imperative 'Now' (hang on a minute mate) or 'Now just you' (hang on a minute mate). In a world of chronically phlegmatic characters, there is an air of determination in the expression, a sign that someone is about to take exception to the course of events. Crump's character Sam Cash, and his alter ego Harvey Wilson, develop the applications of the phrase to that of art. Read and enjoy *Hang on a Minute Mate* by Barry Crump (A.H. & A.W. Reed, Wellington, 1961 and reprinted many times since).

Hangi

What comes out of an umu, or Maori oven. Basically steamed food, heavy on mutton and pork, stacked with vegetables such as kumara, pumpkin and sweet corn. Often served to tourists and marae visitors, complete with the 'ceremony' of opening the hangi. A pit full of stones and firewood starts the process: when the hot stones have fallen to the bottom, embers are scraped out and the food baskets (often wire cages) lowered in. Wet cloth and sacks around the food baskets produce steam when the umu is topped off with earth. Depending on the quantity of food, the cooking may take a couple of hours or more.

Hau Hau

A dreaded religious fervour that inspired Maori warriors opposed to British settlement during the wars in Taranaki, Bay of Plenty and Poverty Bay. Initially the followers believed themselves invincible to bullets. The Upraised Hand, a hand held above the head with palm forward, accompanied by the barking sound 'Hau Hau', was supposed to deflect bullets. In April 1864 Hau Hau ambushed a reconnoitring party in Taranaki, killing six and severing their heads. In March 1865 they killed a missionary, Rev. Carl Volkner, at Opotiki and drank his blood. Hau Hau often carried the heads of their victims on tall stakes, using them as oracles and props in their proselytising. Elements of the faith found their way into the Ringatu religion founded by **Te Kooti Rikirangi** (?1830–1893). The religious service of Pai Marire is still practised in those Maori churches where the influence of Hau Hau was once strong.

The Hauraki Pirates

The people who won back the right for private radio companies to broadcast commercially went to sea for nearly four years to make their point. Aboard the old scow *Tiri* and later *Tiri 2*, the Radio Hauraki pirates broadcast from the waters of the Gulf in the vicinity of the Colville Channel, beyond the range of the law. Their attempts to get going, however, were long frustrated by officialdom. In October 1966 the 'pirates' first went to sea, but had to bounce their mast through the almost-closed Western Viaduct in Auckland, while supporters sat in the bridge-lifting mechanism to prevent it from being lowered completely. The situation finally influenced the government to create a Broadcasting Authority, which in 1970 licensed Radio Hauraki and Radio I to broadcast in Auckland, breaking the State's effectual monopoly of radio broadcasting. See **'Uncle Scrim'** for earlier tangles. *The Shoestring Pirates*, by Adrian Blackburn (Hodder & Stoughton, Auckland, 1974) tells the story of Radio Hauraki's pirate days.

Hawaiki

The location of this traditional Maori homeland in Eastern Polynesia has long challenged the imagination of European scholars. Claims have been made for the Society Islands (Raiatea) and the Southern Cook group (Rarotonga), as possible departure points for migratory canoes. Anthropologists and ethnologists compare material culture and language to make links between old Aotearoa and appropriate Pacific islands with similar culture. Some Maori tribes have independently forged links with the Pacific Islands they favour as their point of origin. There are some scholars who have boldly located Hawaiki as possibly being on offshore islands or places in the warmer north of New Zealand from where later Maori migrated to new tribal lands. They suggest Hawaiki is simply the most recent point in a series of homelands following migration through the Pacific. Yet to Maori the concept of Hawaiki remains a largely spiritual one, referred to in ritual and tradition, as a place beyond this world to which the spirits return. So Hawaiki is frequently referred to on the marae as Hawaiki-nui, Hawaiki-roa, Hawaiki-pamamoa – the great Hawaiki, the long Hawaiki, the Hawaiki of the ancestors. For a modern summary of migration theories see *The Quest for Origins*, by K.R. Howe (Penguin, Auckland, 2003).

The Hawera Republic

On the frontier in South Taranaki, settlers of the Hawera district declared their 'independence' in 1879 because the government would not help them against the Maori. The settlers formed their own volunteer militia and opposed the passive resistance of Te Whiti, whose people ploughed up roads and crops because they believed the land was theirs. Independence was declared after driving the Maori back across the Waingongoro River, which became the only boundary of the 'Hawera Republic'. The people of Hawera rejoined the rest of New Zealand a fortnight later when the government sent troops to support them. See the **White Feather** for another perspective and *Ask That Mountain*, by Dick Scott (Heinemann/Southern Cross, 1975) for a fascinating account of Te Whiti's dispute with the settlers.

Health Camps

Children's health camps date from 1919, when they were set up to help children at risk from tuberculosis and malnutrition. Their 'clients' now reflect changed public health needs, including the treatment of emotional and behavioural problems, along with the establishment of good-health routines for those suffering from asthma or diabetes. Health camps cater for primary-age children, taking the five to 12-year-olds out of their normal environment and teaching them life skills. Camp life includes formal schooling, often of the remedial kind. Besides the 4000 children referred in the year 1992 by health and education workers, there were also 700 adults involved, a step towards helping people cope at home after the camp is over. Health camps are contracted to the government to provide short-term residential care but rely on public fund-raising, too, particularly through the sale of **Health Stamps** that include a donation along with the postal charge. See below.

Health Stamps

To raise money for the **Health Camps** movement New Zealand has issued special postage stamps, annually, since 1929. These include the normal cost of postage plus a premium charge for health camps. The first stamps featured a nurse and the challenge 'Help Stamp Out Tuberculosis'. In 1930 it was 'Help Promote Health'. The rarest Health Stamp is the 1931 'Blue Boy' for, during those early years of the stamps, New Zealand was in the grip of the 1930s **Great Depression** and sales were comparatively low. Recent issues have included postage at 45 cents and a five-cent donation to health camps.

The 'Hell Hole of the Pacific'

Kororareka, now sleepy Russell in the Bay of Islands, deserved this soubriquet in the lawless days before the Treaty of Waitangi. The captains of whaling ships, sealers and traders used the sheltered anchorage as a supply and repair port from the 1820s. Ships that had been up to a year at sea gathered at Kororareka, often taking on local Maori as crew. Deserters, escaped convicts and opportunists added their number to the community that built up about '**The Beach**'. Rest and recreation by the sailors created mayhem. The travelling artist Edward Markham recorded the atmosphere in his *New Zealand or Recollections of It* in 1834. 'The Missionaries hate the Ships to come into the Bay; the Reason is this. Thirty to five and Thirty sail of Whalers come in for three weeks to the Bay and 400 to 500 sailors require as many Women, and they have been out one year. I saw some that had been out Thirty-two Months and of course their Ladies were in great request, and even the Relations of those who are living as Servants with the Missionaries go to Pihere and bring them away in spite of all their prayer lessons. These young ladies go off to the Ships, and three weeks on board are spent much to their satisfaction as they get from the Sailors a Fowling piece for the Father or Brother, Blankets, Gowns & as much as they would from the Missionary in a year. Therefore they prefer going aboard the Ships "kipookys" when they come in, to the annoyance of the Missionaries. I believe the Missionaries are right that They go too young, and are very often barren, and that is one Reason for the decrease of population independent of any disease they may get.' Not surprisingly, it was missionaries who gave currency to the expression 'Hell Hole'. Such lawlessness partly prompted the extension of British government, first from New South Wales and then directly by the Treaty of Waitangi in 1840.

The Heroine of Gate Pa

When the combined forces of British Army and Navy stormed Pukehinahina Pa above Tauranga on April 29, 1864, they had the support of artillery and some 1650 men against 250 defenders. Yet the British were to lose many of their officers and men in the hand-to-hand fighting during what is known as the Battle of Gate Pa. The main pa was defended by Ngai-te-rangi of Tauranga, aided on the wing by a party of Koheriki that included woman warrior Heni-te Kiri-Karamu. Heni had fought in earlier stages of the Kingite wars while carrying a baby on her back. During an apparent lull in the first day of fighting she answered the call of the British wounded outside her trench by taking them water to drink. Then she returned, reloading her single-barrelled shotgun in readiness for another attack. The British, however, were reforming for further fighting on the morrow and the Maori withdrew from their fortifications during the night. Before she left, Heni took water to the wounded again. Later known as Heni Pore, she joined with the government side in subsequent battles. See James Cowan's *Hero Stories of New Zealand* (Harry H. Tombs, 1935).

High Country Runs *see* Run-holders

Hokey Pokey

The nicest ice cream in the world and you cannot get it anywhere else. Vanilla ice cream has added to it lumps of hokey pokey made from golden syrup, sugar and baking soda.

Hokonui

Illegally distilled whisky, the spirit of Southland was produced in sufficiently large quantities to keep the Collector of Customs at Invercargill hot on the trail, particularly through the 1920s and 1930s. The Hokonui Hills were the hiding place of several stills, hence the popular name. The clear-coloured liquor was even sold in some hotels in southern districts. Customs officers and police took part in several big raids on stills, hidden usually on Crown land. The illegal drink escaped the revenue taxes imposed by the Customs Department and thus sold at a more reasonable price to the locals.

The Holyoake Highway

The alternative road past Lake Taupo, along its western shores, opened a mass of back country in the central North Island. It was built during the time that **'Call Me Kiwi'** Sir Keith Holyoake was prime minister of New Zealand. Cynical wits were prompt to point out that the road would speed up the journey between Wellington and the Holyoake family land holdings at Kinloch on the western shores.

'Home'

English settlers in New Zealand long referred to their homeland as Home: the capital letter was deliberately applied. New Zealand being a British colony until 1907 gave the tradition some substance and the habit took a long time to die even in the new Dominion. It tended to weaken, however, with the first and second generations born here who were more familiar with our bush and rivers and manners, and less able to recapture the romance of their ancestors' origins. The idea survived for more than a century, however, with the continuing stream of English migrants who kept refreshing their memories with unkind comparisons and out-of-date copies of British periodicals. Artists felt isolated away from the judgement of London and many sought to work there after the First World War. Probably the apotheosis of this enigma is Alan Mulgan's *Home: A Colonial's Adventure* (Longmans, Green & Co., London, 1927), a sentimental journey back to a much-romanticised England in search of cultural sustenance. The weeping over the first sighting of the White Cliffs of Dover, as the colonial's ship approaches, encapsulates the powerful image of 'Home'. In the period before the Second World War, many writers and artists struggled with what they saw as the philistine nature of New Zealand and their distance from the centres of culture abroad. The European war changed that for most of them. See **Whingeing Poms**, **Old Country**, **Overseas Experience**.

Home Brew

Make your own beer and avoid paying duty on it. Efforts to make liquor at home and the after-effects of some heady brews form the basis of many Kiwi yarns. Modern beer-brewing kits ensure a reasonable tipple, however, at considerably less than bar costs.

The Honourable Roddy

The largest nugget of gold discovered in New Zealand was as big as a man's hand and weighed in at 99 ounces, 12 pennyweights, 12 grains. It was christened the Honourable Roderick Nugget for the Honourable Roderick McKenzie, who was Minister of Mines at the time. The gold was recovered at Ross in South Westland in 1909, in an area that had been mined since 1865. Valued then at around £450, the Honourable Roddy was displayed in many New Zealand towns, and it was offered as a raffle prize at five shillings a ticket, the money to benefit Totara Hospital at Ross. The New Zealand Government then bought the Honourable Roddy from the winner and gave it to King George V as a Coronation gift in 1911. When an enquiry was made of its fate in the 1950s, Buckingham Palace confessed that the Honourable Roddy Nugget was no more – it was melted down to make a golden tea service.

Honours

The traditional system of Royal Honours announced at Queen's Birthday and the New Year now has a distinctive New Zealand flavour. Knights and Dames are no longer created and British honours such as the OBE are no longer granted. Instead there are two New Zealand Orders and an Order of Chivalry. At the top, the Order of New Zealand is limited to 20 living New Zealanders for outstanding service to the people of New Zealand or the Crown. Established in 1987, it does not carry a title. The New Zealand Order of Merit is a chivalric Order established in 1996, with a range of awards that originally ranged from Member (MNZM) to Knights and Dames Grand Companions (GNZM). In 2000, the two levels of knighthood were discontinued and replaced with equivalent ranks that do not bear titles. The Queen's Service Order for public or community services was established in 1975 and includes Companions (QSO) and the Queen's Service Medal (QSM). British awards for gallantry and bravery have also been replaced with New Zealand awards. For example, the Victoria Cross is now the Victoria Cross for New Zealand, identical in design and materials. The George Cross for great bravery by a civilian is now the New Zealand Cross. See also **Queen's Birthday.**

Hot Christmas Dinner

The final test of the heroic New Zealand woman is the cooking of the traditional hot Christmas dinner. Born of the English traditions for hot meals in wintry snows, the Christmas dinner arrived in New Zealand with a set menu, including roast beef and boiled fruit pudding with sauce, Christmas cake and mince pies. While the men gently shelled fresh peas for the meal, enjoying a glass of beer, the heroic woman and her assistants sweated over a hot stove in stifling weather to produce the great feast, usually eaten at lunchtime. The afternoon might be spent sleeping it off in the sun or keeping the kids quiet so they did not disturb the uncles and aunts. The 'rematch' at tea time included the cold portions and such comestibles as cakes, jelly and trifle. Many New Zealanders now recognise that British practices do not always transplant well in our warmer climate. Some have changed the beef for chicken or turkey as such meats have become more available in the past 20 years. Others adapt to the reality of the season and serve salads and lighter accompaniments.

'The House that Jack Built'

A phrase to describe the Labour government's 1935 initiative in building **State Houses** for rental. The State house took this name from the Under Secretary for Housing John A. Lee, a controversial MP later known as the **Man who killed Mickey Savage**.

Hui

A Maori custom that has become increasingly popular in the wider community as a way to discuss issues and reach a consensus. The Maori hui is usually accompanied by a formal welcome or powhiri. Speakers take turns to put forth their views, often arguing vigorously on the marae or within the meeting house. Yet no formal decisions are made and people revise their own position as it suits them. The end result may be general agreement or disagreement, but all views should by then have been expressed and the participants at the hui better informed. Holding such hui and taking note of what is said is part of the process of consultation with Maori interests now built into a number of Acts of Parliament, particularly in the area of resource management.

Huia Feathers

The tail feathers of this remarkable bird, black with a white tip and worn by high-born Maori, were only one of several reasons for its extinction. The feathers were stored in wakahuia, carved wooden boxes, which are among the finest traditional Maori carvings. The female huia had a long curved beak for probing deeply in rotten logs for insects, the male had a differently shaped short beak. Thus a pair of birds could feed over the same ground, taking food from different places. This curiosity attracted European hunters, who killed hundreds of the birds for sale to museums around the world. The clearing of forests by pioneers, coupled with the introduction of rats and mustelids (ferrets, stoats and weasels), increased the intolerable pressure on the birds and none has been seen since 1907. See **Extinct Birds.**

The Inimitable Thatcher or the Goldfields Balladeer

Charles Thatcher was a famous entertainer on the goldfields both of New Zealand and Australia. His forte was popular songs, many of which reflected on the lives of miners and their attitudes:

> *At Home aristocracy seems all the go*
> *Out here we are all on a level you know*
> *The poor men out here aren't oppressed by the rich*
> *But dressed in blue shirts you can't tell which from which.*

Some said he was vulgar, but the audiences loved him. Thatcher wrote his own ballads, often on events of the day, and frequently targeting politicians and officials. He is thus credited with originating the expression 'old identity' in a song about the Otago provincial elections. His story and many of his songs can be found in *Goldfield Balladeer: the life and times of the celebrated Charles R. Thatcher*, by Robert Hoskins (Collins, Auckland, 1977). See the **Old Identities**.

Inter-island Ferries

Originally part of the coastal transport network, passenger ferries are now restricted to the Picton-Wellington run of the Inter-islander. Roll-on, roll-off ferries such as the *Arahura* and *Aratika* carry passengers, freight, cars and trains across the gap in just a couple of hours. Once, passenger ferries operated between most coastal ports but the service had shrunk to linking Wellington with Nelson, Picton and Lyttelton by the 1950s. The extension of the South Island main trunk railway along the Kaikoura coast in 1945 made it easier to get to Wellington via

Picton from Christchurch, though freight ferries still run directly from Lyttelton. See also *Wahine* **Storm**.

The Invincibles

The nickname of The **All Blacks** rugby team of 1924–25 which earned this title by defeating all opposition during a tour of Britain. After winning the provincial games, the Invincibles defeated Ireland and avenged the controversial 1905 loss to Wales by defeating the Welshmen 19–0. In the final match against England, forward Cyril Brownlie was sent off after only eight minutes of play, following a disputed ruling by the referee. Despite playing a man short, the Invincibles still won, 17–11.

'Jack Is as Good as His Master'

Many of the settlers brought this attitude with them and frequently took delight in proving it, as they made good, despite their lack of the advantages of birth or education. Although the new world of free-market New Zealand has begun to put a lie to the theory, there was good reason for holding to it. Settlers often needed each other to survive. Many a privileged person was shortly found to be less practical than a servant, lending credence to the cry. At its worst the idea led to a popular disregard for education and cultural values. The positive aspect was a determination to dispense with privilege in the new colony and enfranchise everyone regardless of background. When Governor Grey set up New Zealand's first Parliament in 1853 only men who owned property could vote – more than 80 per cent of men and all women were excluded. The situation was familiar to those from Britain, where millions were denied the vote well into the 20th century. The right to vote was extended to all New Zealand men in 1879 and to women in 1893. This gave political substance to the claim that 'Jack is as good as his master', though it took until the 1930s for Labour to take advantage of the government benches. See also **Votes for Women**.

Jandals

Third-world sandals found a market in New Zealand from the late-1950s, particularly as leisure wear. Known elsewhere as flip-flops or thongs, the rubber-soled, rubber-strapped jandals are said to be an abbreviation of the Japanese sandals on which they were modelled. Held on by a thong between the big and second toes, they give little protection. Nevertheless, occasional news stories describe inadequately prepared trampers trying to use them in the great outdoors, surely a measure of their continued popularity. Jandals and a beer potbelly over the belt of a pair of shorts are defining visions of the Kiwi male on holiday or behind the barbecue.

'Jap' Imports

Higher motor-vehicle standards in Japan mean cars rapidly become valueless, requiring major replacements to keep them on the road. In the 1990s these vehicles became an easy source of cheap cars for New Zealanders frustrated for years by over-priced locally assembled vehicles. Coupled with the abolition of import duties, car prices fell as second-hand Japanese cars flooded the market. Aged cars rapidly disappeared from the roads with this new generation of under-10-year-olds. These included right-hand-drive European vehicles from quality manufacturers – so the 3-series BMW succeeded the Hillman Hunter in select suburbs. Second-hand vehicles now come from a wider range of countries, including Singapore, South Africa and Britain. Some agents restore their used cars and sell them at a premium. With vehicles so cheap and urban public transport so bad in places such as Auckland, it is perhaps not surprising that New Zealand has more than two million private cars for just over four million people.

Jean Batten

Rotorua-born Jean Batten (1909–82) first flew as a passenger in one of the tourist flights of the *Southern Cross*, the aeroplane that Sir Charles Kingsford Smith made famous on his journey from Australia to New Zealand. She went to Britain at the age of 20 and became a pilot there, learning also the skills of maintenance and navigation. On her second attempt, she became the first woman to fly from Britain to Australia, landing in Darwin in 1934 in a wood-and-canvas Gypsy Moth 1, in a record time of 13 days, 22 hours and 30 minutes. She flew from London to Brazil in a Percival Gull in the record time of 61 hours and 30 minutes, and in 1936 from Britain to New Zealand. Auckland airport was renamed Jean Batten International Airport in her honour in 1990, and the Percival Gull can now be seen in the departure hall.

The Jet Boat

This piece of Kiwi ingenuity has been adopted worldwide. Designed by Sir William Hamilton (knighted for this invention), the boat is powered by a jet of water sucked up by the advancing boat and thrust astern as a high-velocity jet. Hamilton (1879–1978) was a high-country run-holder who became an inventor of heavy engineering equipment, initially through the building of earth-moving equipment for his property at Irishman Creek in the Mackenzie Basin. The jet boat was a response to the difficulty of navigating the swift and shallow high-country rivers. Jet boats may draw as little as 10 cm and are highly manoeuvrable, allowing boats to race up the shallow channels without grounding on river boulders. Such speeding craft now give access to wild rivers for tourists, hunters and thrill-seekers. The Hamilton jet was developed by 1953 and won international recognition when a jet craft conquered the rapids of the Grand Canyon on the Colorado River in the US. Now found on wild or difficult waters worldwide, the Hamilton jet is made in simple single-stage and larger compound forms, one powering a high-speed ferry in Alaska, capable of carrying 150 passengers.

Jogging

Running gently for basic fitness and good health is a craze that swept the world from New Zealand. Olympic coach Arthur Lydiard inspired the Auckland Joggers Club in 1962 as a keep-fit group for businessmen. The movement spread from there. Since 1972, as many as 80,000 keep-fit enthusiasts annually demonstrate what regular jogging can do by running *en masse* in the Auckland Round-the-Bays Race from the city to Kohimarama.

Johnny Jones, Whaler (1809–69)

The sealer lad who saved his pennies and bought a share in three Sydney whalers when only 20. From there he pioneered the practice of **Shore Whaling** in southern New Zealand. In 1840 he brought 11 families from Britain to settle his shore station at Waikouaiti: the farm buildings of Matanaka stand to this day. Jones traded in early Dunedin, printed his own currency notes and owned ships, developing the fleet that became the Union Steam Ship Company shortly after his death.

The Jump Off

A colloquial and not very respectful name for Cape Reinga, also known as the Leaping Place of the Spirits. Traditionally the spirits of Maori dead make a three-day journey to the North, passing along Ninety Mile Beach to the cape, Te Rerenga i Wairua. Here they climb down a pohutukawa tree and enter an undersea cavern, the returning place of the spirits, on the route to the ancestral **Hawaiki** or homeland.

The Kaik

A familiar feature of several southern towns where Maori communities survived into the 20th century on their own reserve land. The expression is short for Kaika, the southern Maori equivalent of the north's Kainga, an undefended village or settlement of the old days.

The 'Kaimai Breeze'

A wind that roars over the Kaimai Ranges between Tauranga and the Hauraki Plains on occasions during winter. Buildings and haystacks in its path can be whipped up. The 'Kaimai Breeze' was blamed for bringing down an NAC airliner near Ngatamahinerua Peak, above Gordon on the Hauraki Plains on July 4, 1963. While the wind blew strong the DC3 aircraft was believed caught in turbulence below the crest of the range. The 25 people aboard were killed in the crash. Details in *Darkest Days*, by Bruce Morris (Wilson & Horton, Auckland, 1987).

Kakapo *see* the Rarest Bird

Kauri Gum

The bleeding gum of the kauri tree (*Agathis australis*) was the basis of a major New Zealand industry from the middle of the 19th century into the 1930s. The gum was gathered by probing 'gumlands', places where ancient kauri trees had fallen, and digging for it. The lumps of gum were scraped and washed for export, finding a ready market in the manufacture of varnishes, some paints and linoleum. Gumdiggers worked the bleak gumlands of the north Auckland region and also entered the forests, where some even bled the trees for quick reward. The practice of 'bleeding' was made illegal in 1905 as good trees became infected and began to die. The great days of the industry were the 1890s to 1910, but many men and women remained on the fields through the Depression of the 1930s, and some were still working there in the 1950s to 60s. For around 50 years, until 1900, kauri gum was the major export of Auckland Province ahead of wool, gold and kauri timber. Synthetic substitutes killed the demand. Yet as late as the 1980s mechanical extraction was attempted on an industrial basis at Kaimaumau Peninsula, Northland. The kauri gum industry attracted people of many races, notably the **'Dallies'** or Dalmatians, many of them Croatians, who came from what was coastal Yugoslavia to make their fortune. Find further detail in Bruce W. Hayward's pictorial history of the gum industry, *Kauri Gum and the Gumdiggers* (The Bush Press, Auckland, 2003).

Keeping Left

Traffic in New Zealand drives to the left-hand side of the road, following the practice of its early source of motor vehicles, Britain. Likewise, pedestrians are expected to walk to the left of the footpath, though this is becoming increasingly confusing in places with heavy immigration and foreign-student populations. In the 1950s, patrolling police would order people chatting on the footpath to move out of the pedestrian way, and there was often a yellow line down the footpath indicating which side to walk on. There was some logic along a muddy, puddled street as the pedestrian faced the oncoming traffic and the man on the outside edge got the first mud flung up by passing vehicles. No more – pedestrians now share with motorised wheelchairs (often illegal), bicycles and skateboards. Many immigrants persist with walking to the right, as do many younger people returning from overseas, expressing their newfound sophistication, probably born of pedestrian snarl-ups from walking to the left overseas. Basically, it seems the best idea is to watch out while still walking to the left.

Kia Ora

A Maori greeting, broadly meaning 'good health', that has returned to wider use in recent years. Although common earlier in the 20th century, its popular use may have reached its nadir with the correction of a telephone operator for using it when answering calls at the manual telephone exchange. Now 'kia ora' is freely used on television when announcing the news, and the politically sensitive may use the plural 'kia ora tatou' – greetings to you all – when addressing public meetings.

Kimble Bent

This reluctant soldier deserted to the Maori side during the war in Taranaki and became a slave. John Cowan wrote his story in *The Adventures of Kimble Bent* (1911), while Maurice Shadbolt drew on his character when writing *Monday's Warriors*. Kimble Bent was an American who, when his wife left him, went to Britain and ultimately joined the 57th Regiment in 1859. He attempted to desert but was recaptured and imprisoned, before serving with the regiment in India and Taranaki. There he deserted to the **Hauhau** who made him slave to several chiefs, but he was not really trusted and lived a difficult life with them. After the wars Bent stayed in the bush for 12 years living the life of a **Pakeha Maori**. In his later life he was regarded by Maori as a tohunga or priest of medicines.

The King Country

Named for the political phenomenon of the Maori King movement. In the late 1850s, several Maori tribes in the central North Island associated themselves under an elected king and parliament to oppose the British settlers who wanted to buy their land. When British and colonial troops responded to their resistance, tribes loyal to the king fought defensive battles against the British, withdrawing up the valleys of the Waikato and Waipa Rivers. As 'punishment' the Crown took the lower Waikato lands, north of the Aukati (Confiscation Line). The Waikato people withdrew onto the remaining lands of Maniapoto to the south, which became the country of the Maori King Tawhiao. **Te Kooti Rikirangi**, too, took shelter there in 1872 after his raids in Poverty Bay, living among the Maniapoto Maori at Te Kuiti, where he developed further his Ringatu religion. So secure were these forests that European settlers could not enter them; the **King Movement** was the government. Some surveyors who crossed the line were murdered. In 1881 King Tawhiao and the chief Wahanui symbolically laid down their arms at the border township of Pirongia and sought settlement of the disputes. During the 1880s things changed as Kingite Maori entered into trade across the border or left to work on farms. Maniapoto leased or sold farms to settlers and the railway pushed down country. Yet the European history of the King Country is comparatively brief, its towns largely dating from the development of the **North Island Main Trunk** in the early 1900s.

King Dick

Richard John Seddon was regarded as the uncrowned monarch of New Zealand during his years as Premier (1893–1906). A populist,

his common-man approach appealed widely as did his government's championing of their causes. Seddon, who was born in Lancashire in 1845, went as a youth to the Australian goldfields, and first made his mark in Westland, becoming mayor of Kumara and a Member of Parliament from 1879. It was Seddon who led New Zealand's creation of its own Empire in the South Pacific, annexing the Cook Islands and Niue in 1901. He successfully held a handful of important ministerial portfolios at once, running departments as personal fiefdoms, and spoke often of **God's Own Country**. Seddon died while in office, aged 61, in 1906.

The King-maker

In the late 1850s Wiremu Tamihana, also known as William Thompson, organised the elections for a Maori king to head a confederation of tribes from Waikato and Hauraki, south to Taupo. Their intention was to halt the sale of land to British settlers. The **King Movement** now selects its rulers from the Ngati Mahuta tribe, descendants from King Potatau and King Tawhiao. Descendants of the first king-maker crown the successor with a Bible.

The King Movement

Formed by tribes in the central North Island during the late 1850s, their confederation under a Maori king and Maori parliament was to oppose demands that they sell their lands to settlers. The idea of the King Movement was to co-exist with the government of Queen Victoria and the new General Assembly set up by the British in 1853. The first king was Te Wherowhero Potatau, who died in 1860. His son Tawhiao (1825–94) headed the tribes during the Waikato Wars of the early 1860s. The confiscation of Waikato land led to their withdrawal to the lands of the Maniapoto in the south, consequently known as the **King Country**. For 12 years the Kingites lived beyond the confiscation line, a state within a state, with Tawhiao at its head. Then in 1881 he laid down his arms and a general amnesty ensued. Subsequent kings have been known in brief as Mahuta (1855–1912), Rata (1878–1933) and Koroki (1909–66). A Maori queen, Te Ariki Nui, Dame Te Ata-i-rangi kaahu (1931–2006), was succeeded on her death by her eldest son Tuheitia. Although there was ultimately some compensation for the taking of Waikato lands, the Kingites were long dependent on the 'hospitality' of the Maniapoto. It was not until the 1920s, under Princess Te Puea Herangi (1883–1952), that they returned to build their 'place to stand', Turangawaewae, by the junction of the Waikato and Waipa rivers at Ngaruawahia. Here there are frequent cultural and sporting gatherings, often involving people from tribes further afield, including annual celebrations marking the accession of the head of the movement. Visiting dignitaries, including heads of state and the British royal family, have made formal visits of greeting to the Kingitanga, which draws core support from tribes in Hauraki, Waikato, King Country and parts of Tuwharetoa, with broader connections as far away as the East Coast.

The Kingston Flyer

This tourist steam train runs on the last remnant of the former Lumsden to Kingston line servicing Lake Wakatipu. The journey now runs only from Lake Wakatipu to Fairlight some 14 km away. Kingston, with its lake steamer terminal, was once the end of a tourist line built from Invercargill and opened just weeks before Dunedin and Christchurch were linked by rail in 1878. Now Ab class Pacific locomotives, with restored carriages in turn-of-the-century railway green, ply New Zealand's shortest commercial route during the summer.

The Kiore or Pacific Rat

The kiore or Pacific rat is a widespread species brought to New Zealand by Maori settlers, along with the **Kuri** or Polynesian dog. The rats became so widespread that Maori kept food in pataka storehouses on poles high above the ground. Pacific rats are short-lived, being about the size of a mouse in their first year, and achieving the size of a small rat before dying in their second. They have largely vanished from the mainland under the spread of introduced Norwegian and ship rats. There are still substantial populations on some offshore islands. Kiore are usually described as seed-eaters, though there is evidence of their taking birds' eggs, lizards and the eggs of tuatara, which makes them a problem in wildlife sanctuaries. Maori trapped and ate kiore. The kiore has previously been known as the Maori rat and the Polynesian rat, names not now favoured for reasons of political correctness.

Kitchen Teas, or Evenings

Before a wedding, women friends and relations call on the bride bearing practical gifts. At a formal tea party, hosted by the bridesmaids, guests offer sufficient kitchenware to equip the bride-to-be's kitchen.

Kiwi, the National Bird

The Kiwi is New Zealand's national bird. Cynics have questioned the wisdom of choosing a creature that 'can't fly, can't see and is bloody near extinct'. Yet these very distinctions are what made it so striking to the pioneers. The expression Kiwi, used to describe New Zealanders, seems to have originated in the First World War. It has since become a synonym for a New Zealander, particularly abroad, and the label is attached to New Zealand enterprises and attitudes from the Kiwi Concert Party that entertained troops abroad during the Second World War to colloquial references to our dollar, and sporting teams. The hairy green Chinese gooseberry became a worldwide luxury when re-presented to the world as the **Kiwifruit**. Foreign companies have also made use of our symbol in their own branding, most spectacularly in the form of Kiwi shoe polish, which is sold into New Zealand by British manufacturers. The kiwi bird belongs to the Ratite order, which includes other flightless species such as the extinct **Moa**. The kiwi has rudimentary wings only 50 mm long, but compensates with its strong legs and scouring claws that help the bird defend itself against some introduced predators. The birds nest in holes underground and come out at night to feed. Nostrils on the tip of the long curving beak allow them to locate food in the dark. Because of its nocturnal habits, the kiwi is more common in some districts than sightings suggest, though it is now sorely threatened by mustelids (ferrets and stoats in particular), possums and dogs. The population halves every 10 years, with 95 per cent of chicks being killed in their first year. There are four species of kiwi, with local variations, the most common being the 'symbol' bird, the North Island brown kiwi. The greater spotted and lesser spotted kiwi are rare and endangered species. A fourth species, called the Haast brown kiwi, has more recently been identified through DNA testing. All kiwi have 'threatened' or 'endangered' status, and are presently the subject of a special recovery plan funded by the Bank of New Zealand.

Kiwifruit

The national delicacy we did not deserve to keep to ourselves. Once known as a Chinese gooseberry, the hairy fruit was refined in New Zealand and produced to perfect size and form for export to the richest markets. The resulting boom was checked by the enterprise of those who made quick cash by exporting the growing stock to less expensive producers. During the 1980s production nearly doubled and kiwifruit became New Zealand's leading horticultural export, worth $659 million in sales revenue in 1990. A centralised agency to market and export the fruit beyond New Zealand and Australia had the usual effect on individual enterprise. Now kiwifruit are no longer a quick way to get rich. Chile is doing quite well, however, out of its exports of kiwifruit. A consequent marketing ploy was to stop calling them kiwifruit and rename the Chinese gooseberry again – it's now a Zespri, and is also available in a golden colour. Sales to 60 countries in 2004 exceeded $1 billion.

The Kokotahi Band (Kokatahi)

A West Coast group that uses scratch instruments to emulate the traditions of a miners' band. Formed in 1910, the group draws members from the Kokatahi district (pronounced locally as cock-o-tie) near Hokitika. Bandsmen wear miners' best clothing – moleskin trousers, red shirts and black bandanas – and make a cacophonous noise.

Konaki

A form of farm cart combining the virtues of a sledge with the mobility of a wheeled vehicle. The konaki was a low, horse-drawn cart with wheels behind and sledge runners in front. Thus it could move more easily over muddy ground while its wheels continued to turn behind. The konaki was ideal for carrying out winter feed, fence posts and cream cans where the ground was rough or wet. Another virtue was its simplicity: it could be home-made. The alternative way of shifting timber and other materials about the farm involved clipping loads onto pack saddles, a horse body-harness, carried by **Pack Horses.**

Korotangi

The Tainui dove is a carving in serpentine executed in a style otherwise unknown in New Zealand. It was exposed when a tree blew over, near Aotea Harbour on the North Island west coast, in the 1880s. Maori pronounced it the lost treasure of Tainui brought to Aotearoa on their canoe. The bird is variously

described as a dove and a prion, descriptions that only approximate its unique form. The carving was formerly in the Dominion Museum, but has since been restored to the care of Tainui people as part of their settlement under the Treaty of Waitangi.

Koru *see* The Springing Fern

Kowhai Gold

The golden yellow flowers of the kowhai tree generally appear in early spring, though in higher inland districts they may flower in early summer. Kowhai has inspired poets and artists as an expression of life in the generally green fabric of the forest. Indeed *Kowhai Gold* was the name given to a collection of indigenous poetry used in schools in the 1940s and 50s. A friend of the English poet Robert Browning, New Zealand premier and poet Alfred Domett, wrote lyrically about it. There are many cultivars of the three major species of kowhai: the straggly shaped *Sophora tetraptera* with its larger leaves, *Sophora microphylla* with tiny leaves and a bushier form, and *Sophora prostrata*. Nevertheless, the poets don't distinguish between them when the flowers form on the bared branches of this semi-deciduous tree. Chiming tui and bellbirds, according to the district, flock to the trees to take honey from the flowers, their drunken song amplifying the temptations to wax poetic.

Kowhai is used along with the **Silver Fern** and the **Kiwi** as a symbol of New Zealand nature, and notably on the logo of the nature conservation body, the Royal Forest and Bird Protection Society of New Zealand.

Kupe

Once credited as the Polynesian discoverer of New Zealand (in AD 950, according to the old schoolbooks), Kupe is now more widely regarded as an early navigator whose exploits are acknowledged in different ways by several Maori tribes. Kupe traditions are strong in the north, for example, where the Hokianga Harbour is named for the departure point of Kupe on his return to **Hawaiki** (Te hokianga a Kupe – the returning place of Kupe). In various traditions Kupe has left place names in Northland, about Wellington, visited the West Coast of the South Island and circumnavigated it before returning up the west coast of the North Island. These traditions are traced in *The Great New Zealand Myth*, by D.R. Simmons (A.H. & A.W. Reed, Wellington, 1976).

The Kuri, or Maori Dog

The Maori settlers of New Zealand brought with them New Zealand's first ground-dwelling mammals, the kuri or dog and the **Kiore** or Pacific rat. The only native land mammals were three tiny bats, one of which is now extinct. The kuri is described by early travellers as a dim creature about the size of a spaniel, with long sheep-like hair. Maori used them for hunting **Kiwi** at night and also as food. Hanks of the hair were tied into superior cloaks for chiefs. As soon as foreign breeds were introduced they began interbreeding with the Polynesian dogs, so the isolated strain was shortly lost. Scientists now consider the last purebred Maori dogs disappeared in the 1830s. There is a specimen of kuri in Canterbury Museum and also a rare carving from Moncks Cave, in Christchurch, which may also indicate the type.

Labour Day

Curiously not the May Day (May 1) of the international labour movement but a New Zealand celebration and holiday on the fourth Monday in October. It dates from October 28, 1889, when unions of watersiders, seamen, transport workers and others joined forces under the banner of the Maritime Council. More trade unions were established and the Council came to represent them as industrial arbitrators with the employers.

The Lady Knox Geyser

New Zealand's most predictable geyser, near Waiotapu south of Rotorua. It is set off daily at 10.30 am by a tourist operator, who primes it with soap. Named in 1904 for the daughter of Governor-General Lord Ranfurly, Lady Knox Geyser looks natural enough but is man-made. Prisoners used to be taken there to wash and their soap caused bubbling eruptions in the pool. So they restricted its surface to a blow-hole by building a cairn above it. The narrowed neck produces an eruption of hot water.

L&P

The combination of lemon flavouring with mineral water from Paeroa in the Thames Valley produced the original New Zealand aerated water, Lemon & Paeroa, which survives as a major brand alongside the imported glamour fizzies. A monstrous bottle stands in the main street of Paeroa to mark its hometown, but the main ingredients of the drink are now mixed to match in a factory elsewhere.

'Ladies a Plate'

The stated price of entry for a woman at many a country dance or local function. The overt expression of this tradition has suffered somewhat with the changing role of women, but in practice many still do bring a plate of food towards the collective supper at community gatherings. The full expression on posters advertising a local event would often read, 'Men a donation, ladies a plate.' In places unlikely to be raided by the police that could be read as 'Men a bottle, ladies a plate.' Until the 1950s women tended to be ladies, or expected to be described as such.

Land Ballots

Because of the Crown's central role in acquiring land from Maori, the job of land development often fell to the Department of Lands and Survey. Other schemes conducted by the Maori Affairs Department involved forming incorporations of multiple owners and developing farm units. 'Wastelands' – lands not under the plough or producing grass – were 'broken in'. 'Marginal lands' were won over for production. Only the capital and faith of the State could have carried this through. On the volcanic plateau of the central North Island, for example, stock simply died until it was discovered that a cobalt deficiency in the land was the reason. Cobalt was then included in the top-dressing and the farms flourished. Once the units were up and running they were sold to eligible young farmers who were selected by a process of balloting. In the early years of the scheme preference for entry to the ballot was to returned servicemen. The scheme was later extended to a generation of trained young men with no chance of inheriting a family farm and who otherwise had little hope of succeeding to their own farm because of the high capital cost in boom years. Young farmers entered ballots conducted by the Crown, often through the Land Settlement Boards. Qualified bidders were allocated a number that was drawn out of a barrel to proclaim those successful. Such a system satisfied the gambling New Zealanders' sense of fair play, an ironic inversion of the historic records of chronic gamblers losing their land on the toss of a coin, or a hand of cards. The winners got the chance to take up the new farms and the rest of the hopefuls waited for the next ballot box. Some never made it before age rendered them unsuited to the heavy manual work of a new farm. Falling farm prices through the 1970s and rising interest rates through the 1980s made things tough for those who borrowed too heavily to get on the land. Land balloting died with the land development division of the Department of Lands and Survey, disestablished in 1987. Now commercial realities determine a young person's chances of getting on the land.

The Land March *see* The Maori Land March

The Land of the Long White Cloud

The romantic translation of the Maori expression Aotearoa is popularly given as the Land of the Long White Cloud. It is said to refer to the vision of New Zealand rising out of the sea, wreathed in cloud, along the horizon. Kura-maro-tini, wife of **Kupe** the early Polynesian explorer, is often credited for this naming. Approaching the shores of New Zealand, from the homeland of **Hawaiki**, she is said to have been first to spot the shore. The Rev. Richard Taylor, who recorded a version of the Kupe myths, wrote in 1868 that Aotearoa is another ancient name that refers only to the North Island 'but is now never used'. Maori then named the North Island Te Ika a Maui – the fish of Maui – and the South Island Te Wai Pounamu – the waters of greenstone. Some Southern Maori still disregard the name Aotearoa as inappropriate for the whole country. Yet many of the biculturally correct prefer to call New Zealand 'Aotearoa', or even 'Aotearoa/New Zealand'. Aotearoa would certainly look better on a postage stamp than 'The Land of the Long White Cloud'.

The Land Wars *see* The New Zealand Wars

Landfall in Unknown Seas

Allen Curnow's poem for the 300th anniversary of the European discovery of New Zealand by **Abel Tasman** on December 13, 1642. Its expansive lines tell of European discovery with a confidence and pride that is no longer naturally to be assumed:

> *Simply by sailing in a new direction*
> *You could enlarge the world*

Set to music by Douglas Lilburn, *Landfall in Unknown Seas* was released as a gramophone recording in 1959 by Kiwi Pacific.

Large Insects

New Zealand's ugliest insect is also its largest. Describing the weta as a kind of cricket does not make it less alarming. Maori called the giant weta 'weta-punga', an acknowledgment that it was an offspring of Punga, the Spirit of Ugliness. Weta vary in size from a body length of 20 mm (the cave weta) to the rare giant species, up to 100 mm in length and which weighs as much as a mouse. Long springing legs and twitching feelers double the body length.

The Largest Kauri

Alas, among the thousands of hectares of felled trees, it is possible there were a number of kauri bigger than the present 'giant', Tane Mahuta in Waipoua Forest Sanctuary in Northland. Kopi in Omahuta and Toronui at Waipoua outranked Tane Mahuta until blown down by storms. The largest measured tree far exceeded the height and volume of Tane Mahuta. Known as Kairaru, it was measured in the 1860s by the Surveyor-General Stephenson Percy Smith. Kairaru was 66 ft (20 m) around and stood a clear 100 ft (30 m) to its first branches. The tree was 'lost' when fire burned much of the Tutamoe Forest, south of Waipoua, but controversy surrounds its possible recovery as described by J.G. Erne Adams in *Kauri: a king among kings* (Wilson & Horton, 1986).

The Largest One-day Sailing Regatta

For more than 160 years, Auckland has celebrated its 'birthday' with what is claimed to be the largest one-day sailing regatta in the world. At one time, more than a thousand boats, from dinghies to cruisers, entered the races. In 2008 there were just over 400 entries, but it is still a great sight. The regatta, now held on Anniversary Day (the Monday closest to January 29), originated with the foundation of Auckland on September 18, 1840. Then, a flag was raised by officials, followed by toasts, gun salutes, and boat races. According to eyewitness Sarah Felton Mathew, 'the gentlemen got up a boat race among themselves, another for the sailors, and a canoe race for the natives which all came off with great éclat. The amateurs pulled with the Surveyor-General's gig boat against that of the harbour master, for a purse of £5.' Occasional regattas were formalised into an Anniversary Day celebration in 1850 and the competition grew, with whale boats, trading vessels and Maori canoe races. Gradually pleasure craft classes were added and the evolving **Scow** craft added spectacularly to the sight. Although the contest now is largely for pleasure craft and racing yachts, including sailboarders, there are still classes for old-time cutters. Maori canoes have also been seen again following their revival in the sesquicentennial year. Tessa Duder and photographer Gil Hanly have profiled the harbour, its history and craft in *Waitemata: Auckland's harbour of sails* (Century Hutchinson, Auckland, 1989).

The Largest Polynesian City in the World

Auckland's 'largest' claim relates to the comparative size of its Polynesian minorities. Since the 1950s many rural Maori have moved to cities to find work, as have many more Polynesians from the Pacific Islands. The larger number choose Auckland. In 1986 there were nearly 100,000 Maori in Auckland, 24 per cent of the total Maori population in New Zealand. By the 2001 census, 127,629 Aucklanders identified themselves as Maori, 11.6 per cent of the population. Other Pacific people, however, continued to outnumber them at 154,680. In a 2001 population of 1,101,594, people of Polynesian descent accounted for 282,309, maintaining Auckland's claim to be the largest Polynesian city in the world.

The Largest Wooden Building

The Old Government Building in Wellington is often claimed to be the largest wooden building in the Southern Hemisphere (the Japanese Todaiji Temple is larger, destroying the claim for world pre-eminence). Located below Parliament Buildings on Lambton Quay, Wellington, it appears in the classic carpenter style of building from the 19th century, with wood used to resemble stone blocks on the Italianate facades. The building is framed in native rimu and Tasmanian blackwood, floored with matai and clad in kauri. With a floor area of more than 9400 sq m, some 1,100,000 super feet of timber was used in its construction. From 1876 until quite recently it housed government offices, but after restoration it became the Law School of Victoria University of Wellington.

Larnach's Castle

A curious stone palace on Otago Peninsula built by Liberal Cabinet Minister, banker and entrepreneur William Larnach (1838–98), dating from 1871. Larnach named it The Camp. When things went bad financially for Larnach he shot himself in a committee room in Parliament Buildings. The 'castle' is now a tourist stop.

'Last, Loneliest, Loveliest ...'

Believe it or not, Auckland. The perception is that of Rudyard Kipling, poet of empire in his *Song of the Cities* celebrating the colonial cities, from India and Canada to Australia and New Zealand. The last stanza, headed 'Auckland', reads:

> *Last, loneliest, loveliest, exquisite apart –*
> *On us, on us, the unswerving season smiles*
> *Who wonder 'mid our fern why men depart*
> *To seek the Happy Isles.*

The Last Moa

The moa birds inspired many a tale as British settlers discovered that the Maori traditions of a giant flightless bird roaming the countryside were based on fact. Sealers first told tales of large birds reputedly living inland. Later settlers also claimed to have seen the large flightless birds. Alice Mackenzie of isolated Martins Bay, South Westland, wrote of finding a bird in the sandhills near her home in 1880 and stroking it. Claims to have seen the bird, originating from Murchison in 1940 and north-west Nelson in 1963, have kept alive the legend. Hoaxsters abound. A reported find near Craigieburn, inland Canterbury, made world headlines as recently as February 1993. Moa were first acknowledged by science in 1839 when the British anatomist Richard Owen deduced the prior existence of a giant flightless bird from part of a leg bone sent to him in London. The birds belong to the order Ratites (along with the **Kiwi**) and descend from species originating in the ancient continent of Gondwanaland. Scientists argue over the number of species – 12 is a popular figure at present. Moa have been roughly grouped into six types, ranging from the *Dinornis* species, some said to stand up to 3 m tall, through dumpy middleweights, to the smaller bush moas, not much larger than a turkey. Archaeologists have recorded the widespread occurrence of moa remains in the fireplaces of early Maori, practically throughout New Zealand. Enthusiasts have found moa nests, preserved footprints, feather and skin fragments in dry caves, and the skeletons of different species in swamps and caves where the birds have been trapped. Moa are generally believed to have been eaten nearly to the point of extinction by Maori during the 15th century.

The Last Moose

Tales of giant elk or moose in deepest Fiordland arise from their importation from Canada early last century. These giant northern deer have a very large antler spread and were keenly sought by trophy hunters along the remote shores of Dusky Sound, where 10 were liberated. Moose were still 'rare' in 1923 when sport shooting began and it is thought they never spread beyond a few of the fiords because of the topography. Hunters in the years following the Second World War soon began to talk of their hunt for the Last Moose, so few were seen. The last moose shot was in 1952 near the Wet Jacket Arm of Dusky Sound. Although the species is now believed extinct in New Zealand, hunters continue to speculate and explore.

The Lemon-squeezer

The dress-uniform hat of the New Zealand soldier is shaped like a lemon-squeezer. The hat originated during the First World War in France.

Lest We Forget

The blank verse recited at memorial services for the war dead comes from *For the Fallen* by English poet Laurence Binyon:

They shall not grow old as we that are left grow old:
Age shall not weary them, nor the years condemn.
At the going down of the sun and in the morning
We will remember them.

Limited Expresses

There were several such trains operating the main routes of both the North and South Islands in the days of steam. The trains operated on a limited number of stops on their run from Invercargill to Christchurch, and Auckland to Wellington, and return. The South Island Limited was the southern express, racing to catch the evening ferry from Lyttelton to Wellington. It ran from 1949 until **Inter-island Ferry** services closed in 1970. The stops were at Gore, Dunedin, Oamaru, Timaru and Ashburton, to fuel and water both passengers and locomotives. The journey of 594 km was supposed to take less than 12 hours and the prospect of holding up the ship to Wellington helped keep the service to schedule. The South Island Limited was replaced by the popular tourist train, the Southerner. The Night Limited ran between Wellington and Auckland. Sleeping cars were available on this train, but it was everyone for themselves when stopping for **Railway Pies**, block cake and stewed tea at Paekakariki (where steam took over from the electric locomotive), Palmerston North, Taihape, Taumarunui and Frankton Junction en route. Most passengers travelled in Second Class, sleeping two to a seat. The tradition of the tea stops and the characters met on the train were celebrated in story and poem, notably two versions of a poem *Taumarunui,* by James K. Baxter and the folk song *Taumarunui on the Main Trunk Line*. The Night Limited had 14 hours to make the 685-km journey and frequently took more.

The 'Lion of Scotland'

The title of a biography of the Rev. Norman McLeod (1780–1866), founder of the Nova Scotian settlement at Waipu, south of Whangarei. A strong and narrow character, McLeod dominated this Presbyterian community, which began with the arrival of settlers via Auckland in 1853. They were highland Scots who had emigrated first in the early 1800s to Prince Edward Island in Nova Scotia, off Canada. Finding conditions there too harsh the settlers moved on to Australia and New Zealand. Gradually they converged again on Waipu. The schooner *Gazelle* came direct from Canada, followed by the *Gertrude,* the *Spray,* the *Breadalbane* and the *Ellen Lewis*. The *Margaret* and the *Highland Lass* subsequently brought many of those who had gone to Australia over from

Adelaide. The strict morality of the settlement was maintained by the influence of McLeod. The statue of a lion that still stands high atop a column in the main street is said to have had its penis removed because it was deemed 'indecent'. The story of McLeod and Waipu is told by Neil Robinson in *Lion of Scotland* (Hodder & Stoughton, Auckland, 1974). *Pride of the Lion* (Waipu 150 Trust) covers the 50 years following the centennial.

Little Biddy of the Buller

One of the few women goldminers, Bridget Goodwin (1813–99) lived and worked with two men, 'occupying the same hut, having all things in common and saw nothing wrong with it', according to her amanuensis 'Waratah'. Biddy weighed less than seven stone (44 kg) and was only four feet tall (1.22 m), but she worked for 50 years along the Buller River. As the years went by Little Biddy became Old Biddy, outlasting her two mates, to die in Reefton at the age of 86, in 1899. The threesome met on the Victorian goldfields at Ballarat and worked first on the Collingwood **diggings** before moving to the Buller in the mid-1860s. 'It was a hard tough life working all day long up to our hips in water in all sorts of weather,' she told Waratah near the end of her life. When they had gold to sell they bought more 'tucker', then 'knocked down the rest of the money in a long booze.' Their money gone they went back to their hut and began work all over again. She lost her 'best mate' first and was less flattering about 'old Bill', who in his last days relied on her to win their gold and fetch the tucker, which had to be carried from Lyell in the Buller Gorge. In old age, at Reefton, she was consoled with a pension of a shilling a day, from the new Liberals' Old Age Pension Act, and the enjoyment of smoking her pipe. The text of Waratah's interview with Goodwin was republished in *The Adventures of Pioneer Women in New Zealand,* compiled by Sarah Ell (The Bush Press, Auckland, 1992).

The Living Fossil

One of the most spectacular survivors of the Age of Dinosaurs is the tuatara, a New Zealand reptile that looks like a lizard but isn't. The tuatara belongs to a group of reptiles extinct everywhere else for the past 60 million years. Tuatara survive on a few offshore islands where they may share a burrow with **Muttonbirds**, the various species of petrels and shearwaters that nest there. The insect life surrounding these bird colonies provides food for the reptile. The creatures are vulnerable to rats and in some places the only survivors are all mature creatures, which are estimated to live for more than 100 years. Tuatara have what is popularly called 'a third eye', on their forehead, a sensitive area linked directly to the brain, though unable to see.

'Living Fossils'

The expression for ancient New Zealand plants and animals dating back to the Age of Dinosaurs. These animals and plants are the survivors of species that evolved in the late Palaeozoic and early Mesozoic periods, perhaps up to 250 million years ago. They possibly reached New Zealand when it was attached to the southern super-continent of Gondwana, some 140 million years ago. Subsequent separation and isolation of the New Zealand land mass, some 80 million years ago, led to the survival of several animals and plants that evolved before the Age of Mammals. Among our living fossils are a fern-like plant known as *Dicroidium*, the tuatara (see previous entry) and native frogs that hatch directly from eggs rather than developing first as tadpoles. These ancient species have remained in existence through aeons of isolation, although on other land masses they may be traced only as fossils. See also **Dinosaur Forests**.

'Living off the Hind Tit'

Perhaps better known as a form of tax evasion, 'living off the hind tit' was widely practised in those favoured sectors of the economy where subsidies and allowances flourished until the 1980s. In business the cost of commuting, daily meals and entertainment were deducted from income, as were car bills (add magazines and grocery items to the petrol account), corporate yachts and club memberships. With creative accounts keeping the privileges could stretch to members of the family who were said to be 'living off the hind tit'. Farming was a particularly easy area for this practice, hence, presumably, the pastoral metaphor. Domestic bills became part of the cost of farming and thus deductible from income tax. Tax-free petrol, coloured to distinguish it from the taxed item sold at service stations, was stored on the farm to run machinery, but could end up in the tank of the farmer's car. Farmers who habitually complained of low incomes compared their net profit after tax with the gross pre-tax incomes of other groups and felt themselves hard done by. A surprising number of them have managed to survive under more equitable tax regimes.

Local Shopping 'Blocks'

Abandoned and converted blocks of shops in suburban areas recall a time when these served thriving local communities. People walked to the shops until the 1960s and tradesfolk delivered the groceries, eggs, milk, and meat by van or bicycle. A typical shopping block might accommodate a grocer, a dairy or two, a hairdresser, draper, electrician, butcher and perhaps a chemist if there was a doctor nearby. The coming of supermarkets spelt the death of many of the smaller shopping blocks. Some survive, particularly where there is a regional supermarket adjacent. Many are now converted to factories or storage, or as the low-rent base of a specialist business, not dependent on local people for survival. With the passing of the shopping block many of the suburban 'shut-ins' lost a community focus, where they could exchange gossip and pleasantries, *Coronation Street*-style, with their neighbours. People who cannot drive are now handicapped, too, in getting service, hence the frequent advertising of properties suitable for the aged as being but a 'level walk to shops'. Greatly extended shopping hours and the two-income family have taken much of the traditional local base away from shopping 'blocks' and onto supermarkets.

The Log o' Wood

The Ranfurly Shield was once the symbol of rugby supremacy within New Zealand. The top provincial team holds 'the Shield' until a challenger takes it away; the regional unions apply to the New Zealand Rugby Union for the privilege of trying. Named for its donor, a former Governor-General called the Earl of Ranfurly, the trophy is of wood, with a border of silver shields. Auckland was the first winner in 1902. Teams from the old provinces have had most success winning the Shield.

The Lonely Graves

The finding of the body of a handsome young man, lying in a remote spot beside the Clutha River, began the story of the Lonely Graves. In 1865 a miner called William Rigney came across the body near Horseshoe Bend **Diggings**. The dead man's dog stood guard but no one knew the young man, nor could they discover his name. An enquiry established that the young man had died of exposure. Rigney sought permission to bury the anonymous corpse close to where he found it. With regard for the dead man's loved ones, Rigney engraved a wooden tombstone with the words 'Somebody's Darling Lies Buried Here.' Rigney retained his interest in the grave throughout his own life and asked to be buried there, too. The original wooden grave marker is still readable, now encased in glass and incorporated in a later marble headstone. Alongside stands a newer stone that reads 'Here lies the body of William Rigney, the man who buried Somebody's Darling.' The graves may be found on the true left bank of the Clutha, 8 kilometres downstream from Miller's Flat.

The Long Drop

There are still quite a number of homes in New Zealand where the toilet (dunny) is off a back verandah or but lately integrated into the main body of the house. This dates back to comparatively recent times when the 'nightman' called to take away the 'night soil'. Many country communities still have the alternative sewage disposal system in the form of a septic tank. Originally, dunnies were located at some distance from the house, being of the 'long-drop' variety. These work – for they are still common about holiday homes in isolated places – on the principle that flies will not go more than about three metres underground to lay their eggs. A handful of earth cast in occasionally should help with composting. Tales of misadventure, going to, using, and coming from the dunny are legion, as indeed is the penchant for lavatory humour.

The Longest Journey

Thomas Brunner set out in 1847 to find a way to Westland by the way of Nelson Lakes and the Buller River. Earlier, with Charles Heaphy and William Fox, Brunner had got as far as the Buller

Gorge. These men had also tried a northern route, around the top of the South Island, and got as far south as the Arahura River, near what is now Hokitika, a five-month return trip. This time, with two Maori guides and their wives, Brunner set off on a journey that took him 550 days, to Paringa in South Westland and back via the Buller. On the way he was stuck for weeks in the lower Gorge and in want of food ate his hunting dog. There he wrote in his diary on March 21, 1847: 'Rain continuing, dietary shorter, strength decreasing, spirits failing, prospects fearful.' He learned to walk barefoot or in flax sandals, and live off fern root like his companions. At Paringa he injured his foot and began his slow return in December 1847, handicapped for some time by paralysis in one leg. His discovery of coal led to the naming of the Brunner Coalfield on the Grey River. The travellers reached 'civilisation' again at Motueka on June 15, 1848. Brunner soon settled into a quiet life as chief surveyor in Nelson. His greatest support on the journey was the Maori Kehu, of whom he later wrote 'to Ekehu I owe my life'.

The Longest Place Name

In Hawke's Bay, near Porangahau, a small peak bears the longest place name in the world, a total of 56 letters. Like many Maori place names it tells a story, but unlike most it has not lost its object (nor consequently its length). The name appears in a four-deck Automobile Association sign, all in capitals and split up with hyphens in odd places making comprehension even more difficult. The sign reads:

TAUMATAWHAKA-
TANGIHANGAKOAUAU
ATAMATEAPOKAI-
WHENUAKITANATAHU

This is translated as 'the summit where Tamatea Pokai Whenua played his flute to his beloved.' The name is three letters longer than the previous claimant, in Wales, a country also much given to expressive and polysyllabic place names.

Lord of the Rings

Despite the hype, the massive three-movie series made in
New Zealand originally stems from a very English story that
draws heavily on ancient British folklore. The production gives
a New Zealand physical background to foreign mythology.
Interestingly, in the 1970s conservationists took place names
from the author J.R.R. Tolkien's fantasyland and applied them
to New Zealand landscapes at risk in the forests near Karamea,
in northern Westland. A Maori member of the Geographic Board
successfully objected to the superimposition of British mythology
over a traditional Maori landscape.

Lord Rutherford of Nelson *see* The Man Who Split the Atom

The Lost Tribe, Fiordland

The lost tribes of south-west New Zealand may not have been as
lost as they looked. Many of the tales spread from the observations
of Captain Cook's expeditions in the 1770s, including the romantic
paintings by his draughtsman William Hodges R.A. that show a
Maori family in Dusky Sound, Fiordland. Cook's men recorded
a family group, including a voluble young woman whose accent
they could not follow, headed by a man called Maru. Some have
argued that the people Cook saw were refugees from a tribal
war. Others observe the seasonal visits that Maori made to
places such as this for hunting and fishing. As Maori themselves
have begun recording their traditions in writing a clearer view of
personalities in this region emerges. The Maori painted by Hodges

now have names and
possible relationships
with people in other
fiords. Both Maori and
archaeologists have
located Maori camp-
sites in the Sounds.
Drs Charles and Neil
Begg, co-authors of
Dusky Bay, believe they
found the bodies of the

folk Hodges painted in a cave at Cascade Cove. They describe them as the last of the Kati Mamoe tribe. Kati Mamoe were the tangata whenua of the south before the coming of Kai Tahu, though there are still people today who claim descent from both tribes and indeed their predecessors, Waitaha. Although the romance of a lost tribe is inevitable, given the vastness of the region and its disturbing history, the facts are just as exciting as can be read in *Dusky Bay* by A. Charles Begg and Neil C. Begg (Whitcombe and Tombs, Christchurch, 1966).

The Lost Tribe, Murchison

Settlers in the remote Buller district of Murchison during the 19th century spoke jocularly of there being a lost tribe in the even more remote headwaters of the Matukituki River. Folk there were supposed to have only one eye, on their forehead. As a child in the late 1940s, I stayed awhile with distant relatives on the Horse Terrace goldfield, and consequently believe this tradition to be untrue.

Lotto *see* Gambling

Lovelock's Mile

Actually a 1500 m running race when New Zealander Jack Lovelock clipped a second off the world record with 3 minutes 47.8 seconds at the 1936 Berlin Olympic Games. The result, the equivalent of running a mile in 4 minutes 4 seconds, set the pace for a post-war battle to run the mile in less than 4 minutes. A Rhodes scholar, Jack Lovelock also represented New Zealand at the 1932 Olympics in Los Angeles, and also at the second Empire Games, held in London in 1934. At Princeton in 1933 he won the first American Mile of the Century Race with a world record time of 4 minutes 7.6 seconds. Lovelock continued to live abroad and was killed when he fell in front of a train in New York in 1949. His enigmatic personality has inspired varied sports journalism, a short film and the novel *Lovelock* by James McNeish (Hodder and Stoughton, Auckland, 1986).

The Mackenzie Country

Named – though misspelled – for **James McKenzie**. McKenzie was said to have used the great mountain basin to hold sheep, allegedly stolen from a farmer on the Canterbury Plains. Most travellers now enter by way of Fairlie and Burke Pass, but McKenzie's entry was through the pass, further south, which now bears his name.

Mackenzie, the 'Sheep Stealer'

A Robin Hood-like glamour surrounds the exploits of James McKenzie (now spelt Mackenzie), who was said to have stolen 1000 sheep from George Rhodes of the Levels and driven them to the huge high-country basin that was named after him. A Highland drover who spoke Gaelic as his first language, McKenzie discovered his 'country' in the infant days of settlement in Canterbury (though his pass was known to others). McKenzie was apprehended by Rhodes' overseer James Sidebotham and two Maori, Taiko and 'Seventeen', on March 4, 1855, but escaped the same night. The memorial on the spot describes McKenzie as 'the freebooter'. Tried and sentenced to five years' imprisonment, McKenzie made several escapes from the Lyttelton gaol before he was pardoned five months later. McKenzie claimed to have been helping a James Mossman to drove the sheep when they saw Sidebotham's party approaching. Before running away, Mossman admitted to McKenzie that the sheep were stolen but asked McKenzie to stay with them as he was innocent. In allowing a pardon, the Provincial Superintendent accepted that McKenzie's silence in defence was born of the Gael's incomprehension of the English language in which he was tried. McKenzie's story has inspired many local legends, as did his dog which was said to have a prodigious memory for mustering instructions, allowing the dog to take sheep long after McKenzie had moved on to some other place of safety. The affair so fascinated the writer James McNeish that he wrote a novel, *Mackenzie* (Hodder & Stoughton, Auckland, 1970) and a subsequent 'historical detection', *The Mackenzie Affair* (Hodder & Stoughton, Auckland, 1972), which reviews what he called 'perhaps the most glaring miscarriage of justice in New Zealand history'.

The Main Drag

Most of New Zealand's smaller towns grew up by an anchorage, around a crossroads, or by a river crossing. As roads linked these towns, settlement spread along the main artery. The main road became known as the main drag, possibly because of its potential for local hoons to race each other there at 2am, but also perhaps a recognition of its dreariness. When driving through the countryside motorists are frequently instructed to reduce speed while passing through such boring ribbon developments. Hamilton is a classic example. Bypasses solve the long drag but can ruin local businesses dependent on passing trade.

The Mainland

An honorific assumed by the South Island. While the North Island was troubled by war with Maori through the 1860s the South prospered, a growth helped by the discovery of gold and the relatively easy pastoral country. Consequently Dunedin became the financial capital, a position in shipping, commerce and industry not lost until after the Second World War, when many of its national companies moved north to be nearer the growing markets. Christchurch in those days assumed the role of cultural capital. The wild North Island was considered 'Pig Island', a reflection on its introduced wildlife and the widespread extent of pigfern in the wake of the bush burns.

'Man Alone'

The classic Kiwi tradition of the loner, isolated even among company in the pioneer wilderness, appears in many New Zealand books. The 'man alone' is self-contained, self-reliant, expecting nothing and giving nothing. He drifts from place to place, incident to incident, and dies with his walking boots on.

John A. Lee and Frank Sargeson described him in their stories; John Mulgan recognised the archetype and made the expression the title of his 1939 novel. The plot traces a loner called Johnson from his arrival as an immigrant in the 1920s, his experiences in the Auckland region and the Depression riots, a murder and a cross-country escape through the central North Island forests. According to Joan Stevens in *The New Zealand Novel 1860–1960*, Mulgan's *Man Alone* is 'the fullest prose rendering of what the New Zealand twenties and thirties felt like'. Loners continue to crop up through the indigenous heroes of the 1940s, 1950s and 1960s, from Guthrie Wilson's *Strip Jack Naked* to the hero of C.K. Stead's *Smith's Dream* (1971), and also in some of Barry Crump's and Maurice Shadbolt's earlier characters. The type is not quite a stereotype, even though the 'outsider' pose attracted so many writers seeking a hero in our more insular past; there is something about the back country that breeds such self-reliant melancholy. Try *Man Alone*, by John Mulgan (Selwyn and Blount, London, 1939). Pick from such real-life 'loners', too: **The Shiner, Arawata Bill** and **Mr Explorer Douglas** are examples noted in this volume. See also **Mates**, **Mateship**.

The 'Man-of-war Without Guns'

James Busby was appointed British Resident to New Zealand in 1832, before the signing of the Treaty of Waitangi effectively annexed the land. For six years he tried to keep the peace between British adventurers and Maori, presenting the chiefs of the Confederation with a flag that is still flown today, that of the United Tribes. Yet with no lawful authority and few resources he was considered by Maori as a 'man-of-war without guns'.

The Man Who Killed Mickey Savage

As the near-sainted first Labour prime minister Michael Joseph Savage approached death from cancer, Labour radical John A. Lee MP continued to argue about his dictatorial style. Lee's *Psychopathology in Politics* pamphlet was written 'to let the Labour movement know that we are being dominated from the bedside by a sick tyrant'. When Savage died Lee's enemies tried to put the blame on him. Ousted from the official Labour Party in 1940, Lee stood successfully as Leader of the Democratic

Soldiers Labour Party, still pressing the Socialist view. Lee was a colourful orator who wrote some excellent social novels and later political commentaries largely based on his own experience. His *Children of the Poor* (1934 and often republished), is based on youthful experiences in borstal, as is the autobiographical *Delinquent Days*. *The Hunted* tells of life as an escaper. Lee's experiences in the First World War (in which he lost an arm and won the Distinguished Conduct Medal) inspired *Civilian into Soldier*. Lee turned to folk history with his excellent humorous book about **Sundowners**, particularly Shiner Slattery in *Shining with the Shiner*. *John A Lee's Weekly* chased the coat-tails of the post-war Labour government. Lee wrote some controversial accounts of the first Socialist government and got his own back with regard to the accusations about the death of Mickey Savage in his *Simple on a Soapbox* (Collins, Auckland, 1963). Lee prefaces the book with the words: 'The internal workings of a party is as worthy of study as its policy.' In a foreword, Frank Langstone, who was Minister of Lands in the 1935–40 Labour government, wrote 'Had the death of the Prime Minister … occurred prior to Conference in 1940, or had the death taken place at a later date, there would have been no motion for Lee's expulsion …'.

The Man Who Split the Atom

The most famous alumnus of Canterbury University, Ernest Rutherford (1871–1937) was born at Brightwater in rural Nelson and attended country schools. From dux at Nelson College he went on to take three degrees at Canterbury, then worked in Britain and Canada on his theories about the structure of the atom. His theoretical analyses led the way to the discovery of atomic energy and the splitting of the atom. The basement room where he first worked on research at Canterbury has been set aside in his honour, in the old buildings of the university, now the Old Arts Centre in Worcester Street, Christchurch. Rutherford's honours included 20 university degrees, the Nobel Prize, a knighthood, the Order of Merit (one of only two New Zealanders to date), creation as Baron Nelson and election as President of the Royal Society from 1925 to 1930.

Mansion House

On Kawau Island, once the hideaway of governor and politician Sir George Grey (1812–98). Mansion House dates from 1841, built originally to house the manager of a copper mine, the remains of which are still Kawau landmarks. Grey bought the place in 1862 and added a new wing, verandah and bay windows. This was the time of Grey's second governorship and when the term ended he became devoted to creating a private kingdom on the island. His imports of wallabies and kookaburras still flourish, though the kangaroos, antelopes, deer, monkeys, zebras and emus have gone. The library formed here was later donated as

the basis of the Auckland City Library. Grey continued to base himself on Kawau during his career as a politician, serving as Superintendent of Auckland (1875–76), Premier of New Zealand (1877–79) and a Member of Parliament until 1890. Mansion House was for many years a hotel and popular calling place for cruising yachties. House and grounds were acquired for the Hauraki Gulf Maritime Park in 1969 and since restoration in 1979 Mansion House has been a showplace for the public.

The Maori All Blacks

Representative teams selected on a racial basis are a feature of New Zealand sport. The players argue this is not apartheid; instead it expresses racial pride and independence, and often reflects a focus on a local church or marae. Thus Maori tribal sports teams compete in inter-tribal games at gatherings such as those celebrating the accession of the Maori Queen. Maori rugby players first formed a 'Native' team (with four white players) to tour New Zealand, Australia and Britain in 1888–89. The first New Zealand Maori team toured Australia in 1910. With Maori excluded from touring South Africa because of its 'colour bar' policy, Maori All Blacks nevertheless played them when the Springboks toured New Zealand in 1981. See **No Maoris, No Tour** and **Stop the Tour**.

The Maori Battalion

In the First World War Maori volunteers served in the Maori
Pioneer Battalion that also included Niueans and Cook Islanders.
In the Second World War the 28th Infantry Battalion was formed
by Maori and served in Greece, Crete, North Africa and Italy.
Its marching song *Maori Battalion* was written by Private Anania
Amohau of Whakarewarewa, Rotorua, initially for a guard of
honour formed for the 1940 centenary celebrations, then adapted
for use by the Maori Battalion itself.

The Maori Dog *see* The Kuri

The Maori Land March

In 1975, Maori people concerned about loss of their lands joined
together in Te Ropu o te Matakite, marching from Te Kao in the
Far North to the steps of Parliament Buildings, to petition the
government. Their leader, the future Dame Whina Cooper (see
the **Mother of the Nation**), was 80 years old at the time. Her
lean figure, stooped over a walking stick, became an icon of the
journey as its import gradually gathered weight through the
media. The hikoi, as it was known, was the first pedestrian group
to cross the Auckland Harbour Bridge since its opening in 1961.
The long-term achievement was to bring Maori land grievances
before a new generation, creating the atmosphere in which the
Treaty of Waitangi Tribunal could be established to review Maori
claims on public land and investigate their complaints about
abuse of other traditional rights.

Maori Point

This point on the Shotover River takes its name from two Maori
gold prospectors, Dan Erihana and Hakaraia Haeroa. They
bravely swam the river there to rescue a dog and found gold.
The men collected 25 lbs (around 11 kg) of the precious metal in
one afternoon.

Maori Time

Not as derogatory as it may at first sound. The expression
is used by Maori, too, to describe their programme of events.
Things happen 'when the time is right'. Attendance at a Maori

function is the best way to experience the phenomenon. Take your watch off or suffer from increased blood pressure if you expect to make progress to a formal timetable. Things get done when appropriate, and not before. This is because things work out best this way.

The Maori Wars *see* The New Zealand Wars, etc.

Maori Woman and Child

Gottfried Lindauer (1839–1926) painted his favourite Maori woman and child picture so many times that it has become one of the most recognised of New Zealand images. The Maori woman wears the tattooed lips and chin favoured by women of her time; the baby peeks over her shoulder from a carrier on her back. The subjects are Ana Rupene of Ngati Maru, a familiar figure in the early mining centre of Thames on the Coromandel, and her child Huria or Julia. Lindauer often worked from photographs, this accounting in part for the strict accuracy in depicting Maori moko or tattoo. Photography also made it possible for Lindauer to return to his favourite subjects, sometimes many years later. According to Leonard Bell in *The Maori in European Art* (Reed, Wellington, 1980), Lindauer painted her about 30 times. See also **Goldie's Maori.**

Maoriland

Once a popular name and reference to New Zealand. It crops up in book titles and writings, particularly late in the 19th century. At that time, as the Maori population and its impact dwindled, so did the habit of describing Kiwis as Maorilanders.

Marion du Fresne's 'Treasure'

A bottle containing a French claim to sovereignty was buried on Moturoa Island in the Bay of Islands by a French expedition in 1772. Despite ensuing hunts no one has admitted finding it, though the ground in Waipao or Treasure Bay has been well dug over. The bottle was buried by the captains of the ships *Le Mascarin* and *Marquis de Castries,* two vessels in an expedition commanded by Marion du Fresne. The French expedition spent over a month at the island and became familiar with the Maori.

Too familiar – for the French became concerned with pilfering by the Maori, and abused a high chief and his son. Du Fresne also failed to take sufficient precautions against attack when he went ashore fishing. Thus, Marion du Fresne, two officers and 24 of his men were killed. The remaining French retaliated, burning buildings and killing Maori before planting their bottle and sailing away. Later attempts to rediscover the bottle were fuelled by the specific 'treasure map' instructions recorded by the French: 'The bottle ... is buried on the left bank of a stream where we obtained our water and fifty seven paces from the place where the sea comes up at the new and full moons in rising, and at ten paces distance from the said stream at four feet deep.' Add to these words the subsequent movement of the foreshore through erosion, and there is a wide margin of error for people willing to dig down 1.2 m somewhere in the sand.

Massey's Cossacks

The conservative prime minister William Ferguson Massey (1856–1925) turned the mounted might of the Farmers' Union onto the workers to break the 1913 General Strike. Sworn in as special constables, the farmers supported mounted police who overcame pickets with long batons and got the wharves open again. In Wellington the mounted farmers made several charges against strikers. Some called it the **Battle of Featherston St**. But although the farmers had the advantage of horses, they also stood to lose the most, as their produce lay on the wharves. For details of the 1932 'rematch' see the **Queen Street Riots**.

Mates, Mateship

The New Zealand male was not always a '**Man Alone**'. In pioneering days heavy work often required a mate to get things done. On the goldfields, here and in Australia, a digger usually had his mate, to the point that diggers alone were known as Hatters – often 'mad as'. In the 19th century, when men outnumbered women by a large proportion, the idea of men living and working together as a couple was not unusual nor sexual. Men in working pairs moved about the country together seeking work, often a younger man and his older mentor. There is an attendant code of loyalty: a bloke doesn't 'split' or 'scab' on his mate or mates. Barry Crump's tales are full of 'mates'. The expression is also a useful reminder that we are all 'mates' under the skin and is often applied in place of the more servile 'sir' when doing business across the economic classes. Jock Phillips examines male bonding in *A Man's Country?* (Penguin, Auckland, 1987).

Me and Gus

The unglamorous lot of the pioneer dairy farmer was humorously captured in the books of Frank S. Anthony (1891–1925). In cow country there were no grand traditions such as the mustering of stock from vast mountain landscapes, only the constant demands of the cows; milking twice a day at dawn and dusk, seven days a week and more than seven months a year. Frequently it rained; mud and muck was the common environment on farms too small to pay their way and provide a comfortable living. Anthony's first book *Follow the Call* tells of a soldier-settler on a 20-ha farm in Taranaki. *Me and Gus*, later to become a popular radio serial scripted by Francis Jackson in the 1950s, was a collection of tales about hard-pressed small farmers. The anti-hero Gus Tomlins is the antithesis of the capable, self-reliant man of the land. Frank S. Anthony saw the humorous side of the small-farmers' predicament, but like many others on uneconomic units he was finally forced to abandon his own farm.

Meatsafe

A common feature of New Zealand homes before the refrigerator. The metal cupboard stood to the south of the house and was punctured with a sieve-like pattern of holes to allow cool air to circulate while keeping blowflies out. Often the structure opened directly from the kitchen or pantry through to the outside wall, its wooden frame roofed with metal and its sides of wire mesh. This traditional way of keeping meat cool and away from flies is still used by many New Zealanders 'keeping house' away from power points. Campers and hunters often hang their meat and perishables in muslin-covered frames from the branch of a shady tree.

The Middle Island

An alternative name for the South Island in early days. The present name appears on maps more often from the 1860s. More southerly Stewart Island, however, was never the South: its renaming from Rakiura to Stewart was an earlier recognition of Captain William Stewart, who not only charted it in 1809 while first officer of the *Pegasus* but also returned in 1826 to establish a trading centre at Port Pegasus.

Milkbars

Perceived in the 1950s, before coffee bars and pubs, as a centre of juvenile decadence, milkbars provided a place away from home for the young to gather, listen to the juke box and drink milkshakes. A few still survive in country towns down south, often within the context of a **dairy.** In many a New Zealand town in the 1950s and early 1960s the milk bar was the only form of night life, providing a focus for the adventurous, a place outside which to 'rev up' the motorbike. The combination of motorbike and milkbar led to the expression 'milkbar cowboy', evoking images of a leathered lad and his leathered chick living dangerously in places such as Oamaru and Eketahuna.

The Milford Track *see* The Greatest Walk in the World

Mitre Peak

Celebrated icon in paintings and tourist photographs since Milford Sound received its first tourists more than a century ago. The sheer triangle of Mitre Peak (1692 m) was shaped by glaciation. To some Maori it represents the genital organs of a mythological figure in the founding of the land. The name Piopiotahi, meaning a single native thrush, recalls the flight there, to mourning seclusion, of a bird that witnessed Maui crushed between the thighs of his ancestor Hine-nui-te-Po.

MMP

New Zealand abandoned first-past-the-post voting for Parliament with the election of 1996. For the first time, voters used the MMP system – a helpful acronym for the obscurely named 'mixed member proportional' voting system. Each voter, 18 and over, has two votes – one for an electorate MP and the other for their preferred party. If a political party wins an electorate seat, or reaches five per cent of the party vote, it is allowed to appoint further MPs in proportion to their support. Thus in 1999, voters elected 67 MPs to represent electorates and the parties used their 'party votes' to appoint a further 53 'list' MPs. There are usually 120 MPs in the one-chamber House of Parliament. MMP was originally chosen from a range of proportional voting systems following a national referendum after voters tired of two-party wrangling. To achieve a majority to govern, parties needed to form coalitions. In January 2000 there were 28 registered political parties and little sign of improved behaviour in the House.

Moa Hunters

The popular name given to early Maori who relied in part on the hunting of moa birds for food. Once believed to be a primitive race who preceded Maori, the moa hunters are now known to be early Maori people who relied on the gathering and hunting of food, including moa, for survival. Tools and ornaments found with the cooked bones of moa show their material culture to be closely related to the islands of Eastern Polynesia from whence they originally came. The expression Archaic Maori is now applied more often to these people. Moa are believed to have been hunted out in the 1400s and 1500s. The later Classic Maori culture developed as the emphasis moved to growing food in gardens as well as seasonal gathering, hunting and fishing. Moa hunter lifestyles are well explained in *When All the Moa Ovens Grew Cold*, by Atholl Anderson (Otago Heritage Books, Dunedin, 1983). See The **Last Moa**.

The Moeraki Boulders

The boulders are scattered along the beach at Moeraki, between Oamaru and Dunedin. Maori traditions describe them as food baskets spilt from the cargo of the ancestral canoe *Araiteuru* that wrecked there. Veined patterns on the near-circular rocks resemble a woven net surrounding a gourd. A walk along the beach reveals future Moeraki Boulders still eroding out of the low cliffs. The boulders, up to four metres in circumference, are concretions formed on the sea floor some 60 million years ago. Calcite crystals make up the veining.

Moko *see* Tattooing

The Molesworth, New Zealand's Largest Station

This sheep and cattle station covers 1800 sq km of high country between Canterbury and Marlborough. Its epic proportions and mountainous landscape have inspired several books and made heroes of those who worked there. Founded in 1852, the Molesworth was almost destroyed by the high-country tradition of burning off, coupled with over-stocking and rabbit plagues. It was taken over by the Crown in 1938 and redeveloped as a cattle run. Access is limited beyond the southern entry in the Upper Clarence Valley, where a historic cob building, the Acheron Accommodation House, dates from 1862–63. During summer the Department of Conservation may issue permits for four-wheel-drive vehicles to make the journey from Canterbury to Marlborough through the great station. *Molesworth*, by Lance W. McCaskill (Reed, Wellington, 1969), tells of farming redevelopment by the State. *Musterer on Molesworth* by Bruce Stronach (Whitcombe and Tombs, Christchurch, 1953) recreates the worker legends. Stronach quotes a musterer's rhyme:

Land of rocks and rivers deep
Lousy with dogs and merino sheep
Squatters' paradise, musterers' hell
Molesworth Station, fare you well!

Mooloo

Beloved mascot of Waikato, originated with rugby supporters in the 1960s. The imitation cow is carried out at games and Mooloo (street) parades when the Waikato team plays a big match.

Moonlight, George *see* George Fairweather Moonlight

Moriori, Maruiwi

New Zealand was long believed to have been settled at first by darker people from Melanesia, then conquered by the Maori from Polynesia. The idea fitted with Victorian concepts of settlement by successive waves of conquerors and helped explain why much of the land was said to be occupied when the present Maori owners took it from 'The People Before'. Other tales told of fairer-skinned people with reddish hair who occupied remote areas, such as the Children of the Mist in the Urewera and the fairy patupaiarehe. Others have argued for shipwrecked Spanish sailors and Tamil traders affecting the make up of the original people. In recent years, studies of common Polynesian languages and traditions, of arts and crafts and of human forms, have all served to underline the Polynesian ancestry of the first settlers. Differences in material culture between the earliest settlers and later Maori simply reflect changing times. The original Eastern Polynesian culture, common to several island groups, developed later on our shores into the distinctive form of classic Maori culture. The name Moriori now properly attaches to the original culture and people of the Chatham Islands, who also developed a distinct culture after a Polynesian beginning, but were conquered by mainland Maori tribes in the 1840s. See *Moriori: a people rediscovered*, by Michael King (Viking, Auckland, 1989). To dispense with Spanish and other settlers see the modern settlement story outlined in *The Quest for Origins*, by K.R. Howe (Penguin, Auckland, 2003).

The Mother Country

A.k.a the '**Old Country**'. A reference to Britain, homeland of many immigrants and also the source of many institutions. See **Home**, the **Thousand Pound Cure**, and the **Ten Thousand Dollar Cure**.

The Mother of the Nation

English translation of a Maori title conferred on Dame Whina Cooper (1895–1994), the correct expression of which is Whaea o te Motu. Dame Whina, was leader of the 1975 **Maori Land March** from Te Kao to Parliament and long a matriarch of the northern tribes. She was founding president of the Maori

Women's Welfare League (1951–57) and the land march organisation Te Ropu o te Matakite (1975). A leader of Maori opinion for more than 60 years, she remained based with her people at Panguru, Hokianga. Her other honours included the Order of New Zealand, the membership of which is limited to 20 outstanding New Zealanders at any one time. Michael King has written *Whina: a biography of Whina Cooper* (reprinted Penguin, Auckland, 1991).

Mr Asia

The codename given to New Zealand drug lord Christopher Martin Johnstone, to avoid charges of libel, in a series of stories by Pat Booth and his investigative team for the *Auckland Star* in the late 1970s. Their exposé of Mr Asia and his organisation climaxed with the murder of Mr Asia himself, found nude and weighted below the waters of a quarry pool near Chorley, Lancashire. Booth tells of his investigation in *The Mr Asia File* (Fontana/Collins, Auckland, 1980).

Mr Explorer Douglas *see* Douglas, Mr Explorer

Mullet Boats, Mulleties

A class of sailing boats once common about the Hauraki Gulf and used for commercial fishing before the widespread use of motorised fishing vessels. Mullet boats have a broad beam and carry around 92.9 sq m (1000 sq ft) of sail, making them fast and spectacular sailers. Measuring just under 8 metres, these sailing cutters have a centreboard and very shallow draught so they can sail over harbour shallows and into tidal creeks. Their racing qualities showed as they returned from the Hauraki Gulf, with skippers anxious to be first in port for the best price for their catch. Usually there were two crew for fishing. The boats became popular as racers after the fishermen entered their mulleties in the old-time regattas. The class, labelled L on its sails, still races in Auckland with several new mulleties built in recent years to keep the competition alive. The sponsoring Ponsonby Cruising Club was able to obtain the truly magnificent Lipton Cup as a class trophy from Sir Thomas Lipton, the international tea magnate and British challenger for the America's Cup. Tradition has it that the club executive had their picture taken outside the Edwardian facade of the Esplanade Hotel in Devonport, so impressing Sir Thomas with the apparent magnificence of their 'clubhouse' that he matched it in style with a superb cup. See *Little Ships of New Zealand*, by Paul Titchener (A.H. & A.W. Reed, Wellington, 1978).

The Murder House

Playground name for the School Dental Clinic. Here, beginning in 1923, school dental nurses checked children for cavities and filled their first teeth with amalgam, using a gross treadle drill that threatened terminal pain. The dangers of 'Bertie Germ' were brought painfully home, along with advice to eat lots of fruit and always brush teeth after eating. With the addition of fluoride to most water supplies from the 1950s the threat of false teeth in one's twenties retreated. Dental nurses continue in schools, with the emphasis on preventative work, under the new title of dental therapist.

Murderers' Bay

Dutch explorer Abel **Tasman** gave the name 'Moordenaersbay' to Golden Bay after an incident in which four of his men were killed in December 1642. The first European vessels recorded on the New Zealand coast, *Heemskerck* and *Zeehaen*, were anchored, it is believed, in the vicinity of the Tata Islands off the northern coast of what is now the Abel Tasman National Park. The ships sought water and vegetables following their journey from Tasmania, but approached the land with caution. Tasman's crews first saw smoke ashore on the morning of December 17, 1642, and, running into Golden Bay, could see canoes near the shore. The cautious Dutch anchored well out in the bay, but as night fell two canoes of warriors came out to the ship, the occupants calling and blowing on a conch shell. The Dutch replied with trumpets, but the warriors paddled off. Next morning a double canoe came out, but the occupants could not be enticed aboard the ship despite the offer of knives and white cloth. Tasman called a council of senior officers from both ships aboard the *Heemskerck* and they had barely resolved to sail closer to shore when things went wrong. Seven canoes now lay about the anchored ships and the Maori attacked the *Zeehaen*'s cockboat as it returned to pick up its officers from the council meeting. A canoe with a high prow suddenly rammed the cockboat, then the quartermaster was attacked with a spear and others clubbed. Three men were killed and a fourth mortally wounded. Musketeers and gunners on both ships opened fire on the canoes, but they were swiftly out of range. In the melee the quartermaster and two of his crew swam to the *Heemskerck*. The ships immediately set sail as 11 more canoes put off from the land. The Dutch held their fire until several were within range but the ultimate hail of fire hit none but a man in the largest canoe bearing a small white flag. The Dutch sailed on, missing the passage between the North and South Islands, and failing to find any landing place along the west coast of the North Island. Murderers' Bay was renamed Massacre Bay by the French explorer Dumont D'Urville in 1827; in 1842 it became Coal Bay after the discovery of coal at Takaka, then Golden Bay for the gold strike of 1857. See *Abel Tasman in Search of the Great South Land*, by Gordon Ell (The Bush Press, Auckland, 1992).

The Murders on Maungatapu

Five men were killed on Maungatapu while carrying gold from the Wakamarina field in Marlborough to Nelson in 1866. They were victims of a notorious group of robbers described elsewhere in this book as the **Burgess-Kelly Gang**.

The Musket Wars

The Ngapuhi chief Hongi Hika (?1777–1828) from the Bay of Islands reshaped Maori history in the regions as far south as Waikato and East Cape. A supporter of the missionaries, he visited Sydney in 1814, then went to Britain where he was received by King George IV. He exchanged all the presents he received, excepting protective armour and guns, for more muskets and ammunition.  Then, with the avowed aim of becoming King of New Zealand he made successive raids in 1821–23 against the people of the

Hauraki Gulf, Hauraki, Thames, Waikato and Rotorua. In 1825 he turned on Ngati Whatua, who had few arms, killing 1000 men at Kaiwaka, for his 70 or so dead. His further battles included turning on Ngati Pou of Whangaroa in 1827, when he was shot while not wearing his chain mail. Augustus Earle painted Hongi surrounded by warriors and family as he lay invalided, planning further battles from what became his deathbed. Another chief who used muskets to advantage was Te Rauparaha (?1768–1849), a Ngati Toa chief from Kawhia in the Waikato region. After quarrelling with other Waikato tribes he moved his people south in the 1820s to new land and associations along the Wellington west coast. Using muskets he was able to extend his lands to include the northern South Island, then pushed further south to sack Ngai Tahu pa at Kaikoura and Kaiapoi. The introduction of muskets in the hands of leaders such as Hongi Hika in the north and Te Rauparaha on the Wellington coast changed the balance of political power between the tribes at a time when European settlement also threatened. Further details in *The Musket Wars: a history of inter-iwi conflict 1806–45*, by R.D. Crosby (Reed, Auckland, 1999).

Musterers

The 'knights' of the high-country sheep stations. In former times they were charged with rounding up the sheep from the high tops and bringing them down to the station yards for shearing, dipping and the like. Up before dawn, the musterers rode and walked to the highest ridges of the station, up along the snowline, from whence they could 'sweep' the faces for sheep. With a string of working dogs, the musterer could cover the 'beat', bringing down the sheep from summer pasture to join the mob in the valley below. Now helicopters are often used for the 'ups'. More on the high-country life is noted under **'Wayleggo!'**.

Muttonbird Scrub

Traditional name for the hard-leaved *Olearia* daisy trees and dracophyllum found on exposed coasts and offshore islands where **Muttonbirds** breed. The trees form a sheltering layer of dense foliage, keeping wind off the forest floor, where muttonbirds have their breeding tunnels.

Muttonbirds

Regarded by some as a delicacy, these oily seabirds are traditional food for both Maori and other New Zealand communities. The birds are petrels or shearwaters, which come ashore to nest in burrows, where they or their fat young are taken. Traditionally, muttonbirds are preserved in their own fat, often wrapped in seaweed bags made by splitting the flat 'leaves' of the bull kelp. The southern muttonbird, called titi, is the Sooty Shearwater, taken by designated Maori families from the Titi Islands off Stewart Island. In the north the bird is oi, the grey-faced petrel, though other species of petrel were taken in the traditional harvest. In earlier times muttonbirds occurred in mainland colonies, too, some flying inland from their ocean fishing grounds as far as the bluffs above Lake Waikaremoana in Te Urewera, and Tongariro. Colonies still exist on the mountains of Paparoa and Kaikoura. Muttonbirds may share their burrow with the rare reptilian tuatara, New Zealand's **Living Fossil.**

The Naming of Queen Charlotte Sound

Lieutenant James Cook gave the name of his Queen to this fiord in the Marlborough Sounds, immediately before laying claim to the South Island of New Zealand on January 31, 1770. Cook's *Journal* tells how he explained to local Maori that 'we were come to set up a mark upon the Island in order to shew any ship that might put into this place that we had been here before, they not only gave their free consent to put it up but promise'd never to pull it down … I gave silver threepenny pieces dated 1763 and spike nails with the King's broad Arrow cut deep in them things I thought were most likely to remain long among them.' After erecting a pole and running up the Union Jack, Cook named the place Queen Charlotte's Sound 'and took formal possession of it and the adjacent lands in the name and for the use of His Majesty, we then drank Her Majesty's hilth in a Bottle of wine and gave the empty bottle to the old man (who had attended us up the hill) with which he was highly pleased'.

The Napier-Taupo Road

Following an old Maori trail, the road was built in times of war with Maori. Originally Tuwharetoa people of Taupo used the trail to take seafood from Ahuriri Lagoon, where Napier now stands. The road began as a Hawke's Bay Provincial scheme to reach the Auckland markets, but the government took over in 1869 to secure a link with Taupo Garrison in the war with **Hau Hau** warriors. Military posts, such as that at Opepe, were manned by the **Armed Constabulary** as the road was pushed through the bush. The journey, which now takes some two hours, took two hard days by stagecoach in 1874.

National Anthems

New Zealand has two. Until the 1970s people customarily stood for the Imperial 'God Save the Queen', played before public functions, big sports matches and entertainment, and particularly the movies. Since then, 'God Save the Queen' has become less fashionable, usually replaced, when ceremony demands, by 'God Defend New Zealand'. Usually unsung is the 18th-century second verse of 'God Save the Queen' with its vituperative chauvinism:

> Scatter her enemies,
> And make them fall.
> Confound their politics,
> Frustrate their knavish tricks,
> On thee our hopes we fix,
> God save us all.

Since 1977 'God Save the Queen' has shared official recognition as a national anthem with 'God Defend New Zealand'. The words to the latter were written in 1878 by Otago poet Thomas Bracken (1843–98). The music was produced from a competition won by John Joseph Woods (1849–1934), a schoolteacher, church choirmaster and sometime county clerk, of Lawrence in Central Otago. The words and music of 'God Defend New Zealand' were bought by the government as a national hymn to mark the Centennial in 1940. The soaring tune has lent itself to modern presentation, so every child now hums along with the pop stars. A Maori-language version is often sung first. Mystery phrase: 'Guard Pacific's triple star' – our three main islands, perhaps?

The National Council of Women

The council was established in 1896 by the women who had won the vote. It was to be the co-ordinating body for women's groups, which were losing their focus after the achievement of women's suffrage in 1893. The suffragist Kate Sheppard, who was first president, wrote, 'In Wellington is every year assembled a National Council of men which holds a session, each member of which is not only granted a free pass over all the railways, but also receives a salary sufficient to maintain him throughout the year. That National Council of men ... deliberates on matters which specially affect women and children ... I trust, however, that the day is not far distant when men will no longer exclude women from their deliberations.' Described as radical and part of the International Women's Movement, the NCW faltered in the early 1900s and did not re-form until the First World War. The right for women to stand for Parliament was not won until 1919 and the first woman to enter Parliament was Elizabeth McCombs in 1933. See also **Suffragists, Votes for Women, Women on Top.**

The National Death *see* The New Zealand Death

National Parks and Reserves

The gift of the summits of Mt Tongariro to the nation, by Te Heu Heu Tukino IV in 1887, initiated New Zealand's magnificent series of national parks. A network of parks and reserves now protects around 33 per cent of New Zealand's land area. These include 14 national parks, with the prospect of more as land once held for other government uses is reassessed against the national park criteria. The test of national-park values is 'land containing scenery of such distinctive quality, or natural features or ecological systems so important, scientifically, that their preservation is in the national interest'. The original gift of his ancestral mountain by the paramount chief of Tuwharetoa has since been expanded into Tongariro National Park. The park has also been recognised internationally as a World Heritage Area along with south-west New Zealand (Te Wahi Pounamu) and the sub-antarctic islands. The largest park is Fiordland, established in 1952 and over 1,251,924 ha. Kahurangi National Park in north-west Nelson was formerly forestry reserve, but in 1996 became the second-largest national park at around 452,000 ha. The 14th park, Rakiura, was created in 2002 and protects 85 per cent of Stewart Island, also known as Rakiura. Altogether there are more than three million hectares of national park, nearly 170 forest and conservation parks covering a further 1.3 million hectares, and about 3500 reserves for scenic, nature, scientific and recreational purposes. A number of marine reserves and protected areas have also been created in recent years.

Native Otters

Despite the fact that no one has ever found a skeleton, the legend of the New Zealand otter persists, particularly in the back country of Southland. In her book *New Zealand Mysteries*, Robin Gosset has collected a wealth of anecdote from witnesses, including Maori traditions of a small otter-like animal called the waitoreke. Some of the European sightings are possible to explain as small seals or large rats, while others test the imagination, such as an account of eating a waitoreke while out eeling with Maori on the Waiau River in Southland. The European records begin with Captain James Cook, who anchored in Pickersgill Harbour at Dusky Sound, Fiordland, aboard the *Resolution* on his third voyage here in 1773. Cook observed that for three or four days, while they set up tents ashore, several people saw a four-footed animal about the size of a cat with short legs and a mousy colour. Beyond that none could agree on the description. The two naturalists of the expedition, father and son J.R. and George Forster, were not convinced, suggesting one sighting was simply a ship's cat hunting birds. New Zealand has only two native land animals, both tiny bats. Our isolation from other land masses began in the Age of Dinosaurs and land mammals simply did not evolve here. Follow the evidence in *New Zealand Mysteries*, by Robin [Jenkins] Gosset (The Bush Press, Auckland, 1996). Bernard Heuvelman dismissed the possibility of a native otter in his book *On the Track of Unknown Animals* (Rupert Hart-Davis, London, 1958) with a chapter entitled 'Waitoreke, The Impossible New Zealand Mammal'.

Nelson's Notional Railway

In the days of State-subsidised everything, Nelson had no railway, so the privileges that applied to places served by this service were extended to the region, notionally. Freight and passenger charges on services to Blenheim were subsidised in 1957 to make them like the cheaper rail services available elsewhere. Nelson in fact had a railway for years, but it went nowhere. An intended connection with the West Coast was abandoned in the 1930s **Great Depression** short of the upper Buller River. A link to Marlborough, reached by the South Island Main Trunk as late as 1945, was never begun. The possibility of despatching goods by rail effectively stalled at Glenhope (1912 to 1954), though tunnels and track beds ran beyond Kawatiri Junction (Hope Junction) at the gateway to Nelson Lakes and Upper Buller in the 1930s. The Nelson railway functioned on a local delivery basis through the orchards, hop farms and tobacco fields of the Waimea Plains and Valley. When authorities ruled that the line be taken up in 1954, local folk sat on it, in one of the first New Zealand examples of a full-scale community protest against central decision-making. See also the **Dun Mountain Railway**.

New Chum

Usually from the **Old Country**, possibly named for the way the English old-timers spoke of 'chums' not 'mates'. The 'new chum' was often the butt of jokes, when the gang set an impossible task, or found great mirth in seeing a beginner stumble through lack of familiarity with their own limited world. One example: the new chum is sent to buy a left-handed screwdriver. The new chum stereotype often appeared in 19th-century cartoons confronting the true colonial with innocence or ignorance, and just occasionally satirical guile. His spirit survives in back-country yarns about officials and other unfortunates sent to deal with good keen men.

New Edinburgh or The Edinburgh of the South

Founders of the Free Kirk of Scotland settlement of Otago at first planned to call their town New Edinburgh. William Chambers suggested changing the name as early as 1843, to avoid adding to the list of colonial town names beginning with 'New', and in 1845 the Lay Association of the Free Kirkers did so. The settlement was then renamed Dunedin, an ancient Gaelic name for the Scottish capital. Yet Dunedin folk still describe their city as the Edinburgh of the South and on a cold day it can seem just as dour.

New Munster, New Ulster

On December 23, 1847, when George Grey was governor in the capital of Auckland, a charter was signed dividing New Zealand into two provinces, New Ulster and New Munster. Grey established a deputy, Edward John Eyre (1819–1907), as

Lieutenant Governor of New Munster, based in Wellington. The Province encompassed the whole South Island and the lower North Island to the Patea River. Eyre had been an outstanding explorer in Australia and he shortly went walkabout without telling his Executive Council when he would return. Grey remonstrated, for the men regularly bickered, then moved himself to Wellington for 18 months, making Eyre superfluous. In Auckland, Lieutenant Colonel Robert Henry Wynyard became Lieutenant Governor of New Ulster in 1852. Eyre left New Zealand when Grey introduced his constitution in 1853. It included the new system of Provincial governments and divided New Munster into Wellington, Nelson, Canterbury and Otago.

New Zealand

This was the name given to Aotearoa by the Dutch, when it was discovered not to be a coastline of the fabled Great South Land. When first encountered by Abel **Tasman** in 1642 it was called by him Staete Landt or **Staten Landt**, for he hoped this coast linked across the southern ocean to the Staten Landt discovered off Cape Horn, South America, by Le Maire in 1616. Spelled variously Nieuw Zeeland (Dutch) or Nova Zeelandia (Latin), it means the New Land of the Sea, though others believe it was named after the low-lying Dutch region of Zeeland, just as Australia became New Holland and old New York, New Amsterdam. The new name appears on maps from 1657. See *Abel Tasman in Search of the Great South Land*, by Gordon Ell (The Bush Press, Auckland, 1992).

The New Zealand Christmas Tree

The pohutukawa (*Meterosideros excelsa*) flowers in the three or four weeks up until Christmas and loses its colour shortly after. The giant coastal trees fringe many a northern bay, tumbling over the cliffs with straggling arms. Their existence helps define the ethos of summer holidays by the sea. A powerful metaphor for Christmas in high summer, pohutukawa have inspired not only poets and painters but also the authors of New Zealand Christmas carols. The tree also stands mid-stage as a central metaphor of historical relations between Maori and European settlers in Bruce Mason's play *The Pohutukawa Tree*. Pohutukawa trees are vulnerable to fire and the depredations of introduced possums. Thousands have died about our coasts in recent years and efforts are being made to replant what was once a widespread symbol of New Zealand summertime. South Islanders do not miss out altogether. In the same season the forest tree southern rata, related to the pohutukawa, also flowers, bringing patches of warm red to the olive-green canopy of the rainforest. More pohutukawa lore is in *Pohutukawa and Rata: New Zealand's iron-hearted trees* by Philip Simpson (Te Papa Press, Wellington, 2005). Project Crimson is a commercial sponsorship dedicated to saving the pohutukawa and rata species.

The New Zealand Cross

Arguably the rarest of decorations for bravery, awarded for military actions during the armed conflicts of the 1860s. The pioneer artist and guerrilla leader Major Charles Heaphy won the Victoria Cross in 1864, but generally the British were loathe to give their award for valour to colonial troops not under their command, hence the introduction of the New Zealand Cross for an equivalent act. In all, 23 New Zealand Crosses were awarded, some several years after the bravery they commemorated and including some for actions before the institution of the

decoration. New Zealanders again became eligible for the Victoria Cross in 1867 and 21 people have now been awarded that honour, including Captain Charles Upham who won it twice during the Second World War. It has now been replaced by the Victoria Cross for New Zealand (see **Honours**). The name 'New Zealand Cross' has been revived to replace the British George Cross for 'acts of great bravery in situations of extreme danger.'

New Zealand Day *see* Waitangi Day

The New Zealand Death or the National Death

Death by drowning was so frequent in pioneer times that it became known as the New Zealand Death, or the National Death. With shipping the quickest way about the country and few bridges on land, people were frequently exposed to the risk.

Sudden squalls and rogue waves tipped over many a boat caught in breaking surf or entering a river mouth. The risks were high as settlers tried to load goods or mail through the surf or used boats in marginal conditions to cross harbour mouths. Ashore, 'flash floods' made travel across normally low streams unexpectedly dangerous. Goldminers, in particular, were exposed to risks as rivers rose suddenly and swamped their camps. Heavily laden miners were caught, too, when makeshift rafts or canoes were swept away as they attempted to cross swollen rivers. Searches for drowned bodies, at certain corners of the river, became a recognised way of looking for missing people. G.O Preshaw observed in *Banking Under Difficulties* (Capper Press, Christchurch, 1971) that, 'Since my arrival there has been on average one death per week through drowning' at a single ford of the Teremakau near Hokitika. After discovering the alpine pass that now bears his name, John Henry Whitcombe, in the company of Jacob Lauper, became impatient and drowned  trying to cross the flooded Teremakau in 1863. The explorer Charles E. Douglas is quoted in *The Bad Old Days* by Tony Nolan as writing, 'A lonely grave on the South beach is a gentle hint to all that Westland rivers are not be played with. These graves are a feature at the mouth of every river in the country.' In Otago, floods before the Great Snow of 1863 are believed to have taken 100 lives. The writer Samuel Butler lost a visitor in the Rangitata River one Christmas Day. Butler records in his *First Year in the Canterbury Settlement*: 'On their first experiences of one of these New Zealand rivers, people dislike them extremely; they then become very callous to them, and are as unreasonably foolhardy as they were before timorous; then they generally get an escape from drowning or two, or else they get drowned in earnest. After one or two escapes their original respect for the rivers returns, and for ever after they learn not to play any unnecessary tricks with them.' For a more modern example of the barriers that wild rivers pose consider Mona Anderson's title for her autobiographical book about high-country life across an unbridged river in the Rakaia Valley – *A River Rules My Life*.

The New Zealand Wars

Formerly known as the Maori Wars, an expression now racially unacceptable, these wars on New Zealand soil have successively become the Land Wars (too simplistic), the New Zealand Wars and the New Zealand Colonial Wars (too general) and latterly 'the armed conflicts of the 1860s' (the preferred description for passing university examinations). Conflict began, however, with the **War in the North** (1845) and incidents about Wellington in 1846, Waikato Wars (1860–64), various Taranaki Wars, fighting in the Bay of Plenty in 1864–65, and campaigns against **Te Kooti Rikirangi** in Poverty Bay, Te Urewera and inland Bay of Plenty-Taupo (1870). Nineteenth-century historian William Pember Reeves took stock of the situation at 1871 in his *The Long White Cloud* (1898): 'Out of a multitude of fights between 1843 and 1870, thirty-seven (exclusive of the raid in Poverty Bay which was a massacre) may be classed as of greater importance than the rest. Out of these we were unmistakably beaten nine times, and a tenth encounter at Okaihau was indecisive. Of twenty-seven victories, however, those of Rangiriri and Orakau were dearly bought; in the double fight at Nukumaru we lost more than the enemy, and at Waireka most of our forces retreated, and only heard of the success from a distance. Two disasters and six successes were wholly or almost wholly the work of native auxiliaries. The cleverness and daring of the Maori also scored in the repeated escapes of batches of prisoners.' Reeves added: 'The killed alone amounted to 800 on the English side and 1800 on the part of the beaten natives. Added to the thousands wounded, there had been many scores of "murders" and heavy losses from disease, exposure and hardship. The Maori were for many years left without hope and without self confidence.' For the historical background refer to *The Origin of the Maori Wars*, by Keith Sinclair (Auckland University Press, Auckland, 1961) and the work of later scholars including *I Shall Not Die: Titikowaru's war, New Zealand 1868–69* (Allen & Unwin/Port Nicholson Press, Wellington, 1989) and *The New Zealand Wars* (Auckland University Press, 1986), both by James Belich. James Cowan made a technical record of the battles in his two-volume *The New Zealand Wars and the Pioneering Period* (Government Printer, Wellington, 1922–23). There are also the novels from the 1960s of war in the Waikato by Errol Braithwaite, and a trilogy of more recent novels by Maurice Shadbolt: *Season of the Jew, Monday's Warriors* and *The House of Strife*.

Niagara's Gold

A sensational sea disaster in 1940 was then followed by a spectacular attempt to recover a cargo of gold, worth more than £2.5 million. The *Niagara* was nearly 50 km off Whangarei Heads, bound from Auckland for Vancouver, when she struck a German mine on June 19, 1940. The ship went down in a couple of hours but all 338 passengers and crew were rescued. The cargo of gold attracted an Australian syndicate to what would then be a record for deepwater salvage, around 70 fathoms. Risking the German minefield, the vessel *Claymore* was used to locate the wreck and service a diving bell from which the salvagers worked. A hole was blown in the hull of the *Niagara* and into the strongroom. Ten tons of gold was salvaged, leaving 35 bars behind. Of these, 30 were recovered by another expedition in 1953, leaving only five still in the wreck. The story of the original recovery, done under the cloak of official secrecy, was told in *Gold from the Sea: the epic story of Niagara's bullion,* by James Taylor (Harrap, London, 1943).

Ninety Mile Beach

In fact only 64 miles long, stretching north from near Kaitaia up the east side of the Aupouri Peninsula to **Cape Maria van Diemen** (103 km of beach). Maori spirits are said to travel along it on the way to Cape Reinga, bound for the ancestral world of Hawaiki. The broad sand beach has long been used as a road, serving at one time the gumfields of the Far North and today providing tourists with the thrill of a high-speed drive beside the sea in tourist coaches. Quicksands have grabbed some vehicles. The beach is also part of the national walkways system.

The 'Nit Nurse'

An unflattering reference by children to the public-health nurses who visit schools as part of the preventive health system. Nurses regularly intervene in cases where special health or emotional problems exist, recommending at-risk children for treatment at residential **Health Camps**. Public health nurses also provide support in the home environment, but most pre-school care is carried out by **Plunket** nurses. Inspection for 'nits' – head lice – and the role nurses played in cleaning up an epidemic at school spawned the nickname.

'No Maoris, No Tour'

The battle cry of those opposed to South African apartheid in 1960, who believed that a New Zealand touring rugby side should include Maori players or the tour be cancelled. Previous All Black tours of South Africa had excluded Maori in deference to South African sensibilities, or racism; some liberals even suggested that South Africans should consider Maori to be 'honorary whites'. When it came time to select the team no Maori players made the grade and the tour went ahead. Not surprisingly the arguments over racially selected teams soon matured and rallied to the cry of Halt All Racist Tours. New Zealand rugby still fields a national team known as the **Maori All Blacks** – at Maori insistence, which apparently makes it acceptable. See **Stop the Tour**.

The North Island Main Trunk

This 685-km railway linking Wellington with Auckland was not completed until 1908. Coastal shipping was the more direct route until then. Construction was in part frustrated by the existence of the **King Country**, where Maori dissidents, who had lost the war for the Waikato, had gathered behind the Confiscation Line. Negotiating access and surveying the line southward took time and initially involved an armed force of volunteer engineer-militia in the Waikato. There were engineering difficulties, too, including building nine major viaducts and the **Raurimu Spiral** in the central North Island. The line entered the King Country in 1885 and the two ends eventually met near Makatote Viaduct (78-m high) near the middle of the North Island, on November 6, 1908. Settlement of the bush country between Marton and Te Awamutu followed the construction towns on the line. Electrification of the route from Palmerston North northward, during the 1980s, also involved enlarging tunnels and replacing bridges, but stopped short at Hamilton when the true cost was realised.

The Nor'west Arch

The föhn-like winds of Canterbury shape life and farming on the plains. The hot, dry winds may blow for several days at a time, heralded by the Nor'west Arch, a high arch of cloud poised over the Southern Alps. The wind originates out in the Tasman, full of blustering rain that is dropped on the West Coast as the winds rise up the barrier of the Alps. That climb increases its temperature by 1 degree Centigrade for every 100 m of altitude, plus the effect of condensation on temperature. The wind descends to the plains by way of the gorges of the great rivers, spilling out in a column of dust that marches down the braided shingle riverbeds like an angry cloud. The enervating effect of the wind wears tempers. The consequent wind switch to a cold south-westerly is not much more cheering, but it is a relief.

Nova Scotian Settlers *see* The 'Lion of Scotland'

Now Is the Hour

New Zealand's *Auld Lang Syne*, sung widely at the departure of ships and in sentimental situations of impending separation: even the end of Maori concerts. Written by a Maori composer, Maewa Kaihau, under the title 'Haere Ra' and instantly popular during the departure of troops to the Second World War.

Number Eight Wire

The heavy gauge of steel wire from which any ingenious Kiwi is said to be able to manufacture something useful. Originally used for heavy-grade fencing, number eight wire can be worked into pegs and catches, coat hooks, bindings and candle holders. It is tough enough to drive in as a makeshift nail or staple. In combination with a piece of '**Four by Two**' (timber) most **Practical Kiwi Jokers** can use number eight wire for solving their backyard construction problems. Add a few sheets of **Corrugated Iron** to keep it dry and you have a **Do-it-yourself** building system.

Okiato, Old Russell

In 1840 the capital of New Zealand was briefly at Okiato, close to where the Opua car ferry now deposits its passengers on the way to Russell in the Bay of Islands. The site was bought from the trader and US Consul James Clendon and renamed Russell after the Secretary of State for the Colonies. The capital was never built there, however, for Governor Hobson briefly set up his administration at Kororareka, before selecting Auckland as his capital instead, from 1841. The name of Russell was assumed by Kororareka, while Okiato is only sometimes referred to as 'Old Russell'.

Old Age Pensions

A reward for the pioneers who had worked hard but made little money. Old age pensions were introduced in 1898, by '**King Dick**' Seddon, the Liberal premier. They benefited men over 65 and women over 60 of little income but who were sober, respectable and moral – and able to prove this in court. Right from the start doomsayers predicted the country could not afford such largesse, but the system lasted nearly a hundred years in varied forms. The scheme was redeveloped by the Labour government of 1935 to become the Universal Super – or superannuation – available to all without a means test and supplemented, for those who were 'hard up', with additional benefits. The age limits for the old age pension were subsequently lowered to 60 for men and 55 for single women. In 1977 a National government gave universal superannuation equivalent to 80 per cent of the basic wage to all at 60. Only the economic collapse of 1987 alerted governments to the fact that New Zealand's population was rapidly ageing and the country would shortly be unable to pay the bill. Now the minimum ages for national superannuation are 65, as the 'baby boomers' reach full maturity, and the population balance becomes more geriatric. The pension for a married couple has also fallen to 65 per cent of the average wage.

'Old Blue' *see* The Black Robin

The 'Old Country'

A.k.a the **Mother Country**. Frequently heard reference to Britain. Also known to more recent immigrants as **Home**. See also the **Thousand Pound Cure**, and the **Ten Thousand Dollar Cure**.

Old Government House, Auckland

Now the luxurious Senior Common Room of Auckland University, Old Government House on Princes Street and Waterloo Quadrant has been the setting for many interesting events in New Zealand history. Built of wood cut to model stone, the building dates from 1856, when it replaced an earlier Government House destroyed by fire. Governor George Grey lived here during the period of the wars with Maori in the Waikato and Taranaki. In happier times it was a meeting place between the races. When the capital of New Zealand shifted to Wellington the Governor went, too, though the Auckland house remained a summer residence for Vice Regals until the 1960s.

The Old Identities

This phrase, attributed to the goldfields balladeer the **Inimitable Thatcher**, was used to distinguish between the founders of the Otago Settlement and the later comers. Charles Thatcher saw fit to refer to the differences between Old Identities and the **New Chums** in a satirical song about the provincial council elections of 1862. As gold-miners from around the world rushed to Otago, Edward Bowes Cargill (1823–1903) son of the leader of Otago Settlement, had implored the original settlers to stick together to preserve their identity.Thatcher satirised:

A Representative Old Identity.
(From a Drawing by Jas. Brown.)

> *Mr Cargill on the Council*
> *Made such a funny speech;*
> *He got up and he stated*

> *That it devolved on each*
> *Of all the early dwellers*
> *To preserve as safe as could be,*
> *Amid the Victorian influx,*
> *The Old Identity.*

Sung to the tune of 'Duck Leg Dick', the number was so successful that Thatcher wrote another version including the lines:

> *The Old Otago Settlers,*
> *That came here long ago,*
> *Are distinguished for their being*
> *So very dull and slow,*
> *The greater number of them*
> *Have a Scottish pedigree*
> *and by Thatcher they were christened*
> *The 'Old Identity'.*

The Old Stone Store

On Kerikeri Inlet, Bay of Islands, two of New Zealand's oldest buildings survive in good repair and public hands. The Stone Store was built by missionaries in 1832–35 to replace a wooden store of 1819. Bishop Selwyn used the top floor as a library and there is still a shop on the ground floor. The Kerikeri Mission House next door is the oldest building in New Zealand, dating from 1822, and lived in by the Kemp family from 1832 until its gifting to the Historic Places Trust in 1974. For many years early in the 19th century, Miss Gertrude Kemp kept alive a family tradition by setting a light in a window to guide boats up to the river basin. It remains known popularly as the Kemp House, and rightly so.

The Oldest Hotel in New Zealand (Rebuilt)

The Duke of Marlborough Hotel on the waterfront at Russell, Bay of Islands, claims the oldest liquor licence in the land. That dates from July 14, 1840. The hotel site was purchased in 1827 and the present hotel is the fourth there.

The Oldest Hotel on its Original Site

Reputedly the Thistle Inn, 1846, on the corner of Mulgrave and Sydney Streets in Thorndon, Wellington.

One Man, One Farm

The idea of owning one's own farm is deeply entrenched in the New Zealand psyche. Immigrants came here in the 19th century to get their own land, largely an impossibility in their homelands. Consequently politics in New Zealand, from the earliest conflicts between the New Zealand Company and its settlers and the British Government, were about land, its price and availability. The early role of government as the only agency allowed to buy land from Maori gave the State such a central role that, even after recent divestments, the Crown still owns in the vicinity of 40 per cent of New Zealand's land area, some 30 per cent of that in the conservation estate of protected parks and reserves. The key to establishing new provincial settlements was the allocation of land, at a price sufficient to fund the roads and services to reach and develop it. Soldier-pioneers were lured to some districts, by the promise of land, in return for securing the frontiers with Maori. Early on, rich landowners set up huge sheep runs, some adopting the Australian practice of **Grid-ironing** the Canterbury Plains to monopolise access to essential water, and thus render the country in between uneconomic except as an adjunct of their own runs. The pleas of the small farmers and those unable to find land were heard by the Liberal governments of the 1890s. Sir John Mackenzie (1838–1901), while Minister of Lands in 1892, purchased the 34,000-ha Cheviot Estate in North Canterbury, for the Crown to subdivide into smaller properties of 40-200 ha to get more people 'on the land'. Mackenzie would quote in argument for land subdivision: 'Yet millions of hands want acres, And millions of acres want hands.' His laws against aggregation of land and the compulsory subdivision of vast land-holdings made the sometime Scots shepherd a popular hero and knight. When he died poet Jessie Mackay recognised the sense of national mourning in *The Burial of Sir John Mackenzie*:

A wider clan than he ever knew
Followed him home that dowie day

And who were they of the wider clan?
The landless man and the No Man's man,
The man that lacked and the man unlearned,
The man that lived but as he earned;
And the clan went mourning all the way.

Mackay went on to write of Mackenzie:

He found her a land of many domains,
Maiden Forest and fallow plains:
He left her a land of many homes,
The pearl of the world where the sea-wind roams.

For most of the 20th century New Zealand farms were family-owned with one property each. Land Settlement Boards allocated Crown-developed properties by **Land Ballot** to families without land. Only in recent years have farming companies been allowed back into the market, allowing investors from overseas to threaten the hard-won New Zealand tradition of people farming their own land.

One Tree Hill

This Auckland landmark is the volcano known to Maori as Maungakiekie. At its summit a lone pine tree replaced the original totara from Maori times. The earlier tree gave the summit a similar name in Maori, te Totara i ahua. According to a tradition quoted by David Simmons in *Maori Auckland*, the sacred tree was said to originate from a stick on which was cut the umbilical cord of the ancestor Korokino about 1600. It was cut down by vandals about 1853 and the pine tree planted in its place. Several efforts to replant with a totara were unsuccessful and there is a saying that when a European succeeds in growing a totara there, then they shall be truly tangata whenua, people of the land. The pine tree that did grow was attacked with a chainsaw by a Maori activist in 1994. Attempts to save it suffered another blow in 1999 when the tree was further damaged by Maori protestors. After a severe storm it had to be cut down in 2000. Replacement trees, both totara and pohutukawa, have been raised from local seed but not planted out because the area is presently under a Treaty of Waitangi claim by the local tribe, Ngati Whatua. Maungakiekie is terraced and walled in an extensive pattern of Maori defences. From the summit at 183 m the view encompasses the whole of the Auckland isthmus and far into the Hauraki Gulf. The 21-m obelisk that stands on the top, adjacent to the site of the vanished tree, was erected by Sir John Logan Campbell, known as the **Father of Auckland**, to honour the Maori connections with the land. Traditions of the volcanoes and early Auckland are recorded in *Maori Auckland*, by David Simmons (The Bush Press, Auckland, 1987).

'Onward'

Once the motto of New Zealand but removed from the coat of arms in 1956. It looked challenging on the service hats of soldiers abroad and exuded some confidence of a brighter future at home. The motto on the arms now simply reads 'New Zealand'.

Opo the Dolphin

During the summer of 1955–56, a bottle-nosed dolphin made friends with the people of Opononi on the southern shores of the Hokianga Harbour. At first dubbed Opononi Jack, the dolphin was then identified as a half-grown female; thence she was known simply as Opo. Newsreels of the time made Opo world famous as she swam with local chidren and adults, tossing balls and playing a form of water polo. People rolled up their trousers and tucked skirts into bloomers to walk out into the shallow water of the harbour to be close to her. Soon, busloads of visitors came to see the dolphin, sorely stretching the local community. At length, after some months, Opo disappeared only to be found a few days later washed up on nearby rocks, some said deliberately killed by dynamite blasts placed in the water. Opo inspired musician Crombie Murdoch to immortalise her in popular song, with references to taking a 'fishy back ride'. Author Maurice Shadbolt used elements of the story in the plot of his novel *This Summer's Dolphin,* re-set on Waiheke Island. See also **Pelorus Jack.**

The Originals

The expression is used of the 1905 New Zealand rugby team that toured the British Isles with devastating effect. They won all but one game and that loss arose from a controversial decision not to allow Bob Deans a try against the Welsh at Cardiff Arms Park. Deans claimed to have been dragged back over the goal line by the Welsh after scoring, but the referee did not see. That decision is now part of rugby legend and still sufficiently debated to have loosely inspired a movie, *Old Scores*, in which the game, or something like it, is replayed. The defeat by the Welsh was avenged by the **Invincibles** of 1925.

Overseas Experience (OE)

Not so much a qualification as a rite of passage; a young New Zealander's version of the Grand Tour. Originally undertaken by sea, such journeys '**Home**' were a cultural necessity for writers and artists through the 1920s and 1930s. As the world opened up in the 1950s, more young New Zealanders made the journey, usually to Britain and Europe, to explore their past or, more often, to escape the stultifying narrowness of New Zealand at the time. As aeroplanes brought cheaper fares, overseas travel became much more attainable and the proportion of young people seeking Overseas Experience burgeoned. In London through the 1960s they gathered, with Australians, in the district of Earls Court, adopting a hedonistic lifestyle celebrated by Australian Barry Humphries, in his 'Adventures of Barry Mackenzie', originally published in *Private Eye*. As the world became a more accessible place, New Zealanders extended their OEs to Asia and Africa, perhaps returning from Britain through Europe, India and Asia by road. A similar adventure trail went through Africa. From the mid-1990s, as student loans debts became heavier, and the value of the New Zealand dollar fell drastically, young New Zealanders often went abroad to make more money and try to repay their debts.

The P-Class

The smallest competitive class of yacht. Most of New Zealand's world-class yachtsmen learned to sail in this 2.1-m sailing dinghy designed by Harry Highet. Also known as the Tauranga Class, Ps have been raced by under-16-year-olds since the first inter-provincials in 1940.

Pa Sites

A distinctive feature of the New Zealand landscape is the Maori pa or fortress. Defined by the lines of abandoned ditches and banks, these pa mark the defensive sites of Maori times. Once, they were topped by palisades of logs with fighting platforms above. Inside, Maori stored valued crops of kumara and protected the honour of their bloodlines, both reasons for raiders to attack. Many Maori lived outside the pa in undefended kainga villages, but retreated inside when the warning conch shells or gongs sounded. There are more than 5500 recorded pa sites, mainly in the North Island of New Zealand, but with more than 100 in the South Island. Look for the lines of them on small hills, such as the highly defended volcanoes of Auckland, and on cliff tops and points of land surrounded by sea or swamp.

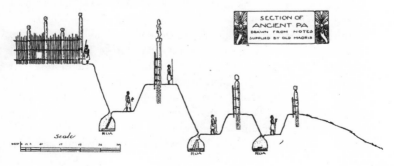

SECTION OF ANCIENT PA
DRAWN FROM NOTES SUPPLIED BY OLD MAORIS

Pack Trains

Strings of horses were used to carry heavy loads over rough country in pioneer times. Horses carried loads in bags tied to a pack saddle. In this way it was possible to carry loads over the high mountain passes of the South Island before roads were cut to the goldfields. At the head of the pack train rode the packie, in charge of a string of such horses. The practice continued in the high country and back country generally until the helicopter took over the job.

Pakeha Maori

This expression was once used of those Europeans who were naturally at home with Maori people, speaking their language and observing their customs. In the days before the Treaty of Waitangi the population of Europeans in New Zealand was fewer than 2000 and some accepted the local way of life to the extent that they lived to all intents as Maori. Whalers and sealers were the first to adopt Maori ways. Some escaped prisoners from the Australian colonies stowed away, or otherwise reached New Zealand, hiding away with Maori tribes. Those who married into a tribe sometimes went to battle in their cause. Among notable Pakeha Maori was **Kimble Bent** (1837–1916), an American adventurer who joined the British Army only to desert to the **Hauhau** during the wars in Taranaki. John Rutherford was known as the **White Chief** or the Tattooed Sailor. On his return to Britain he exhibited himself as a travelling stage show, telling wild yarns of his days among cannibals. The most notable user of the description 'A Pakeha Maori' was Judge Frederick Edward Maning (1811–83) of the Hokianga. In 1863 he published his experiences in *Old New Zealand*, one of the classic accounts of life in those formative days, using the name as a *nom-de-plume*. Maning came from Tasmania to settle at Onoke on the Hokianga, where he was a trader. He married a woman of Te Rarawa and identified with Maori interests, arguing against the effects that British ways would have on them. At the signing of the Treaty of Waitangi he was one of those who translated for the chiefs. Then, during the **War in the North** he supported Hone Heke and wrote an account of it from the Maori side. From 1865 Maning was a judge of the Native Land Court, where his deep knowledge of Maori custom won wide respect. His book regrets the passing of the 'good old times'. Once published, Maning then tried to suppress its first edition, gathering up copies and burning them beside the Hokianga River. The scholar T.M. Hocken speculated in 1906 as to why Maning destroyed the books, perhaps 'for respectability and his children's sake to obliterate every glimpse of those old times ... in which they had been born'. Alternatively he was incensed 'with Mr Julius Vogel, then editor of the *Southern*

Cross for printing, unauthorised, one thousand copies of the book'. Maning also burnt the original of a sequel, *New New Zealand*, with the intention of rewriting it, but died before he could. The original *Old New Zealand*, amended and expanded, has been reprinted many times.

Pakihi

The Maori word for a clearing in the bush; in common usage pakihi describes a particular class of land, its trees felled and only wetland fern and low scrub growing in its place. Under the surface a hard clay pan stops water draining away and new plantings from taking satisfactory root. Pakihi lands abound in Westland. In parts of Northland the old gumlands, once kauri forest, are similar.

Panning for Gold

A broad shallow pan was the working tool of the gold prospector and the alluvial miner. A shovel full of shingle from a likely bed was swilled about in water. The dross was floated off and tipped out, leaving the gold-bearing black sand or 'pay-dirt' at the bottom of the pan. Tell-tale specks of gold remained in the bottom, heavier than anything else in the wash. When mechanical devices such as cradles and riffles were set up to catch larger quantities of gold, the final 'wash-up' was often done by swilling the gold-bearing sand in a pan. Prospectors found the pan useful even in 'hard rock' districts. Usually there would be some sign downstream of gold-bearing country, where alluvial gold dust had washed from the quartz reefs nearby. Thus when Charles Ring and his brother found alluvial gold at Coromandel in 1852, the disappointing quantities in the creek were but a sign of the wealth discovered much later, locked up in the quartz hills above the town. Getting gold from quartz involved a different process, using at first mercury and subsequently cyanide to separate grains of gold from the crushed rock flour.

Pantry

Traditionally the room where food was kept, adjacent to the kitchen. Separated from other rooms, it contained open shelves for the storage of food in bulk, including hung meat such as bacon, and drying vegetables. The room was supposed to be secure against pests. Larger, older homes may still have such spaces used for storage, though convenience shopping and refrigerators have disposed of the need for a bulk food store beside the family kitchen.

Parker and Hulme

Two Christchurch schoolgirls killed the mother of one in a murder that made international headlines in 1954. There were parallels with the Loeb case in New York (filmed by Alfred Hitchcock as *Rope*). The newspapers introduced psychological terms such as *'folie à deux'* and the concept of lesbianism to many of the public. The *Press* of Christchurch, indeed, prides itself on publishing every word of evidence, in transcript. Pauline Parker and Janet Hulme went to prison for several years, but their case remains a celebrated one, marked by a stage play and several books, including *Parker and Hulme: A Lesbian View*, by Julie Glamuzina and Alison J. Lawrie (New Women's Press, Auckland, 1991, Auckland). The story was also filmed as *Heavenly Creatures* by Peter Jackson, who went on to make the **Lord of the Rings** trilogy. At the time, the girls wrote fantasy stories. In adult life, Hulme has become a popular author of Victorian mysteries, under the name of Anne Perry.

Party Lines

The manual telephone system often placed a number of subscribers on one line, their incoming calls distinguished from each other by a Morse code signal rung on a bell, (e.g. 42S, 42R, 42M, etc.). One telephone line and number, with distinguishing code signals, frequently served a whole country valley. The caller rang an exchange operator by winding a hand-generator and was then connected by plug to the person called. On a party line the operator rang through with a Morse code signal, for example three short bells for an S, so the owner of the telephone with that suffix should answer. The system could be abused by gossips who simply listened in to their neighbours' calls, but an unusual pattern on the phone sometimes served as a warning that all was not well nearby. The country telephone exchange operator became a central figure in the district and a key source of information and co-ordination in a civil emergency. The system persisted until the upgrading of manual telephone exchanges to automatic, which took place through the 1970s. The last party lines disappeared when the exchange on Great Barrier Island was automated in 1991. Party lines also occurred in the city, but were usually more secure. When two or more parties shared a line through an automatic exchange they could not hear each other, only share the frustration of frequently finding the telephone engaged.

Pastoral Leases *see* Run-holders

Paua Shell Jewellery

Jewellery featuring the glowing colours of the abalone, or paua, shell is a traditional New Zealand art form. The shell itself is usually encrusted in sea growths which must be ground away to reveal the beauty underneath. Paua shell jewellery was for long a by-product of the paua-fishing industry; slivers of the iridescent material being incorporated into silver ear-rings, brooches, stick pins and tie pins, sometimes in the form of the national symbols, **Kiwi** and **Silver Fern.** Paua shell was traditionally used by Maori, too, to provide eyes on carvings of the human form.

Pavlova

The epitome of tradional New Zealand cuisine, rich in sugars and filled with fats. The pavlova, named it is said for the lightness of the ballerina, is a confection of sugar and whipped egg white, topped with cream and fresh fruit. Some cooks use the separated egg yolks along with the cream for a richer filling, stacking two layers of the meringue before topping with cream and strawberries, or raspberries, kiwifruit or sliced apricot. For a good recipe consult *Classic Kiwi Recipes,* by Sheryl Brownlee (Beckett, Auckland, 1991).

Peggy Squares

Using left-over balls of wool, the beginner knits a little square; sewing together a patchwork of squares produces at first a doll's blanket, then one big enough to cover a full-sized bed. A competition to knit such blankets for Bosnia produced in the *New Zealand Herald* the story of Mrs Peg Cook of Te Puke, who claimed to be the original Peggy. As a four-year-old in 1930 she knitted some practice squares and sewed them together for a doll's rug. A family friend promoted the idea on radio and the popular blanket of the **Great Depression** years was born.

Pelorus Jack

The tradition of Pelorus Jack began when a white Risso's dolphin began to accompany ships on the Nelson-Wellington run, across the entrance to Pelorus Sound. The dolphin was first noticed in the late 1880s and greeted passing ships by rubbing along the hull and cavorting in the water. The creature seemed to favour steam passenger vessels and became internationally famous through travellers' writings. In 1904 it became 'the only fish in the world protected by an Act of Parliament' though this description on the souvenir postcard only reflected the confusion the marine mammal posed. In fact an Order in Council forbade 'the taking of the fish or mammal known as Risso's Dolphin in the Cook Strait and Marlborough Sounds area' for a period of five years. The protection was renewed twice before Pelorus Jack vanished in 1912. See also **Opo the Dolphin**.

The Petrified Man

Traditions of a petrified man found in a limestone cave in remote Fiordland have been confirmed and explained by the authors of *Port Preservation*, Drs Charles and Neil Begg. The tales begin with the discovery of a man turned to stone by dripping limestone, found by Walter Traill at Cavern Head, Port Preservation, in 1877. When Traill returned to cut out the body for a museum the petrified man was gone. The Maori crew of the whaler *Splendid* admitted moving it, presumably to save their ancestor. In a fascinating piece of historical detection, the Beggs link the petrified man with Maori traditions of the last battles between Kai Tahu and the remnant Kati Mamoe. Recounting the mid-18th-century battles in Port Preservation, the Beggs named the petrified man as Tarewai, leader of the Kai Tahu war party, who lost his life there. His body was placed in the cave along with a mere made of tangiwai **Greenstone**. This was recovered later by goldminers, who found the club embedded in the limestone. See *Port Preservation,* by A. Charles Begg and Neil C. Begg (Whitcombe and Tombs, Christchurch, 1973), and the **Lost Tribe, Fiordland**.

The Phantom Canoe

There are many Maori tales of the portents of the **Tarawera Eruption** in 1886, but the phantom canoe was seen by several European travellers, too. The sighting occurred just 11 days before the mountain, west of Rotorua, erupted, killing 153 people and devastating the district. Accounts by Maori guides and travellers tell variously of a canoe crewed by unknown Maori wearing flax cloaks and the symbolic feathers of huia and white heron. The canoe was of a design never before seen on the lake and when the guides challenged its crew, the phantom simply continued, heading in the direction of the traditional Maori burial grounds on the slopes of the dormant volcano. The sighting of the Phantom Canoe added to feelings of growing unease among the people of the Tarawera villages. The ancient tohunga Tuhoto of Wairoa was also involved in laying curses and making prophecies of disaster at that time. He survived the eruption, dug out of his tiny house after four days of burial under the ash. He was taken to Rotorua, where he died a few days later in hospital, aged over 100, claiming still to have invoked the wrath of the mountain. The eruption of Tarawera is documented by Geoff Conly in *Tarawera: the destruction of the Pink and White Terraces* (Grantham House, Wellington, 1985).

Phar Lap

The horse the Aussies 'stole' from New Zealand. The internationally famous Australian thoroughbred was actually born in New Zealand, at Timaru, in October 1926. Australian Hugh Telford bought 'Australia's Big Horse' at the Trentham Yearling Sales of June 1928 for 160 guineas ($336). Phar Lap won more stake money than any other horse at that time, winning 37 of 51 starts during three years in Australia. There was mystery and allegations of poisoning when the horse died shortly after success in North America. Phar Lap's hide became an Australian icon, the stuffed horse once put on display at the entrance to the National Museum in Melbourne. Sensitivity over which country can claim the horse is expressed in the foreword to *Phar Lap* by Isabel Ray Carter: 'Phar Lap is referred to in this book as an Australian horse. This is to avoid confusion in the narrative. Phar Lap was, of course, bred in New Zealand, and no disrespect is intended to that home of great thoroughbreds.'

Pig Hunting

A rural sport that pits hunter and dog against wild pig (or **Captain Cooker**). Dogs hunt out wild pigs in the scrub or 'pig fern' otherwise known as bracken. Dogs hold the pig, often by the ear, at considerable risk of being torn by tusks. The hunter has to kill the pig by sticking a knife in its heart. Predominantly a male sport, pig hunting nevertheless includes many women amongst its devotees. Kim Swan of Rai Valley has made a book of her hunting stories called *The Grunter Hunters* (Halcyon, Auckland, 1992).

The Pigroot

This was the name of an old miners' route into Central Otago, which turns inland at Palmerston and follows the Shag River to Dunback, Waihemo and on, by Highway 85, to the site of the old Kyeburn **Diggings** and the Maniototo goldfields. Buildings from the old coaching days can still be seen in modern guise along the way. Over the years there has been some argument about the origin of the name, but in the old days wild pigs were plentiful along the trail, and a nearby Pigroot Hill was named by surveyor John Turnbull Thomson in 1857. Thomson also named many of the local streams after animals, such as the Hogburn and Sowburn.

Pikau

An improvised backpack popular for carrying loads, or **Swags**, in old New Zealand. It was made from a sugar sack or similar. The bottom corners are secured by tying a rope around a stone pushed into the corner to lock the knot. The ropes then run up to the neck of the bag, thus forming carrying straps. When the idea caught on in Australia it was known as a collar-fashioned pack, 'tied New Zealand-style'. Source: editor's footnote to a poem in *Australian Folklore*, compiled by W. Fearn-Wannan (Lansdowne, Sydney, 1977).

The Pink and White Terraces

Advertised as the Eighth Wonder of the World, the Pink and White Terraces on Lake Rotomahana attracted tourists to the Rotorua region as early as the 1870s. These great volcanic landforms, built by nature from silica, cascaded down to the shores of the lake in two formations. The White Terrace (Te Tarata) fell 240 m in steps, expanding to the same width, from a giant hot spring 30 m above the lake. Basins on the platforms provided natural hot swimming pools, getting hotter as the bather climbed up the giant steps closer to the crater at the top. The Pink Terraces (Otukapuarangi) were across the lake, having smoother steps and popular bathing platforms near the top. Both can be seen today only in the paintings of Victorians such as Barraud and Hoyte, or in the photographs of pioneers such as the Burton brothers. In the darkness before dawn on June 10, 1886, an eruption of Mt Tarawera buried the surrounding countryside, including the Pink and White Terraces, with volcanic debris. The story of the **Tarawera Eruption** is well told in *Tarawera: the destruction of the Pink and White Terraces*, by Geoff Conly (Grantham House, Wellington, 1985). See also **Buried Village** and **Phantom Canoe.**

Playlunch

The morning and afternoon breaks at New Zealand schools where children may eat a sandwich or snack, while teachers pause in the staff room. From 1937–1967 the State provided half a pint of milk at morning playtime and, during the Second World War, also an apple a day. Alarmingly, more and more children now come to school without playlunch or even lunch. A 1993 survey revealed that 75 per cent of primary children get only two meals a day. Things haven't got better in the 2000s, with schools in poorer areas reporting children arriving at school without having had breakfast.

Plimmer's Ark

A conspicuous establishment in early Wellington, this Ark was the upturned hull of a ship. In 1850 the 460-ton vessel *Inconstant* went ashore on rocks near Pencarrow Head. An early trader, John Plimmer, had the hull towed off and beached where Lambton Quay now meets Willis Street. Plimmer's Steps connected his house, still standing in Boulcott Street, with the Ark on the old foreshore. The building was then known as Noah's Ark, trading as a warehouse, bondstore and auction rooms for 32 years. See its remains, exposed in the basement floor of the Old Bank Arcade in the redeveloped former BNZ building.

Ploughing Championships

Do anything boring long enough and the mind makes a ritual of it. Turning over the furrow has become a high art to farmers who compete in local and national ploughing championships. Competitors take turns to show how they can lay down a straight furrow. Since 1956 national ploughing championships have been held for the Silver Plough, a replica of the one used by the missionary Rev. J.G. Butler, who on May 3, 1820, turned the first sod at Kerikeri in the Bay of Islands. Winner and runner-up become New Zealand entrants for international ploughing championships.

The Plunket Shield

Long the symbol of cricketing supremacy between the provinces. Donated by Governor-General Lord Plunket for the 1906–07 season, it has been played for between the North and South Islands since 1975, when the Shell Series superseded its inter-provincial role.

The Plunket Society

The brainchild of pioneer paediatrician Sir Truby King (1858–1938), 'Plunket' was founded in 1905 'to help the Mothers and save the babies'. Breast-feeding was a fundamental tenet. Originally known as the Society for the Promotion of the Health of Women and Children, it became 'Royal' in 1916, having as its first patron Lady Plunket, wife of the Governor-General of the time. The Plunket Society provides much of the advice and help needed to keep babies healthy in pre-school years, with what is now the Royal New Zealand Plunket Society as focus for volunteer fund-raising, and support for professional nurses and their clinics. A related service, Karitane nurses, provides domestic support for mothers in need of help with children at home. Karitane nurses take their name from the Plunket training hospitals, named in turn for Karitane in Otago where Sir Truby King lived as medical superintendent of Seacliff Mental Asylum. Later, he combined the jobs of Inspector-General of Mental Hospitals with Director of Child Welfare. King was the author of popular guides including *The Feeding and Care of the Baby*, *The Natural Feeding of Infants*, *The Expectant Mother* and *Baby's First Month*. Lady King actively supported this work, writing mothercraft pamphlets and syndicated newspaper columns to promote the Plunket ideal. King's work included tables of growth and weight with matching advice to reach these 'norms' of childhood development. While some complained that a child's failure to achieve perfection could discourage a young mother, the overall impact was to raise mothering skills and mothercraft to a high art. Despite all this New Zealand has never enjoyed a good record in the area of infant mortality, though recent work on cot deaths has somewhat improved the statistics against the international scale.

The Pohutu Geyser

Tourist stop and largest of the surviving geysers in New Zealand, Pohutu is the temperamental queen of the Whakarewarewa geothermal field at Rotorua. At its foot other geysers, including the Prince of Wales Feathers and Mahanga (the Boxing Glove) belch and spurt more consistently. Pohutu's regularity and pressure have improved considerably in recent years, following constraints on nearby city residents, who took so much hot water from the underground field that the geothermal performance of Whakarewarewa was weakened.

Pohutukawa *see* The New Zealand Christmas Tree

Poi Dancing

Maori dance form in which women twirl balls of flax on short or long strings in time to music; beloved of concert parties. An old school instruction book illustrates the movements, but basically counsels the beginner to first learn the words, then the song, then the actions, by doing them with someone who already knows how. Confused? Then try stick games.

Polio Epidemics

The frequent summer disease that killed and maimed many young New Zealanders before the invention of the Salk vaccine in 1956 and the Sabine oral vaccine in 1961. Known as infantile paralysis the disease was fought against by quarantine, washing hands and wearing a sunhat. In 1947–48 schools throughout New Zealand were closed for four months and all children took correspondence school lessons at home to avoid contact with the disease.

Pommies, Poms, *Prisoners of Mother England*

The etymology of the term Pommie, as a description of the English, has long been debated. Arguments vary, from a French judgement on English eating preferences, to the poetic title of a play about migrants by Roger Hall. The play ascribes the meaning Prisoners of Mother England to the acronym P.O.M.E. To a New Zealander its characters display many of the attitudes that surfaced in the persona of the **Whingeing Pom**. The play has a wistful twist, typical of the migrant experience, when a character returns **'Home'** too late to see a dying parent. See *Prisoners of Mother England*, by Roger Hall (Playmarket, Wellington, 1980).

Poppy Day

In the week before **Anzac Day**, April 25, returned servicemen and women sell artificial red poppies to raise funds for war veterans' aid. The same poppies may reappear on lapels on Anzac Day, when people gather to remember the fallen of New Zealand's foreign wars.

Postage Stamps

New Zealand issued its first postage stamps in 1855, featuring a full-face picture of the younger Queen Victoria in her Coronation robes, engraved from a painting by Challon. The rarest stamp, printed but never issued, is a 1949 threepenny featuring HMS *Vanguard*. Only three are known to have escaped destruction when King George VI became ill and the issue prepared to mark his Royal Visit to New Zealand was cancelled. A rare misprinted stamp is the 'Taupo inversion', a 1904 penny stamp with its scene printed upside-down, which was passed in at auction in 1993 at $155,000. See also **Universal Penny Post.**

Poverty Bay

Local people who resent the name point to the region's riches, but James Cook looked on the darker side when he first reached New Zealand with the *Endeavour* in 1769. The ship needed fresh water and food. Cook wrote 'I have named (it) Poverty Bay because it afforded us no one thing we wanted.' He reprovisioned his ship in the Bay of Plenty.

The Practical Kiwi Joker

This is not about practical jokes. Kiwi jokers can do anything. They are famous for coming up with a simple solution to a complex problem. Unlike Pommies and other useless jokers the Kiwi is able to cut through the bullswool and come up with a simple answer. The practical Kiwi joker can slap together most things if he has the raw materials; **Number Eight Wire**, a length of **Four by Two** timber and perhaps a sheet of **Corrugated Iron**. (Lord Rutherford of Nelson, The **Man Who Split the Atom**, undertook his first experiments at Canterbury University using a battery he built during working holidays on his father's Taranaki farm.) The practical Kiwi joker doesn't have a string of letters after his name, though. He can sense an expert at 50 yards and not only show him up in front of his mates but live to tell the tale again and again in the pub. Nor does he need flash tools. You can often tell a practical Kiwi joker by the pile of useful things lying round his section yard. The more pre-occupied practical Kiwi joker usually doesn't worry much about keeping the garden up to scratch and his wife's probably been waiting eight years for him to fix the lock on the bathroom door or knock up a few shelves. On the other hand, practical Kiwi jokers have been known to use their ingenuity to lay concrete all over the yard to save mowing lawns, also creating noticeable gardens decorated with home-made gnomes or old cars. The tradition lives because of successful practical Kiwi jokers. They may be seen on television, occasionally, working on such things as revolutionary engines fuelled by water or sunlight, and building better possum traps. Notable successes that prove the ingenuity of Kiwis are the aeroplane and engine built by Richard Pearse in South Canterbury between 1898 and 1902 using scraps from round the district. See also the **First Man to Fly** and the **Taranaki Gate**. Less successful was the attempt by a wartime Minister of Works to convert his crawler bulldozers into fighting tanks by the addition of an iron shell.

Preventing Car Sickness

A strap of rubber or leather, attached to the underside of a car and dragging along the road, was widely believed to stop car sickness during the 1950s and 1960s. A section of bicycle tyre or a leather belt was often used. This piece of folklore may still be observed occasionally about New Zealand roads.

Prison Escapers *see* George Wilder

Prohibition

Abuse of alcohol by male settlers in the 19th century was a matter of considerable concern, particularly among women and the families who suffered. Thus women gathered in organisations such as the Women's Christian Temperance Union in lobbying for prohibition of the sale of alcoholic liquor from the 1880s. Their organisational strength may be judged in the critical role that the WCTU played, in winning for women the right to vote, in 1893. With links to prohibitionists in the all-male Parliament they continued to press both for votes and the suppression of liquor. Organisations such as the Band of Hope encouraged children to sign 'The Pledge' never to drink liquor and many thousands did. In a 1911 referendum, 55.83 per cent of votes were cast for prohibition but a three-fifths majority was required to change the law. A further referendum was sought by an association promoting prohibition, the New Zealand Alliance, which presented its case with 242,000 signatures. The liquor industry responded with 306,826 petitioners, who wanted a third referendum option called State Control. When a special liquor referendum was held in March 1919 a majority wanted prohibition and only the late votes of soldiers returning from the First World War kept the hotels open. At the General Election a third option of State Purchase and Control effectively split the vote three ways, thus making a clear majority for change more difficult to achieve. Nevertheless Prohibition came within 3000 votes of winning and 13 'dry' electorates were declared. Most of these went 'wet' during the 1950s and 1960s, but large areas of urban Auckland were without local hotels until the establishment of licensing trusts, owned by the community, during the 1970s. The liquor referendum was usually held in conjunction with a General Election. See **Dry Towns**.

The Prophet Rua

A tohunga of the Urewera, Rua Kenana came to believe he was the reincarnation of John the Baptist and on occasions the Holy Ghost. Building what he called the New Jerusalem at remote Maungapohatu, he was frequently at odds with the Crown, placing himself apart from the law. Charges of sly-grogging against him led to a series of events involving contempt of court charges and the subsequent 'invasion' of Maungapohatu by armed and mounted police on April 2, 1916. As police moved in to arrest Rua, his supporters in the scrub opened fire. The gun battle lasted half an hour. Two Maori, including a son of Rua, were killed. Several more Maori were wounded as were four police. Rua was sentenced to prison for a year for resisting the police, but the jury could not agree on charges of counselling to murder and bodily harm. Rua remains a distinguished prophet of the Ringatu church and has been the subject of study, including *Mihaia: the prophet Rua Kenana and his community at Maungapohatu*, by Judith Binney (Oxford University Press, Wellington, 1979) and *Rua and the Maori Millennium*, by Peter Webster (Price Milburn for Victoria University Press, Wellington, 1979).

Puha, Puwha

The common sow thistle found and eaten in most parts of the world. *Sonchus oleraceus* is a popular Maori vegetable finding its culinary expression in such dishes as puha and pork. It is rich in vitamin C.

Pukeko, Recipe *see* Cooking a Pukeko

Quarter-acre Sections

The standard size for a New Zealand suburban section was formerly the quarter acre, i.e. 40 perches or around 1000 sq m in modern measurement. The quintessential nature of such subdivision is captured in the title of Austin Mitchell's social commentary on New Zealand life *The Half-Gallon, Quarter-Acre, Pavlova Paradise* (Whitcombe and Tombs, Christchurch, 1972). The quarter acre made room for growing vegetables, an essential part of the domestic economy of most New Zealand famiies until the 1960s. A more basic reason for this size of plot was that it could accommodate a septic tank whereby toilet waste was 'treated' within the confines of the section (before there was a mains sewage system). Many quarter-acre sections are now being subdivided for 'in-fill' housing. Ironically, this is creating overload on the sewage systems that made such further subdivision possible.

The Queen of New Zealand

New Zealand became a colony of Britain when Maori signed the **Treaty of Waitangi** with the representative of Queen Victoria, William Hobson, in 1840. Self-government followed in 1852, and independence as a Dominion in 1907 but the royal link remained. Efforts to discard the royal connection have been half-hearted, partly due to the very real trade advantages of belonging to the British Commonwealth before the rise of the European Economic Community, and the large number of British-born Members of Parliament in the 1950s. When the young Queen Elizabeth II toured New Zealand in the summer of 1953–54 towns everywhere vied with each other with displays of their fervour. At the time, New Zealand was simply the 'food basket' of Britain, and in return gave British goods a competitive advantage over those of other nations. The changing national mood was reflected when the Queen of Great Britain and Northern Ireland and Head of the British Commonwealth became, separately, Queen of New Zealand in a major sort-out of constitutional laws in 1986. The Queen is represented in New Zealand by a Governor-General appointed for five years on the recommendation of the prime minister. The job is largely symbolic, but constitutionally involves giving the Royal Assent to legislation (on the advice of the government ministers) and in calling on the leader of the major political grouping in Parliament to form a government. There have been rumbles of republicanism in recent years, but there is a very good reason for maintaining a link with the British Crown. Although political scientists now generally define the Crown as 'the will of the people expressed through Parliament', some Maori leaders tend to view the Queen personally as the other party in the Treaty of Waitangi; severing links creates difficulties for them. A further concern related to the right of appeal to the judicial committee of the British Privy Council. This link was severed in 2004 and replaced with a New Zealand Supreme Court.

Queen Street Farmers

The expression has also been used in reference to Hereford Street, Christchurch, and perhaps to other places where urban investors, professionals and businessmen such as stockbrokers, lawyers, accountants and the medical fraternity, do business. Their money-market savvy has allowed them to invest in farms and run them from the city. The absentee owner has often been an unpopular figure in the countryside, stemming from the tradition of the family farm. Their 4WD vehicles are known variously as Remuera or Fendalton tractors, named for the suburbs where many live. Improvements in roads and cars over recent years have led to many more urban people not only owning country property but also living on it. These commuters are more often known as **10-acre Block** people.

The Queen Street Riots, 1932

A march by Post and Telegraph workers, protesting at proposed wage cuts, was the trigger for rioting in Queen Street, Auckland, in the depths of the **Great Depression**. They were joined by hundreds of unemployed who turned on police with stones and batons. Looting broke out and even mounted police could not control the situation. Shop windows along Queen Street were broken and stock taken, while theatregoers looked on. Sailors and volunteers were called in to help restore order. More than a hundred injured were taken to hospital. When trouble looked likely to continue, the following night in Karangahape Road, 1200 special constables were sworn in. Many were mounted farmers, others naval volunteers and servicemen. The incidents deeply divided the community. There is a lively account of the events of the time in John Mulgan's novel *Man Alone* (Paul's Book Arcade, Hamilton, 1950).

The Queen Street Riots, 1984

A large, free concert in Aotea Square, Auckland, attracted thousands of young people on a Friday night in 1984. When crowd control broke down, young people rioted, breaking windows of shops in adjacent Queen Street. Police used riot gear and batons to restore order.

'Queen Victoria', Takiora (1842–93)

Soldiers' nickname for Lucy Lord, or Takiora, a Maori woman who fought with the Colonial troops against the **Hau Hau** in Taranaki. She was also known as 'Queen Victoria' and Wikitoria of Nukumaru (her tribe), Lucy Grey after her mother and, in later life, as Louisa Dalton. Born in the Bay of Islands to a Maori woman of Taranaki ancestry and a European whaler, Takiora acted as guide to government troops unfamiliar with the terrain and locations of Taranaki. Both she and her husband Te Mahuki acted at times as guides to Major Gerhard von Tempsky VC and his Forest Rangers. The brilliant water-colours of the Taranaki campaign, executed by von Tempsky, include several paintings of Takiora in action with the **Forest Rangers.**

Queen's Birthday

A public holiday set on the Monday following the first weekend in June. The pattern was set by the birthday of King George VI. Queen Elizabeth was actually born on April 21, 1925. In New Zealand the Queen issues an **Honours** list to mark her official birthday and another at New Year.

The Queen's Chain

Valued right of public access along river banks, lake shores and the sea front, generally assumed by New Zealanders. The width of this marginal strip is 22 yards (equalling the length of a cricket pitch). The Queen's Chain contrasts with the privatised waters of Britain (and the relatively easy access to their countryside through the use of frequent rights of way across private land). The theory of easy access to the New Zealand countryside is confounded, however, by many waterside landowners claiming riparian rights. A Labour government in the 1980s insisted that such riparian properties be opened up when subdivided by the creation of esplanade reserves. The matter rankles with landowners and recreationalists however. With the buy-up of Crown high-country leases by overseas interests in recent years, the question of public access has become hotly contested. Gaining permission to cross Crown-leased land and walk up its rivers is no longer easy to get, as hunting and fishing is effectively privatised, particularly on 'safari' properties. The tradition of free access across Crown land, inherited from pioneer days, is fiercely defended for, without it, huge tracts of country may be closed to the recreationalist. Also, access to public lands in the back country can be blocked by landowners bordering the Crown estate. Debate on the ownership of the foreshore and seabed has also touched on public access. It was then revealed the Queen's Chain applied to only about one-third of all foreshores and riverbeds.

Quid

Slang for a pound (20 shillings or 240 pence) before it was turned into two dollars with decimalisation in 1967. 'Fivers' and 'tenners' were worth twice as much then, too. Some quid pro quo?

The Raetihi Bushfire

In March 1918 a combination of cyclonic winds and bushfires devastated the district around Raetihi in the upper Wanganui region. The fires destroyed nine timber mills and the forest lands they depended on, burning from Horopito to Raetihi and from Ohakune westward to the Wanganui River. The people of Raetihi jumped into the river to save themselves from the flames that destroyed much of the town. The concurrent cyclone took its toll in the town centre, too. Smoke spread so far, darkening the daylight, that the ferry entering Wellington had to take soundings to find its way in. In all more than 120 homes were burned. See *New Zealand Sensations*, by Rex Monigatti (Reed, Wellington, 1962).

Railway Cups

Heavyweight white china bearing the device of New Zealand Government Railways was a distinctive feature of the railway cafeteria of steam passenger days. The thick china was hard to break even in the accidents that accompanied the push of people pressing to be fed. (See **Railway Pies**.) The manufacture of railway cups, saucers and plates was the protected preserve of the New Zealand china industry based at New Lynn. Such Crown Lynn 'heavies' have now become collectables and are also sold as reproductions.

Railway Pies

Customary fare at railway tea rooms for travellers in the days of steam trains. Usually comprised of scalding hot meat and fluids inside flaky, breakable pastry. The alternative menu, or the complementary one, was a block of plain cake, damp sandwiches and a cup of railway tea. Passengers descended at irregular intervals from the mainline expresses at isolated stations, rucking for food at long counters, then struggling back through the massed passengers to have yet another late supper. In New Zealand fashion, people did not queue, they pushed. On the North Island main trunk there were tea stops at Paekakariki, as the engines were changed from electric to steam, at Palmerston North, Taihape and Taumarunui through the night, and at Frankton Junction (Hamilton) for breakfast. In the south, Springfield, Ashburton, Timaru, Oamaru and Dunedin were among similar facilities.

The *Rainbow Warrior*

The sinking of a Greenpeace protest vessel at the Auckland wharves by French secret agents hardened New Zealand opposition to French nuclear testing in the Pacific. On July 10, 1985, an explosion aboard the 40-m *Rainbow Warrior* sunk her alongside Marsden Wharf, drowning a Greenpeace photographer. Subsequently, police traced the perpetrators, some of whom were arrested and tried and imprisoned in a special camp. The consequent political row had finally to be sorted out by the Secretary-General of the United Nations. The *Rainbow Warrior* now lies off the Cavalli Islands, where it was deliberately sunk as a place for divers to explore.

The Ranfurly Shield *see* The Log o' Wood

The Rarest Bird

The ground parrot kakapo is the rarest of New Zealand's several species of rare and endangered birds. It is also the world's largest parrot, the average adult specimen weighing in at 3.5 kg. During the 1970s the last kakapo appeared restricted to an isolated valley in Milford Sound and the number of known birds fell to only three. Then a population was rediscovered on Stewart Island and these birds have gradually been transferred to safer island habitats. The kakapo is a long-lived bird with a complex breeding cycle that includes such rituals among the males as building tunnel systems through the scrub and creating courtship bowls where they make booming sounds by night to attract females. Breeding is infrequent, possibly one nest in two years, but success appears to depend on the productivity of fruit-bearing food trees. The population of kakapo slumped to 51 in 1995, but close observation and supplementary feeding has led to a small increase in numbers since then. A kakapo recovery programme supported by Comalco has spent $3 million, with island populations now transferred to Codfish Island/Whenua Hou off Stewart Island, and a new colony on Chalky Island, Fiordland. A prolific fruiting of rimu in 2001–02 led to 21 birds nesting, pushing the population from 62 to 86 (still the population in 2008). None of them bred in 2002–03. Details of kakapo and earlier days of its conservation are recorded by David Butler in *Quest for the Kakapo* (Heinemann Reed, Auckland, 1989).

The Rarest Decoration *see* The New Zealand Cross

The Rarest Plant

The rarest plant to be found in New Zealand is probably the climbing plant *Tecomanthe speciosa,* a single plant of which was discovered on Great Island of the **Three Kings Islands**, off Northland, in 1946. No further plants have ever been found in the wild, but the species was propagated at Mt Albert Research Centre in Auckland in 1956 and the greenish-tinged flowers may now be seen in mainland gardens. For similar stories consult *Rare and Endangered Plants of New Zealand*, by David R. Given (A.H. & A.W. Reed, Wellington, 1981).

Ratana

An influential Maori religion, membership of which was for a long time critical in selection as a Parliamentary candidate for the Labour Party, which has historically dominated the Maori seats. Tahupotiki Wiremu Ratana (1870–1939) was the founder, a faith healer who began having visions while ill during the 1918 influenza epidemic. Ratana was active in trying to reclaim lands he believed were taken unjustly, and visited Britain in 1924 to bring these grievances before the King. His religion was established in 1925, at Ratana Pa near Wanganui, but its churches may be seen widely through New Zealand. Their twin towers are respectively marked with the words Arepa and Omeka – 'I am Alpha and Omega, the beginning and the end.' Ratana's son

Haami Tokouru Ratana was elected as Member of Parliament for Western Maori in 1935. He was succeeded by his brother Matiu in 1944. Iriaka Ratana (1905–81) was the first Maori woman in Parliament, serving as a Labour member for 20 years after the death of her husband Matiu in 1949.

The Raurimu Spiral

In this spectacular feat of railway engineering the North Island Main Trunk railway line turns completely around on itself to clamber up onto the Volcanic Plateau, north of Mt Ruapehu. The railway line below can be seen as the train curves up the hill, using tunnels to redouble on itself. The Raurimu Spiral rises a total of 213 m at a gradient of 1 in 50, spiralling up through two tunnels, doubling the straight-line distance up the hill to just over 7 kilometres.

'Ready Money' Robinson

One of the richest Canterbury **Run-holders** – he first made a fortune selling stock in South Australia. Robinson (1814–89) owned the great Cheviot Estate, which was cut up by the government in 1893 so smaller farmers could each have a piece. (See **One Man, One Farm.**) He is said to have paid cash for the Cheviot estate, paying with a wheelbarrow-load of bank notes when his cheque was questioned. See also the **Blood-stained Tombstone.**

The Red Feds

The internationally inspired leaders of the infant Federation of Labour were described as the Red Federationists by their opponents in 1912. Although most of the infant trade unions sought to negotiate for better wages and conditions, the young FOL opposed the Industrial Conciliation and Arbitration Act, preferring to strike in an attempt to destroy capitalism. The Red Fed leaders made their stand with the Waihi Strike, which led to brawls between opposing factions of the Labour movement. Among the FOL leaders were future Labour Ministers W.T. Armstrong, Paddy Webb and Bob Semple, along with unionist Pat Hickey. The Red Feds earned their name from their 1912 Constitution lauding the principles of Marx and Engels and reflecting the philosophies of the International Workers of the World movement, in passing: 'The working class and the employing class have nothing in common. Between these two classes a struggle must go on until the workers of the world organise as a class, take possession of the earth and the machinery of production, and abolish the wage system …. It is the historic mission of the working class to do away with capitalism.'

The Rediscovery of the Takahe

One of the most romantic of New Zealand traditions was that which spoke of a hidden mountain valley in Fiordland where there might be a surviving population of the extinct takahe bird, or Notornis. Guided by Maori traditions of the bird occurring in the Murchison mountains by Lake Te Anau, Dr G.B. Orbell rediscovered a colony living in a high montane valley in 1948. For 50 years takahe had been believed extinct and even then there were only four records from European times, all from remote Fiordland. In Orbell's Takahe Valley the birds were found to be feeding on snow tussocks and forest fern. Eventually a population of about 200 pairs of birds was found in high valleys of the Murchison and nearby Kepler and Stuart mountains, though this number has fallen in part due to competition for food from deer and the depredations of stoats. In an attempt to save the species the birds are being bred in captivity. Takahe are flightless birds, looking a little like stocky pukeko, but weighing two or three times more.

The Redoubtable Bill Fox

Bill Fox won his nickname through his exploits as a gold prospector in Central Otago and Westland during the 1860s. Patrick William Fox learned mining in California and so recognised rocks in the Arrow River as similar to rock forms that bore gold in America. In secret he and three partners gathered a fortune in gold. When they came to bank it at Dunstan (Clyde), others tracked them back through the gorges of the Arrow. Hundreds, then thousands rushed to the Arrow, called briefly Fox's. The 'redoubtable miner' ruled the gorge with his fists until the official law arrived. He opened hotels in Arrowtown and Arthur's Point, also running a cargo boat on Lake Wakatipu. Fox was sentenced to six months in jail for accidentally wounding a customer in a bar brawl, but was out in time to join the West Coast rushes of the mid-1860s. First it was Fox's Gully in the Arahura catchment; then he led a party to Bruce Bay; he was early at Charleston, but within weeks had found another field at what is now the Fox River: all this in just 18 months. In the 1870s he helped companies and the government to prove that there were quartz seams about Reefton, continuing to capture the public imagination as a man who could find rich gold. From *Gold Rush Country of New Zealand*, by Gordon Ell (The Bush Press, Auckland, 1987).

Redoubts, Stockades and Blockhouses

A number of earthen redoubts built by the British as defences against the Maori can still be traced along the frontiers of the early days. Usually these were stockaded – defended by palisades of logs – behind which soldiers could fire through rifle slits. Blockhouses often stood in the middle of the redoubt, a secure base for defending soldiers or the **Armed Constabulary**. Sometimes farmhouses or even churches were similarly used as defensive positions, surrounded by palisades, or equipped with rifle slits through heavy timbers. A double line of redoubts protected early Auckland from Waikato and Hauraki tribes during the conflicts of the 1860s. The remains of some are preserved on public land such as Fort Alexandra on the Waikato near Waiuku. Others survive as earthworks only, including Fort Miranda on the Firth of Thames. In suburban Auckland there are ruins at Howick and an intact blockhouse in Onehunga. The Confiscation Line set up between Waikato and the **King Country**, when the Maori Kingites withdrew there in the 1860s, was marked by the Alexandra Redoubt at Pirongia on the border. There are other examples in the Waikato and Taranaki, also in the Murupara and Taupo regions, and in the Hutt Valley.

Remittance Men

Living off a regular 'remittance' from families in Britain, on the condition that they never return from the colonies. Often ne'er-do-wells, many such remittance men affected upper-class English manners and were consequently unpopular in bush camps and on the goldfields. Remittance men are often the butt of colonial yarns. Read of them in *Colonial Outcasts: a search for the remittance men*, by Nell Hartley (Arrow, 1993). She writes of such as the Marquis of Grandy, the Duke, the Sweep, Sydney Bill, Jim the Devil and Randolph Figuero, who, as Don Bucks, gave his name to a road near the Waitakere Ranges of Auckland, where his camp was a gathering place for outcasts.

Rewi's Last Stand

The battle at Orakau was the last in a chain of battles fought in the Waikato, this time against a large war party from the Tuhoe of the Urewera, 50 Maniapoto under Rewi and others from western Taupo. They dug into a defensive fort 24 m by 12 m: 310 Maori, including women, against six times as many troops under General Cameron. For three days, from March 31 to April 2, 1864, the battle raged. The defenders became short of water and used manuka and apple plugs for night firing as their ammunition ran low. When Cameron challenged them to surrender, on the third day, Rewi's spokesman replied, 'Peace will never be made, never, never … Friend I shall fight against you for ever and ever.' When the interpreter Mair asked that the women and children at least be allowed to come out, the chieftainess Ahumai Te Paerata called out, 'If the men are to die, the women and children will die also!' The defenders would not surrender, but with their last ammunition loaded they left Orakau in a compact body, surrounding the women and children, and retreated into the scrub by the Punui River. Many were shot as they retreated. More than half the Maori defending Orakau died and were buried where they fell. The resounding phrase of Rewi's reply 'E hoa, ka whawhai tonu ahau kie a koe ake, ake' was adapted as the defiant motto of the later **Maori Battalion** in the Second World War: 'Ake Ake Kia Kaha.' The battle of Orakau was the subject of two pioneer motion pictures called *Rewi's Last Stand*, both made by Rudall Hayward, one silent and the other with sound. Source: accounts by historian James Cowan, whose father's farm included the site of the battle. Cowan personally interviewed some of the Maori survivors early last century.

Rimu Beer, 'Spruce Beer'

Beer was first brewed in New Zealand at Dusky Sound by the second Cook expedition aboard *Resolution* in 1773. James Cook was noted for his concern about the health of his crews and an insistence that the men ate fresh vegetables to counter scurvy. Beer based on the leaves and branches of rimu trees had a similar effect. Although Cook took 1200 gallons of beer with his first expedition, it was all but gone in six weeks, so his crews grew used to such concoctions, sometimes enhanced with brown sugar or spirits. Cook defined the rimu as 'a tree that resembles the Americo black spruce'. His recipe for making beer from it involved boiling the foliage with 'Juce of Wort and Molasses … the Juce deluted in warm water in the proportion of Twelve parts Water to one part Juce made a very good well tasted small Beer.' Later settlers tried their hand at making bush beer too, using for example the sweet gum of manuka and kanuka (**Tea Tree**) as flavouring.

The Rimutaka Incline

The old way by rail over the Rimutaka Ranges, from the Wairarapa to Wellington. Special Fell locomotives worked the section from Cross Creek, Wairarapa, to the summit on a 1 in 15 gradient. The Fell system was used from the line's opening in 1878 until a rail tunnel was opened in 1955. Fell locomotives had an extra steam drive to additional horizontal wheels that gripped a central rail underneath the locomotive. Brakes to the central rail and from special brake cars helped control the train.

The Ringatu Religion *see* Te Kooti Rikirangi

River Cages

Before bridges, and after numerous drownings at river crossings, aerial cableways were strung across many rivers, bearing a metal cage. The technique for crossing involved pulling the suspended cage by wire rope across the river. Cages were the first bridges across many rivers on the goldfields. A few still survive on back-country farms, providing all-weather access to isolated paddocks.

RSA

The lapel badge of the Returned Services' Association was for a generation after the world wars a 'red badge of courage', denoting the service of its wearer on foreign battlefields. Mere home guard, veterans of the occupation of Japan and attenders at minor consequent wars could not at first apply. Local RSA clubs were once popular community gathering places, often providing attendant bowling greens and other facilities. The fact that it was possible to drink alcoholic liquor in an RSA club was an added appeal. Through the 1960s and 1970s the RSA remained a powerful lobby group for active defence, supporting such policies as **Compulsory Military Training** and involvement in the Vietnam War. As the veterans of the First World War dropped away, membership extended to those who had fought in Korea, Malayasia and Vietnam. In the 1980s the declining numbers of veterans saw the RSA open its club doors to 'house members', territorial and regular servicemen and women, police and others who had not been in a war.

The Roadless North

A popular expression that reflected the isolation of Northland even into the 1920s. Existing tracks were deep in mud during the frequent rains. The Whangarei to Auckland route became an all-weather road as late as 1932. Most travelled longer distances by sea or rail. For practical reasons, many northern townships were built at the head of tidal navigation, from Silverdale and Warkworth near Auckland to Awanui in the Far North.

Road-rail Bridges

The cost of spanning the broad-skeined rivers, of the South Island in particular, led to the construction of road-rail bridges. In most cases motor traffic shared the bridge with trains, causing immense frustrations at places such as the Waitaki River, where delayed trains frequently held up cars for an hour or more. At the Awatere River trains ran above the road bridge on a box-like girder structure. A few road-rail bridges can still be found, but they are relatively short and trains are now infrequent. The Waitaki road and rail bridge was one of a number of long bridges crossing the seaward ends of the great braided riverbeds of

Canterbury. The Waitaki Bridge is 1105.9 m long and crosses the boundary between Canterbury and Otago just north of Oamaru. From 1876 trains and vehicles shared the bridge until the present road bridge was opened in 1956.

Roast and Three Veg

The accepted menu for Sunday dinner (eaten at lunchtime) from pioneer times. A roast, put on to cook before going to church, was surrounded by such vegetables as potato, pumpkin and kumara (in the north), or served with peas, cauliflower or cabbage. Changing social patterns and less physical work have tended diminish the popularity of this menu, but it still remains the Kiwi definition for a good, square meal.

Rogernomics

Named for the Hon. Sir Roger Douglas, who brought the free market to New Zealand's conservative socialist politics in the name of the Labour Party. As Minister of Finance from 1984 to 1988 (when he resigned) Douglas demonstrated that New Zealand was living beyond its means and was indeed in hock to the international banking fraternity unto the second and third generations. With admirable single-mindedness he carried support from sufficient of his neo-socialist colleagues to dismantle the public service and began a fire sale of New Zealand's accumulated State wealth: assets in land, railways, forests, finance and energy that had been expensively gathered together through decades of inflationary borrowing and punitive taxation. Among other 'economies' was New Zealand's **Cradle to the Grave Social Security** system, which had made life in a command economy more sufferable. By the time Douglas's political supporters saw the likely effect of this, particularly on the traditional worker support for the Labour Party, it was too late. Tens of thousands more were out of work and crusading officials were writing a revolutionary agenda for selling off more assets and making all forms of government financially 'transparent'. The process continued under a National government, grateful for this lead from the workers' friends, until even the funding of the arts and health became models of competitive free enterprise. The process continued while international consultant Douglas helped less fortunate governments achieve his form of economic Nirvana. With other left-wing colleagues he also founded the Act Party, which occupies the extreme right in New Zealand's political spectrum.

Rua Kenana *see* The Prophet Rua

Rugby

The 'national game'; according to rugby historian Arthur Swan, rugby was introduced to New Zealand from England in 1870. In that year the son of the Speaker of the House of Representatives, Charles Munro, arrived back in Nelson from Sherborne School and persuaded locals to play by the rules of Rugby School. By 1882 there were enough teams in New Zealand to warrant a tour by New South Wales players, with a return tour by New Zealanders in 1884. The British toured New Zealand in 1888. A Maori team, but including four New Zealanders of European descent, was selected to tour New Zealand, Britain and Australia in 1888–89. The New Zealand Rugby Union dates from 1892. See also the **All Blacks,** the **Invincibles,** the **Originals** and the **Ranfurly Shield**.

Rugby, Racing and Beer

The traditional definition of New Zealand culture, now given lie by statistics that show that more New Zealanders visit art galleries than attend matches of the national game. Racing, too, is having its financial difficulties as its following decreases, while the **TAB** betting shops are having to diversify. Beer drinking is also in decline as changing drinking habits and the popularity of wine challenge the old masculine codes.

Run-holders

Much of the South Island high country still comprises leasehold properties farmed by run-holders. The name originates with the concept of a licence to 'run' sheep or cattle on an area of land. These blocks of land date from early settlement when the new country of Canterbury, for example, was divided into 'runs' that were allocated to settlers by the provincial government. Each 'licence to occupy' permits the run-holder to farm the property and erect homes and buildings, but the freehold remains with the government and an annual licence fee is payable. Other freeholds are held by institutions such as the University of Canterbury, which leases its endowment lands for income. The term of a high-country lease is usually 33 years, with a perpetual right of renewal. The lease gives the farmer the right to graze stock and control public access, but Crown consent is required to burn vegetation, to cultivate or to shift soil. A number of farmers are now pressing to freehold their properties in accordance with the normal New Zealand practice of land ownership by the occupier. The Australian tradition of the 'squatter' has a similar meaning to that of a run-holder. In early days a number of Australians earned a bad name in Canterbury by aggregating runs so that they blocked the access of neighbours to the infrequent water supplies on the dry plains: the classic Western plot, the practice was known here as 'grid-ironing'. The run system survives largely in the high country of Otago, Canterbury and Marlborough, with some 2.5 million hectares classified as high-country runs of various tenure. These support 2.5 million sheep (down from 3.2 million in 1993). Changing farming practices have increased other stock numbers (by an unspecified amount) from 100,000 cattle and 30,000 domesticated deer in 1993. A system of tenure review, introduced in 1998, now allows farmers to freehold their farmable land in return for passing lands of conservation or historic value back to the Crown as public reserves. There has been concern among conservation and recreation groups in the 2000s with the sale of high-country leaseholds to foreign investors who have paid up to three times the valuation to obtain an iconic landscape. Foreign ownership is said to affect formerly assumed (traditional) rights of public access. By blocking access, run-holders can effectively privatise game shooting and fishing on these properties: another blow to Kiwi traditions.

Rural Delivery

Contractors carrying mail and parcels service most country roads in New Zealand. Once, grocery stores provided a similar delivery service, but now such everyday items are also carried by the rural postal contractor. With the re-creation of the Post Office as a State-owned enterprise, Rural Mail Deliveries have been a subject of contention among farmers who object to paying a premium service fee for having their letters delivered to the gate. The address R.D. designates a property on the Rural Delivery service, usually followed by the route number, e.g. R.D.2. (earlier R.M.D.).

The 'Russian Scare'

'Russian scare' forts are a feature of old harbour defences about the New Zealand coast. The forts, developed during later wars, were never used against the Russians. In fact the fear that an expanding Russian empire would reach down the Pacific from Vladivostok never materialised. Constructed from 1885, the forts include those at Ripapa Island in Lyttelton Harbour and on North Head above Auckland Harbour, with further defences at Wellington and Port Chalmers. The fear of the Russian 'Bear', then testing its might against Britain in Afghanistan, did bring home to New Zealanders their vulnerability without British troops and ships. Militia units were formed, the **Armed Constabulary** divided into soldiers or police, and arrangements were made to pay for two British warships to be based in New Zealand. Concrete bunkers still seen along the shore and on coastal islands largely date from Second World War and Home Guard defences. Preserved defences on Ripapa Island in Lyttelton and Fort Takapuna in Auckland have their origins in the 'Russian scare'.

Salting the Claim

A technique used by the dishonest to create the impression that a poor gold claim was a great one. Gold dust recovered elsewhere was sprinkled into the earth of the claim to show a rich 'colour' when some mug came along to buy. An unintentional scam occurred in Hokitika when gold was found in the main street. Soon, people were digging up Revell Street to get at it. In fact, the return was tremendous – up to an ounce (about 30 g) a pan – and the sites of nearby buildings were threatened by the 'rush'. The source of the gold was later traced to a shipment dropped in the street by a passing packhorse – a bag containing 230 ounces (6 kg) had been scattered while being transported from the bank.

Scandinavian Settlers

Names such as Dannevirke and Norsewood indicate where Scandinavian settlers made their homes in the Seventy Mile Bush of Wairarapa. Brought to New Zealand from Norway, Sweden and Denmark in 1872, the settlers were to cut a highway through the dense forest and break in the land. The road is now State Highway 2 and much of the bush, which stretched from Masterton nearly to Takapau, was burned in a huge fire in 1888.

Scarfies

The name applied to students of Otago University. To keep warm in that testing climate students (and others) frequently resort to wearing scarves. In the student milieu, these are banded in the gold and pale blue colours of the university. An amusing movie called *Scarfies*, about Dunedin students and released in 1999, has given the expression wider currency, even in warmer towns where a scarf would be a hindrance.

School Cadets

Once being a cadet was part of every high school boy's experience, parading in 'sandpaper suits', the khaki uniforms of the School Cadet Corps. Usually the first week of a new school year involved endless parades in the hot sun, wielding rifles from the First World War. The system dated from then, but died out in schools through the 1960s and early 1970s, along with **Compulsory Military Training**. In 2005, there were still 3095 cadets in 107 voluntary units of the Army Navy and Air Force.

School Holidays

The pattern of more than a century was broken in the mid-1990s as schools moved to a four-term year. From the beginning of free, universal education in primary schools in 1877, educators took heed of the realities of rural life. Pioneers needed their children to help with harvests during the six weeks at Christmas; in May people shifted properties; and in August there were newborn animals to care for. The consequent concentration of holidays in this more urban age has meant congested facilities and holiday crowds. Spreading the holidays through the year has latterly been resisted, not for its rural economies but for the difficulty of getting a family together, when different levels of education fail to co-ordinate their plans.

School Milk

Free milk to build up children's bodies was supplied in half-pint bottles from 1937 until 1967. It was received and doled out at morning playtime by milk monitors. Until it was drunk no one could move about or play. Some suggest the scheme was largely born from a need to get rid of surplus milk in the days before casein plants. The apple industry also profited from the free disbursement of apples in playgrounds during the Second World War, when export shipping was difficult: an apple a day keeps the doctor away.

The School of Hard Knocks

The idea of being adequately educated by life rather than in formal classrooms has been a long-popular aspect of the New Zealand tradition. Indeed, populist politicians often made a virtue of their lack of educational attainment – it showed them to be just like the other bloke, a **Practical Kiwi Joker**, not some kind of rarefied professor. Prime minister **'Call Me Kiwi'** Keith Holyoake often boasted during the 1960s of his leaving school at 12 and a later Labour prime minister, Norman Kirk, received much respect for his attainments despite leaving school at an early age. It is a far cry in just a generation to the situation now, when some Members of Parliament use their spare time to take higher university degrees in disciplines such as Public Policy. Universal and free, secular education through primary school was introduced in New Zealand in 1877. Until recently, even university education has been practically free; yet many people viewed the opportunity as elitist. The lessons from better-trained nations abroad are now being learned.

Scott of the Antarctic

The heroics of Captain Robert Falcon Scott and his four companions who died on their walk back from the South Pole in 1912 are still publicly remembered in the South Island. The expedition's ship *Terra Nova* sailed for the south from Lyttelton and in those pre-radio days, news of Scott's loss was telegraphed from its first landfall on return, the Port of Oamaru. Scott, in a statue by his wife, stands by the Worcester Street Bridge beside the Avon in Christchurch. He looks towards Canterbury Museum, which devotes a whole wing to Antarctic heritage. As headquarters since the 1960s for the American Operation Deepfreeze, Christchurch maintains close links with 'the Ice'. Aircraft fly 3500 km from Harewood International Airport to the United States base at McMurdo Sound, close to New Zealand's own Scott Base.

Scows

These traditional sailing vessels were a feature of coastal shipping in New Zealand from their introduction in the 1870s well into the 20th century. Locally built from kauri logs, they carried huge loads of logs and sawn timber from the northern forests, shingle for construction and sand for the glassworks. Developing from a punt-shaped vessel, scows gradually achieved more rounded bows, but they remained basically a floating platform for the shipping of heavy loads. Varying in length, with a medium length of 20 m and large vessels around 30 m, scows were broad-beamed, carrying their cargo, generally, on the deck. They were variously rigged from the smaller ketches to schooner rigs, with the occasional three-masted topsail schooner. Flat-bottomed, with a centreboard instead of a keel, they could be run ashore at high tide, loaded, then floated off with the next tide. Their shallow draught allowed them to be sailed over river bars, into muddy estuaries and up tidal rivers. The largest scow, *Zingara* (1906), was 30 m long and 10 m broad, yet still drew less than two metres. Scows carried many other cargoes about the coast, from firewood and livestock, to inter-island traffic. In the days of the kauri timber trade a number of scows also plied the Tasman, but they were generally used in the coastal trade. Marine historian Clifford W. Hawkins lovingly documents the development and lore of the scow in *A Maritime Heritage* (Collins, Auckland, 1978); see also Ted Ashby's *Phantom Fleet: the scows and scowmen of Auckland* (Reed, Auckland, 1993).

Seal Ends

The shingle and dirt roads of New Zealand are the bane of visitors and townspeople travelling in the country, not to mention the inconvenience for country folk who use them regularly. The road sign Seal Ends is a warning to slow down, look out for potholes and corrugations and expect dust, mud or stone chips. Several major tourist routes still contain unsealed sections. New Zealand has more than 92,000 km of formed road and streets, but more than 33,000 km remain unsealed.

Selwyn Churches

Name given to churches built during the time that Bishop George Augustus Selwyn was Anglican Bishop of New Zealand. These churches make fine use of timber in place of stone, featuring Gothic details in timber. These often include exterior bracing in black timber over white boards, with natural timbers inside. There are several still in use around Auckland, but the most spectacular is the restored Old St

Paul's (1866), which once served as Wellington's pro-Cathedral. The Selwyn Churches were designed by the Reverend Frederick Thatcher (?1820–90), who was based then at St John's College, Auckland. For a visual appreciation of the style see *The Selwyn Churches of Auckland*, by C.R. Knight (Reed, Wellington, 1972).

Service Cars

Rural buses were known as service cars, from the days when routes were run by large American limousines capable of carrying some eight passengers and freight on the unsealed roads. Luggage was often strapped on the roof or in a large dog box at the back, with longer items strapped inside the mudguards and along the running boards. Service cars carried parcel freight from town to town, often running inter-city as well as local routes. The arrival of the service car was often the high point of the day in small communities, as they received urgent supplies and the daily mail bag. The car-like design of the first service cars was carried into later bus-sized vehicles which had a range of doors down the side, each serving a bench seat for passengers. Freight was carried in a rear compartment. A spectacular aspect of the journey was the driver's technique of rolling a daily newspaper and twisting it slightly, so it resembled a paper boomerang, then flinging it ahead and over the bonnet of the moving car, to land in or more often near the **Cream Stand**, which stood then at the gate of most farms. The heyday of service cars preceded the widespread ownership of reliable family cars. Well-known operators included the New Zealand Railway Road Services, Newmans, Mt Cook and Southern Lakes Tourist Company and White Star. The service car concept persists in a few isolated districts, where parcels, freight and a few passengers may still be carried in a bus divided into two compartments for the purpose.

The Severed Hand

At the centre of an insurance fraud in Christchurch, a hand was discovered by two men fishing at **Taylors Mistake** on December 16, 1885. Police connected the hand with the disappearance from nearby Sumner of a man called Arthur Howard, nine weeks before. A gold ring on this (left) hand bore the initials A.H. The hand turned up at an opportune moment, for Mrs Howard was then trying to convince the insurance companies to pay out on her heavily insured husband. When the hand was discovered to be that of a woman, sawn from a body, Mrs Howard was arrested and her husband sought. He was found, living in disguise, in the North Island. Howard went to prison for two years, but the source of the hand remains a secret. The full story is told in the words of lawyer and later Justice O.T.J. Alpers in his recollections *Cheerful Yesterdays*, first published in the 1920s.

The Shaky Isles

A nickname for New Zealand, where earthquakes are a frequent occurrence in some areas and an ever present risk almost everywhere. New Zealand lies along the collision line of two of the great earth-forming plates, the Indo-Australian and the Pacific. Volcanoes and earthquakes mark this instability in the Earth's crust. Active volcanoes include Tongariro, Ngaurahoe, Ruapehu, Tarawera and White Island. Others, such as Taranaki, which may have last erupted a mere 200 years ago, are barely dormant. Statistically we can expect one Richter 6 earthquake annually, a serious shock of seven once in 10 years and a magnitude eight perhaps once a century.

Sharemilking

The way cow **Cockies** become landed gentry and young farmers earn money and skills to get their own land. The tyranny of milking cows, twice a day, seven days a week, becomes more bearable with an unpaid worker taking a share of the gross profits instead. Some sharemilkers put in their energy only, while others, further on their way to farm ownership, may provide stock and equipment for a larger share. The usual sharemilking deals are 29 per cent, 30 per cent or 50 per cent for the sharemilker, depending on their investment in the deal.

Shearers' Meals

Much farm work is heavily physical, but probably the most energetic is the work of the shearer. The sustained effort of heaving sheep from pen to floor and holding them while swiftly and surely removing their fleece demands regular intake of high-energy food. Traditionally the women of the house prepare the shearer's meals. The day should begin with at least a cup of tea before the 'early morning run', then 'stewed fruit for breakfast, not porridge'. At morning tea, cakes and scones are served with a cooked meal at midday and more food at mid-afternoon. When time is of the essence, a longer day might involve a second afternoon break. Godfrey Bowen, a world champion shearer, warns in his book *Wool Away!* (Whitcombe and Tombs, Christchurch, 1955) not to drink too much, only one or two swallows a half hour, personally favouring 'cold tea or the good old oatmeal and water'. 'Meals must be on time for the shearer,' Bowen warns. 'If he has to stand around waiting he loses the value of the rest period and loses the time necessary to digest or even partly digest his food before bending again.' See also **Shearing**.

Shearing

Getting the wool off the sheep's back has developed its own mystique and tales since the first settlers found it the only sheep product they could export before refrigeration. British farmers tied their sheep up to shear them but the method was too slow in New Zealand, where thousands of sheep ran on some properties. Shortly, shearing sheds were developed, with slatted floors and pens to hold sheep awaiting the shears. The shearers worked 'on the board' catching their sheep from the pens, shearing them of wool and sending the shorn sheep down an adjacent chute to the tally yards. Holding the sheep between their knees, 'gun' shearers could handle 100 or more a day. The shearers were the aristocrats of the shed, supported by 'fleecies' who picked up the wool and tossed it onto the sorting tables. Then the wool was 'pressed' in a wooden press into bales for the journey down country to be exported. In the 1890s, steam-driven shearing machines developed in Australia were introduced to New Zealand sheds and tallies rose. Yet the closer trim achieved with mechanical blades was too much for sheep in the high country and the techniques of hand-blade shearing continue to this day to give the big Merinos more protection against the colder weather there. The work of a shearer is competitive, for they are traditionally paid on performance. The top man among these 'knights of the blade' was the 'ringer' who occupied the number one position and with whom the other 'gun' shearers competed. The slowest shearer was the 'drummer' and below him were the aspirants for a place on the board, sometimes known as 'barrowmen', shed rouseabouts who got to practise shearing during the meal breaks. The 'art and technique' of shearing sheep has been described as a 'romance' by its most famous exponent, Godfrey Bowen, who in 1953 shore the fleece from 456 sheep in nine hours. Bowen describes the work of a shearer in *Wool Away!* (Whitcombe and Tombs, Christchurch, 1955) combining practical hints with the mystique and special vocabulary of his trade. Of it he wrote: 'Shearing is hard work (probably amongst the hardest we have got), work that calls for much more than just physical strength and exuberance – rather for balance, grace, rhythm, suppleness, with eye, brain and hand in smart co-ordination … the ability to work and keep going, mastering with big heart such things as very high temperature … aching back, grease boils, maybe a touch of biliousness or some such ailment … Yes, it is a Man's job (no one with a chicken heart should ever consider taking it on).' The evolution of shearing practices is documented in 'Knights of the Blade', a chapter of *The Forgotten Worker: the rural wage earner in nineteenth century New Zealand*, by John E. Martin, (Allen & Unwin, Wellington, 1990).

Sheep Breeds

New Zealand breeders have produced a number of crossbred sheep more suited to our climates, condition and industries. An early cross, popular in the South Island, was the Corriedale, bred by mating British longhair rams such as the Lincoln, the English Leicester, Romney or Border Leicester with the Spanish Merino. The breed is named for Corriedale Station in North Otago, where the station manager James Little bred them first in 1868. Corriedales now occur in Australia, Uruguay, Argentina, Chile and China. In the North Island Romneys are the traditional breed. At the infant Massey University (Massey Agricultural College) Sir Geoffrey Peren crossed the Cheviot with the Romney to produce the Perendale, an 'easy-care' sheep that can be left to run unattended. William Dry bred the hairy Drysdale, by genetic selection from the Romney to provide carpet wool and, incidentally, good meat. The Coopworth was bred at Lincoln Agricultural College under Prof. Ian E. Coop in the 1950s–60s by crossing Romneys with Border Leicester sheep.

The Shiner

'Shiner' Ned Slattery was more than 50 years 'on the road' avoiding work. John A. Lee recorded the folklore in two books about 'the champion of anti-sweat'. When Lee was a runaway from a boy's home, he met the Shiner, then an old man, and ever after collected yarns about him. Edmond Slattery was born in 1840 and reached New Zealand in time to become a figure on the road during the Otago gold rush of the 1860s; he died aged 87 with a reputation throughout the land, but largely earned in Otago and Southland. Slattery was a 'professional' tramp who bludged his meals and drink wherever he could, usually targeting publicans and others whom he thought above themselves. He would set up elaborate tricks to get a drink, for example pretending to survey a road through a bar and consenting to change direction only when appropriately bought off. Others of his ilk included the Highland Chief, the Gorse Warrior, Piccolo Charlie, Dublin Tommy, the Flour o' Wheat, and Barney Whiterats, who produced white mice from his ears. John A. Lee published the tales in *Shining with the Shiner* (N.V. Douglas, Auckland, 1950) and later expanded on the theme with *Shiner Slattery* (Collins, Auckland, 1964).

'She'll Be Right'

Epitomises the laid-back Kiwi attitude to problems or challenges. At best it reflects the positivism of the American expression 'No worries' or 'Don't worry.' At worst, and more frequently, it reflects a less-than-perfectionist attitude to getting things right. Thus the unmotivated, when challenged on an outcome, may also observe 'She's near enough'. 'She,' incidentally, is an 'It' in this context.

Shore Whaling

The technique of hunting whales from a shore base was widely practised in early New Zealand. A lookout on a headland alerted the crew to a passing whale and the hunters rowed off to harpoon it. Whales were towed ashore where they were flensed of their fat, which was boiled down into oil for lamps. Whalebone was used for shoring women's foundation garments and ambergris in scents. Some of the earliest settlements in the South Island were based on whaling, including Te Awaiti and Cloudy Bay in Marlborough, Kaikoura, Banks Peninsula, headlands of the Otago coast and stations about Foveaux Strait. In the North Island there were stations about the Wellington coast, East Cape and Northland. Te Awaiti, on Arapawa Island in the Marlborough Sounds, was the earliest, established by Jacky Guard in 1827. Several shore establishments flourished into the 20th century and the last, Perano Brothers, inside the entrance to Queen Charlotte Sound in Marlborough, closed in 1964.

The Silver Fern

The official New Zealand plant, used as a motif by travelling national sports teams. The Silver Fern on jersey, tie or jacket was once the badge of **All Black** stature, though it is now worn by many other representatives. Indeed, the national women's baskbetball team is known as the Silver Ferns. The symbol of the silver fern stems from the silver tree fern (*Cyathea dealbata*), which has dark green foliage above and intense silver colouring below. In the bush Maori would turn them over to catch the moonlight and mark the way when travelling by night. Silver fern leaves are now a popular badge, but New Zealand soldiers wore bronze ones on their field caps. Look for them in coats of arms. A popular brand of butter uses the name Fernleaf, while the silver railcars of New Zealand carried the train name Silver Fern for some years. See also the **Springing Fern**.

Six O'Clock Closing, The Six O'Clock Swill

This shame of the New Zealand liquor industry was originally introduced during the First World War to save resources. Until then pubs were open to 10.00 pm, and the early closing of bars was welcomed by the huge **Prohibition** lobby of the time. For the next 50 years New Zealanders were forced to drink against the clock, a practice that led to rapid drunkenness and drinking conditions that resembled a rugby ruck. Several generations of New Zealanders never had the opportunity to learn the habits of moderation and civilised drinking. Food and entertainment were specifically banned from bars, as were barmaids. The public bar was a man's world. The reintroduction of 10 o'clock closing by referendum in 1967 led precisely where its critics said it would. Gradually the rules governing the dispensation of liquor were relaxed and its availability increased to the present liberal combination of hotels, restaurants and corner bars, open largely when it suits the local community, even serving liquor, with food, on the formerly sacrosanct Sunday.

The Slump *see* The Great Depression

Smoko

Tea break on the job; time to roll a cigarette, light up and enjoy a 'smoke'. The general 10 minutes allowed by most employment awards often spread to 15–20 minutes in the days before job competition. An alternative expression, 'taking a breather', meaning to get your breath back after hard work, was somewhat compromised by the cigarette. Laws about smoking at work and in public places have recently reduced the ritual of 'smoko' to a few furtive puffs by the addicted in 'designated places', in doorways or on the pavement outside. 'Smoko', as an expression, has thus become a baseless metaphor for a tea or coffee break.

The Social Laboratory of the World

New Zealand earned this reputation during the reign of the Liberal government in the 1890s and early 1900s. This was the period when women won the vote (1893); when industrial conciliation and arbitration was introduced (1894); when basic standards were set for factories (1894), shops, offices and farm work and regular payment to workers enforced by law; when the State purchased large estates and cut them up for 'the little man'; when old age pensions were introduced (1898); when the State became a lender at low interest, a public trustee, an insurer and a banker, and a coal miner.

'Somebody's Darling Lies Buried Here' *see* The Lonely Graves

South of the Bombay Hills

Once the frontier between the British settlers of Auckland and the Maori of Waikato, the Bombay Hills now symbolise a new border. First there is Auckland, then there is the 'Rest of New Zealand'. One effect of this cultural boundary is that Auckland-based national media tend to regard the news north of these hills as national news and whatever happens to the south as local news, less worthy of notice. Cross the hills from the Waikato and glimpse the spread of more than a million people across the Auckland isthmus.

The Southern Cross

Oriented towards the South Pole, the constellation is formed by four major stars and two 'pointers' conspicuous in the Southern Hemisphere. The New Zealand flag uses the four main stars as symbols, red with white outlines, along with the Union Jack: the similar Australian flag has six white stars.

Southern Cross, Aircraft

Aptly named Australian aircraft in which Charles Kingsford Smith and C.T.P. Ulm succeeded in first flying the Tasman on September 10–11, 1928. The journey, from Sydney to Christchurch, took 14 hours and 25 minutes. The three-engined Fokker aircraft also carried a navigator, Henry Litchfield, and a radio operator. The first attempt to fly the Tasman was made by Lieutenant J.R. Moncrieff and Captain G. Hood in a single-engined Ryan aircraft. They set off from Richmond Field near Sydney on January 10, 1928, but never arrived. Nothing more was heard of the plane after its last signal some 320 km short of New Zealand.

The Southern Lights

On long summer evenings in the south of New Zealand it is occasionally possible to see the effects of the Aurora Australis in the southern sky. This band of light, generated from the ice-clad continent of Antarctica, creates a wall of flickering pink or red above the Southern Alps. The phenomenon occurs during midsummer when the Antarctic region experiences sun at midnight. The Aurora Australis 'plays' in the sky as dusk falls, like a late-persisting sunset, a pinkish flush as if on softly lit theatre curtains.

The Sovereign Chief of New Zealand

The entrepreneurial Baron de Thierry (1793–1864) claimed this title, along with that of King of Nukuhiva, when he took up land in Hokianga in 1837. En route from Britain he persuaded the islanders of Nukuhiva in the Marquesas to have him for their king. Then he moved onto 40,000 acres in New Zealand, bought from the chiefs Hongi and Waikato whom he had met in England in 1822. Despite de Thierry's promises of no taxes and good profits from trade, his kingdom collapsed and his land claims were disallowed. British interests responded, however, fearful of French ambitions (though de Thierry was not French; he was actually English, the son of a French emigré). In 1835 the British Resident, James Busby, encouraged several northern tribes to confederate as the United Tribes of New Zealand and declare their independent sovereignty. De Thierry ended his days as a music teacher in Auckland. His story has been fictionalised by Robin Hyde in *Check to Your King* (republished by Golden Press, Auckland, 1975).

The Spanish Helmet

Dredged up off Petone in 1906, the Spanish Helmet has been the inspiration of many suggestions that Abel **Tasman** was not the first European to discover New Zealand. The headpiece, now in the care of Te Papa Tongarewa/Museum of New Zealand, is of a European type used between 1560 and 1570. The dredge that recovered the helmet also brought up a cannonball and, it is said, some coins, though these have not been sighted since. Spanish ships were crossing the northern Pacific from South America to the colonies in the Philippines during that period, but would have been thousands of kilometres off course to encounter New Zealand. Yet further claims have been made for unexplored Spanish wrecks off the Kaipara coast and even inland in a field in that district. Others quote suggestions in old Maori traditions about 'white ghosts' in sailing ships. The Spanish Helmet has become a symbol of this romantic quest. The real mystery, however, is how the helmet survived so long in the saltwater. See also the **Tamil Bell**.

The Spanish Influenza

An outbreak of Spanish influenza killed some 6716 New Zealanders late in 1918. The worldwide epidemic took millions of lives elsewhere. Some believed the disease was brought into New Zealand by the passenger ship *Niagara* that also bore Prime Minister William Massey and Finance Minister Joseph Ward back from a First World War conference. In the aftermath of the epidemic there were arguments about their need to land promptly and whether that influenced the decision to disembark infected passengers. Historians have discounted this; *Black November: The 1918 Influenza Epidemic in New Zealand*, by Geoffrey Rice with assistance from Linda Bryder (Allen & Unwin/Historical Branch, Wellington, 1998) is a good account of what happened.

Spanish Names

In Doubtful Sound, Fiordland, a number of Spanish place names recall the visit of the explorer Malaspina, more than 200 years ago. The Spanish expedition was five years at sea from 1789, exploring around the world, and mapping part of Doubtful Sound while trying to test the gravity in this part of the world. The two corvettes *Descubierta* and *Atrevida* stood off the sound on February 25, 1793, while the hydrographer Felipe Bauza took a party inside in a ship's boat. His chart includes the Nee Islets at the entrance, named for Luis Nee, botanist on the *Atrevida*, Malaspina Reach, Bauza Island and Marcaciones Point (translated as Observation Point) where he took the gravity measurements. The story of Doubtful Sound is recorded by John Hall-Jones in *Doubtfull Harbour* (Craigs, Invercargill, 1984) and *Supplement to Doubtfull Harbour* (1988).

The Springing Fern or Koru

 The traditional Maori image of the springing fern, known as the koru, has become a traditional symbol of New Zealand in recent years. The lead probably came from Air New Zealand, which carries the koru symbol on the tails of its aeroplanes. The coiled spring of the emerging fern leaf symbolises the life force.

'Spruce Beer' *see* Rimu Beer

Stamper Batteries

These machines were used to crush gold-bearing ore from the hard rock mines, notably of the Coromandel, Westland and Otago-Southland. Their job was to crush the ore into a watery flour from which gold (and silver) was washed onto riffled trays. The minute grains of gold were initially separated out using mercury as a collecting agent, but later a cyanide process was developed, with which New Zealand miners led the world and doubled their gold recoveries. Driven by water-powered giant wheels or steam, the batteries rose and fell with a terrific thumping noise. Individual hammers could weigh as much as 350 kg. These hammers were linked together, side by side in batteries along a revolving shaft, so they were lifted and dropped in quick succession. The din of the stamper batteries dominated the gold towns of the 1880s and on into this century.

Stanley's Boast

Still freshly painted on the stone walls of Stanley's Hotel at Macraes Flat in Otago is a crowing cock and the Stanleys' motto 'while I live I crow'. The motto dates back to the 1880s, when the publican John Stanley engaged in bitter rivalry with Bill Griffin of the United Kingdom Hotel. Here the **Swagger the 'Shiner' Slattery** pulled his trick of offering to pay for a drink with stamps, then stamping his foot, scoring a double against these two publicans who had both dared him to try the trick on the other.

Starkie

The exploits of Private J.D. Stark in the First World War were the inspiration for Robin Hyde's book *Passport to Hell* (Auckland University Press, Auckland, 1986). 'Starkie' was famous for getting into disiplinary trouble, then being released from field arrest to fight with spectacular courage in the battles in France. On one occasion he was recommended for the award of a Victoria Cross, but instead he was excused a five-year prison sentence he faced for striking an officer.

State Funerals

State funerals are usually reserved for governors and prime ministers who die in office. Sir Truby King (1858–1938), founder of the **Plunket** movement, was the first private citizen to receive a State funeral. In 2008, the conqueror of Everest, Sir Edmund Hillary, was also accorded this rare honour. Politicians are more frequently valedictoried. There was national mourning and a funeral journey from Wellington to Auckland for the first Labour prime minister, who died in office. Venerated by most of his followers, Michael Joseph Savage (1872–1940) lay in state in Parliament Buildings for two days before the procession to Auckland. A special train carrying the body and the Cabinet stopped at 20 railway stations for farewells. The last leg was by gun carriage to the Savage Memorial on Bastion Point. See also the **Man Who Killed Mickey Savage** for a less adulatory perspective. William Ferguson Massey (1856–1925), a conservative prime minister from 1912–1925 known as **Farmer Bill**, has a similarly impressive tomb on a headland of Wellington Harbour. See also **Massey's Cossacks**.

State Housing

Owning your own home has always been a desirable end in New Zealand. With readily available freehold land, people looked to have their own property by dint of hard work. For the less fortunate and those in public employment the prospect of a state house was an option from 1937. The idea of good housing at affordable rents gradually deteriorated through the 1950s into mass housing developments by the State, in suburbs with few facilities, giving rise to loneliness and social problems. In July

1991 the Housing Corporation became a State-owned enterprise, demanding market rentals but giving preference to more needy applicants. It still owns or manages more than 66,000 houses, some 20 per cent of the national pool of rental housing.

Staten Landt, Staete Landt

The Dutch explorer Abel Tasman gave this name to New Zealand when he encountered its shores in 1642. He believed he had found the western shore of the Great South Land, said to balance the continents of Europe and Asia in the Southern Hemisphere. The other edge of this great continent he believed to lie just off southernmost South America, where a short coastline was also labelled Staten Landt. The name means not south land but 'the State's Land', a way of saying it was claimed for the Dutch Republic that was ruled by a body called the States-General. Tasman spent a few days in Golden Bay, not noticing the existence of Cook Strait, then sailed north. He named **Cape Maria van Diemen** without landing or discovering that New Zealand was just an island group. Within a year Hendrik Brouwer, a governor of the Dutch East India Company, circumnavigated the South American coast of 'Staten Landt' proving it just an island, still known as Staten Island. In fact, nothing but ocean lay between the east and west coats of the imagined southern land. The Dutch subsequently gave to the presumed western shore of the Great South Land another name, Nieuw Zeeland. See *Abel Tasman in Search of the Great South Land*, by Gordon Ell (The Bush Press, Auckland, 1992).

Stations, Sheep and Cattle *see* Run-holders

The Steepest Gradient in the Southern Hemisphere

Dunedin once had five cable car routes operating, the first opened in 1881 as the Roslyn Tram Co. It was the first cable-car system built outside the United States and prompted a local invention, later used worldwide. The new mechanism allowed cable trams to run around corners. The Maryhill cable-car extension was reputedly the steepest in the world, running on a gradient that varied from 1 in 4 to 1 in 3.5 at its steepest. The last cable car in

Dunedin stopped in 1957. Refer to *When Trams Were Trumps* by Graham Stewart (Grantham House, Wellington, 1993).

The Stephens Island Cat

It is arguable whether it was the cat, or the bird it ate, that deserves to pass into folklore. The little lighthouse island in Cook Strait is a treasure house of rare species, including the **Tuatara,** which has its strongest population there, sharing burrows with hundreds of thousands of **Muttonbirds**. There is also a rare gecko peculiar to the island and once there was a species of wren found nowhere else. The Stephens Island Wren was discovered in 1894 through the hunting prowess of the lighthouse keeper's cat. That animal brought in 11 specimens that were passed to scientists to describe. The bird was said to be semi-nocturnal, living among rocks, and never seen to fly. After a few more captures by the cat, the birds vanished forever. See *New Zealand Birds* by W.R.B. Oliver (A.H. & A.W. Reed, Wellington, 1955).

'Stop the Tour'

The battle cry of those opposed to sporting contacts with the apartheid state of South Africa through the 1970s and 1980s. The organisation Halt All Racist Tours was in the vanguard of the liberal conscience from the 1960s as a growing number of New Zealanders came to oppose sporting contact with South Africa. The evolving arguments grew to encompass all sporting codes and the issue of playing any other countries that had sporting ties with South Africa. Internationally, similar arguments led to the passing of trade sanctions against South Africa and within the British Commonwealth New Zealand's prime minister was persuaded to sign the Gleneagles Agreement that in 1977 banned sporting contacts with the former Dominion. The issues split families with a bitterness of debate that found physical expression in street battles and riots during the 1981 Springbok tour of New Zealand. In 1993, HART disbanded, as South Africa moved through the processes of dismantling apartheid and began fielding representative sports teams selected on a non-racial basis.

Street Parades

Most of these mark local festivals and promotions, notable among them the Alexandra Blossom Festival and the Hastings Blossom Festival. Local businesses, children's groups and good causes mount floats on the back of trucks, bands parade and people have an old-fashioned good time. Occasionally the big cities put on a more sophisticated show such as the long-running Farmers' Christmas Parade in Auckland, and impromptu welcomes home for sporting heroes, such as the ticker-tape parade for KZ7 when the New Zealanders won the America's Cup for yachting.

Suffragists

An expression used of New Zealand women who, in the early 1890s, fought for **Votes for Women**. The description is less sexist than the English 'suffragettes' with its feminine diminutive. New Zealand's suffrage fighters succeeded in getting their voting rights in 1893. Some later joined the battle in Britain on behalf of their 'sisters' there.

Sugarbags

Hessian bags containing 44 lbs (20 kg) of sugar were widely recycled in pioneer and harder times. They were useful hold-alls. Tied at the corners, with light rope, they made a **Pikau** or pack. Split open down one side they made a rain hood and jacket. The hard-wearing material also produced rough clothes, aprons and oven cloths. Sewn together sugarbags made curtains and interior doors and screens. Along with the larger wheat sacks, sugarbags might substitute for a mattress wire or even, stuffed with straw, make the mattress, too. The softer cottons used by flour manufacturers for their bulk bags were popular materials for shirts and girls' dresses. Tony Simpson took the image and called his history of life in the 1930s **Great Depression** *The Sugarbag Years* (reprinted Penguin, Auckland, 1990).

Sunbathing

Getting a 'good tan' or a 'healthy tan' was a hedonistic ambition of most young New Zealanders in summer, until quite recently. The risks in terms of skin cancer, however, have now been noted by the health conscious. The habit dies even faster as the hole in the ozone layer makes cancerous outcomes even more likely. Sunlight in New Zealand is particularly strong as the protective layer of atmospheric ozone, which filters out some of the ultra-violet light, thins away each summer over the Antarctic.

Sundowners

In farming country, **Swaggers** who arrived at evening in search of work, expected a meal and a bed in the barn at least.

The Surville Cliffs

The northernmost point of New Zealand, where the bluffs fall directly some 200 m into the sea was rounded by the French expedition of Jean-Francis-Marie Surville on December 16, 1769, just as the first expedition of Lieutenant James Cook in the *Endeavour* passed in the opposite direction. The *Endeavour*, heading westward around North Cape, was swept further offshore in huge westerly swells, while the *St Jean Baptiste* was swept in the opposite direction around the cape by the same wind. Though close, the ships passed each other unseen in the storm. The area is now a scientific reserve for its strange botany, evolved to survive on the windswept plateau of serpentine rock. The miniature plants include several found nowhere else in the world.

Surville's Anchors

Cast off in Doubtless Bay, Northland, during a storm, the anchors of the explorer's ship are tangible reminders that the French were in New Zealand at the time of Captain Cook. The Frenchmen under Jean-Francis-Marie Surville sheltered and refreshed themselves in Doubtless Bay, but nearly lost their ship when its anchors dragged in a storm on December 28, 1769. As the *St Jean Baptiste* was driven towards a reef below Rangiaohia, her crew raised sail and slipped the anchors. The loss of the anchors was a factor in Surville's decision not to stay and explore New Zealand. His sad voyage ended with the seizure of ship and crew in Peru and Surville's death in the surf there, trying to get help for his scurvied crew. Undersea explorers Kelly Tarlton and Wade Doak traced and recovered the anchors of *St Jean Baptiste* more than 200 years later. One anchor is in the Far North Museum at Kaitaia, the other at Whangarei.

Swag

A backpack carried by a **Swagger** or swagman, an itinerant 'gentleman of the road', tramp or '**Sundowner**'. Later, what a soldier carried en route. Now colloquially applied to the backpack of the overnight tramper, for it contains the sufficiency for survival outdoors.

Swaggers, Swagmen

Men who carried their 'swag' on their back were a feature of early New Zealand, as seasonal labourers moved from farm to farm in search of work. In *Shiner Slattery*, writer and sometime Labour MP John A. Lee distinguishes between them and the 'army' of the unemployed who roamed the countryside in the Great Depression of the 1930s. The swaggers were on the road for a purpose, not because there was nowhere else to go. Harvesters and shearers in particular travelled in a broad circuit, some moving from Queensland to New South Wales then Victoria before crossing to New Zealand in an annual migration following the demand for skilled workers. In the 20th century, mechanisation did away with much seasonal work. Farmers could also find labour more efficiently by advertising and workers could telephone them instead of calling at the door in search of work.

Swamp Kauri

The remains of giant kauri trees are occasionally recovered, preserved in the peat of swamps, and still usable after 30,000–50,000 years. Such trees often show signs of having been flattened, with surrounding forest, by phenomenal wind blasts. The timber may still be used if carefully dried, otherwise it crumbles after removal from the earth. 'Fossil forests' of kauri can be viewed in the gumlands of Lake Ohia on the Karekare Peninsula of Northland. Here altered lake levels have exposed the vast stumps of trees decapitated by some vast blast 30,000 years ago.

Swanndri or 'Swanny'

A trade name and a nickname for a coarse shirt, made of rain-rejecting woollen material, which sometimes extends all the way from hood to knee. Often loudly checked, the over-all garment is popular among outdoor workers on cold days. The product dates from 1913.

The TAB

In 1907 betting on horse races was made illegal except at the racetrack. (See **Bookies** and **Gambling**.) Legalised off-course betting dates from 1951, when a national referendum led to the establishment of State-controlled betting shops, under the Totalisator Agency Board. From the 1990s, the TAB runs betting on and off the racecourses of New Zealand, and on other sports, here and abroad. Bets can be placed on horses or greyhounds six days a week and there is also provision for eight days of racing on Sundays each year. The government taxes the betting turnover; some money goes to facilities and clubs and the rest is paid out as dividends. The 2006 TAB turnover exceeded $1.04 billion. (Statistical detail from the *New Zealand Official Yearbook 2006,* published by the Department of Statistics, Wellington.)

Taihoa

Often pronounced 'tai ho', this Maori expression has been popular in English since the early days of settlement. As an alternative to 'Hold on' or 'Wait on' it seems to suit the idea of **Maori Time**, waiting until the time is right. Taihoa, however, may also serve for that more commanding expression so memorably articulated in the book *Hang on a Minute Mate*, by Barry Crump.

The Tail of the Fish

The Aupouri Peninsula stretching to the Far North of New Zealand is often known as the Tail of the Fish. This comes from the Maori legend of Maui fishing up the North Island, retold as **Te Ika a Maui,** the Fish of Maui. The region is known as Te Hiku o te Ika, for it resembles the tail of a skate fished up from the sea, with its head about Wellington and its fins on the capes east and west of the North Island.

Tailings

Rock piles left behind by alluvial gold-miners of the 1850s and 1860s. Heaps of spoil were left, both by the miners using monitor hoses and hydraulic lifts, and by mechanical gold dredges. Chinese goldminers often profitably re-worked the rough tailings of careless European miners, leaving their characteristic neat piles of stones. In the 1980s mineral boom, modern-day miners often did well reworking the tailings yet again, with the added efficiency and volumes possible by machine. Some large rock tailings are now used as a source for stone-crushers producing road metal.

Takahe *see* The Rediscovery of the Takahe

Taking Possession of New Zealand

Maori traditions tell of tribal tohunga priests taking up the earth of the new land and blessing it. Often they buried a symbol of tribal life force, a mauri, in some significant place. European traditions involved erecting a flagpole and raising a flag. Both English and French did this at various times, often more than once to make sure the claim was full and complete. See **French Akaroa**, the **Naming of Queen Charlotte Sound**, **Marion Du Fresne's Treasure**.

'Taking the Waters'

A fashion from the 19th century that continues with people going to the old spa baths to bathe. Many springs have health-enhancing effects, and the fashion led to the establishment of a 19th-century tourist industry, notably at Rotorua but also along a chain of hot springs, including Miranda, Te Aroha, Matamata and Okoroire on the way to Rotorua from Auckland. In the far north, Ngawha Springs offers hot mud pools with curative effects. The Armed Constabulary Baths at Taupo have been redeveloped as a public facility. Outside the volcanic zone further hot springs include those where ground water, after penetrating to the hotter interior of the earth, is forced to the surface again as springs. Thus it is possible to get a hot bath from the earth deep in the forests of the South Island mountains at places such as Maruia Springs and on the Copland Track in Westland, across the Main Divide from Mt Cook. Hot pools using water direct from underground may contain a fatal meningitis virus, hence the fashion for using heat exchangers to warm ordinary water with underground supplies. It is the natural pools that have the mineral benefits however. New Zealand's spas began attracting tourists from overseas as early as the 1880s, a story included in *Taking the Waters*, by Ian Rockel (Government Printing Office Publishing, Wellington, 1986).

Tall Poppies

These are the victims of the **Clobbering Machine**. People who are different have always troubled New Zealanders, particularly people of foreign cultures. So have people who excel; such tall poppies can expect to have their heads chopped off as they rise above the Kiwi pasture. In a tiny country it doesn't take long for word to spread about the human frailties of the interim great. We all know that **'Jack Is as Good as His Master'** and excelling in something tends to erode that principle. The people most likely to survive the syndrome are sports people, who tend to be more down to earth in their manner, though they still fall victim to their human foibles. About the only person apparently immune to this process was Sir Edmund Hillary, who climbed higher than anyone else.

Tamaki-makau-rau

The traditional Maori name for the Auckland isthmus is now more broadly used by Aucklanders, who include it on signs welcoming air passengers at Mangere. It means Tamaki of a hundred lovers or Tamaki of the many lovers, a much sought-after and fought over place even in Maori times. The transliteration of Auckland itself is Akarana, preserved notably in the name of the Royal Akarana Yacht Club.

The Tamil Bell

This bronze ship's bell inscribed with Sanskrit characters is a favourite of myth makers. The bell was recovered by the missionary William Colenso about 1836, from an inland Maori group who were using it as a cooking pot. Since then there have been several attempts to translate the inscription, generally agreed now to read 'the Ship's bell of Mohammed Buks'. Some attribute it to early Tamil traders based in Java coming ashore in New Zealand or to Portuguese traders who found the style useful. Still others argue it may have been taken by traders to the Pacific Islands and then have been brought on to New Zealand by Maori. The bell is in the collection of Te Papa Tongarewa/the Museum of New Zealand in Wellington.

Tangi, Tangihana

The Maori ritual of mourning lasts three days or more. The body may lie on the marae surrounded by relatives and friends, while mourners gather to make their farewells. The tangi approximates the time taken for the spirit to move northward to Cape Reinga, Te Rerenga i Wairua, point of departure for the other world.

The Tangiwai Rail Disaster

On Christmas Eve, 1953, 151 people were killed when the Wellington-Auckland express plunged into the Whangaehu River. A sudden surge of water from the Crater Lake of Mt Ruapehu washed away the bridge supports at Tangiwai. The Maori name of 'weeping waters' found literal expression as the nation mourned. For many years after, on Christmas Eve, passenger trains slowed to cross the river and left a floral tribute on its waters.

Taniwha

A Maori spirit, frequently appearing as a shaper of land or waterway, and as a guardian. Such monsters may be good or fearsome. Tainui are said to have them at every bend of their river Waikato. Not seen by European settlers, but respected all the same.

Tar White, Tarwhite

Te Awaiti, the **Shore Whaling** station on Arapawa Island in the Marlborough Sounds, was established in 1827–28 by the whaler Jacky Guard. Said to be the first European settlement in the South Island, Tar White was later operated by Dicky Barrett, who guided the first Wellington settlers to Petone in 1840. John Guard, born 1831, is said to be the first European child born in the

South Island. In 1836, the Guards shifted to Kakapo or Guards Bay on Port Underwood to continue whaling. See the **Wreck of the** *Endeavour* for details of earlier, if unintentional, settlement.

The Taranaki Gate

A wonderful invention combining barbed wire and fence stakes to make a low-cost and flexible gate. Several strands of wire are strung across a gap and nailed to stakes that provide vertical rigidity. The wires are drawn tight when the end stakes are held by loops of wire attached to the top and bottom of the gate posts. Stock avoid the barbed wire. The farmer simply lifts up the top loop, to free the tension, and peels back the 'gate' to open it up. The best of Kiwi ingenuity, originating it seems in Taranaki.

'Taranaki Wool'

During the 1880s and 1890s, when times were tough on the land, a Chinese merchant in Taranaki, Chew Chong, developed an export trade in fungus. Farm families scoured the bush looking for the ear fungus, which was a delicacy in China. In the 1880s the fungus sold for four pence a pound, the same price as butter, and this 'Taranaki wool' was a major income for the settlers.

The Tarawera Eruption

New Zealand's largest volcanic eruption since settlement. Before dawn on June 10, 1886, this mountain near Rotorua exploded – not for the first time – and blanketed the surrounding countryside (over 4800 sq km) with mud and dust. The peak eruption of Tarawera's craters lasted four hours. After 23 hours the volcano subsided into gushing steam vents and occasional bursts of ash and scoria. The explosions were heard as far away as Auckland and Napier, Hokianga, Nelson and Marlborough. Near the mountain itself rocks, scoria, ash and mud smothered several villages and the world-famous **Pink and White Terraces**. The settlement of Moura slipped into Lake Tarawera; people in the village of Ariki were buried alive. The tourist village of Wairoa was also buried under several feet of ash and its hotel collapsed. In all, 153 died in the eruption. The ruins of Wairoa have been excavated and visited for many years as the **Buried Village**, a haunting spot in a deceptively quiet countryside. The Tarawera eruption is documented in *Tarawera: the destruction of the Pink and White Terraces*, by Geoff Conly (Grantham House, Wellington, 1985). See also herein under the **Pink and White Terraces**, and the **Phantom Canoe**.

The Tarndale Slip

Still slipping after more than 50 years, the Tarndale mud slide on the Mangatu Block in Poverty Bay is a moving symbol of what deforestation can mean in the hills. Triggered by heavy rains in 1938 the slip flowed for 20 years until reafforestation began to halt it, but its head is still slipping. The spoil buried farms and fences, raising the level of riverbeds downstream by up to 30 m. Later storms, such as Cyclone Bola in 1988, have wrought continued devastation to the bare hills of the East Coast.

Abel Tasman (?1603–1659)

The first Europeans recorded as discoverers of New Zealand were members of an expedition mounted by the Dutch East India Company under the command of Abel Janszoon Tasman. With two ships, the *Heemskerck* and *Zeehaen*, Tasman's expedition set out from the company's headquarters at Batavia (Djakarta, in Indonesia) in 1642. They were commanded to find the Great South Land or Terra Australis Incognito, long believed to lie in the southern oceans in counter-balance to the weight of the continents north of the equator. This journey took them west to Mauritius, then south of Australia through the Roaring Forties, to find Tasmania and the west coast of New Zealand, then north to Tonga and northern Fiji and back through the Indies to Batavia. Thus they sailed some 30,000 km around roughly a quarter of the globe, circumnavigating the only substantial unknown land, Australia, without seeing it. Tasman and his men did not land in New Zealand, though they spent nearly four weeks off our west coast and lost four men in a mêlée with Maori in Golden Bay. See **Murderers' Bay**. See *Abel Tasman in Search of the Great South Land*, by Gordon Ell (The Bush Press, Auckland, 1992).

The Tattooed Sailor *see* The White Chief

Tattooing

The practice of tattooing the body is popular in several New Zealand communities. Maori, Samoans, Tongans and European sailors all favoured forms of tattoo in the 19th century. Modern forms include the traditional body tattoo of Samoa and New Zealand, along with commercial designs. Facial and other tattoos recording prison terms are worn by some. Traditional Maori tattoo was known as moko. Two forms were noted by the first British visitors to these shores. In its puhoro form ta moko consisted of punctured skin with the colour stain rubbed in. By contrast the whakairo carved form was three-dimensional, cut into the flesh. Face and body tattoos were popular during

the armed conflicts of the 1860s, after which Maori men largely abandoned the practice. During the early 20th century many Maori women received chin and lip tattoos using the needle technique. Modern designs are made by electric needle. Maori tattoo designs and their meanings are the subject of several readily available books. See the **White Chief**.

The Taupo Eruption

Several monstrous eruptions in fact, the last reputedly being reported by Chinese recordists, and by Roman observers who wrote of a darkening of the Mediterranean sky. Some 330,000 years ago an explosion thought to be the world's largest plastered 2500 sq km of land with up to 200 m of debris. Variously estimated to have exploded last in 130 BP and 186 BP (coincident with the Chinese and Roman records), the last Taupo eruption is said to have reached 50 km in height, dropping pumice and ash to a depth of 5 metres, then collapsing to push out a layer of ignimbrite rock over a radius of 15 km. The crater is now drowned by Lake Taupo. The volcanic story of the region is well told in *Volcanoes of the South Wind*, by Karen Williams (Tongariro Natural History Society, Turangi, 2001).

Taylors Mistake

Over the bluff from the seaside suburb of Sumner in Christchurch. It is said a Captain Taylor brought his ship into the cove, mistaking it for Sumner or Port Lyttelton on either side of it. The mistake would be relatively easy with a fog, for there is a visual similarity among the drowned harbours around Banks Peninsula. Germans mined the entrance to Sumner during the Second World War believing it to be Lyttelton. During the black-out conditions of the Second World War, and in a heavy fog, an inter-island ferry fetched up in nearby Port Levy by mistake. For more than 90 years various authorities have been trying to get some control over the curious baches in Taylors Mistake. These consist of buildings in caves and crevices beside the sea, dating back more than a hundred years.

Te Ika a Maui

The fish of Maui is a traditional Maori name for the North Island. It originates with the myth of the Polynesian demi-god Maui who is credited with fishing the island up from the sea. Maui was regarded as a trickster and his brothers were reluctant to take him out to sea fishing. So he hid under the floorboards of the canoe. Offshore he revealed himself, then led them to a good but distant fishing ground. Still they would not give him bait for his enchanted hook, so Maui bloodied his own nose and smeared the hook with it. When he fished up the North Island it was smooth and flat. Maui asked his brothers not to cut up his fish until he had fetched a priest to bless it and offer a portion to the gods. The brothers did not wait and the giant fish writhed and flapped, creating mountains and valleys, breaking the perfect land. Maori tradition notes the resemblance of the North Island to a skate or stingray with its tail in the Far North and mouth about Wellington Harbour. Curving Cape Kidnappers at the southern end of Hawke's Bay resembles the enchanted hook with which Maui fished up the island. Maui appears in Hawaiian legend, too, fishing up the island named for him there. See *Polynesian Mythology*, by Sir George Grey (Whitcombe and Tombs Ltd, Christchurch, 1961 edition).

Te Kooti Rikirangi (?1830–93)

This often-maligned warrior, against whom the last pitched battles were fought in 1870, spent his last 20 years in seclusion developing his faith of Ringatu. The religion is still widely practised in Maoridom, particularly on the East Coast. Te Kooti actually fought against the **Hau Hau** with the colonial forces in 1865, but was arrested as a suspected spy and shipped without trial to the Chatham Islands. His resentment, coupled with his powers of leadership, led to his leading an escape of Hau Hau prisoners who sailed back to New Zealand aboard a captured schooner. Te Kooti's religious fervour and leadership were enhanced when he sacrificed a relative to placate an ocean storm en route. Authority was awaiting the escapers and there were ensuing battles in the Poverty Bay hills. From there Te Kooti led his force against those whom he believed had wronged him. They murdered 33 British and 27 Maori in Poverty Bay before carrying the war through the Urewera country and on to Taupo. Te Kooti escaped the final fight at Te Porere beneath Tongariro in 1870 and in 1871 took shelter behind the Confiscation Line, in the **King Country**, with the Maori King. From there he exercised his influence as a religious leader of the Ringatu cult, a faith derived from Hau Hauism, Christianity and Judaism, which is still practised today. A Ngati Maniapoto house built in his honour still stands by the southern railway crossing at Te Kuiti. Te Kooti was pardoned in 1883. His story is in *Te Kooti Rikirangi: general and prophet,* by W. Hugh Ross (Collins, Auckland, 1966).

Te Reo (Maori)

The Maori language has undergone a renaissance over the past 30 years, particularly since being declared an official language of New Zealand in 1987. At the 2001 census, 26 per cent of Maori claimed to speak Te Reo Maori. For Maori aged over 70 this reached around 55 per cent. The kohanga reo movement has seen Maori language restored for many pre-school children (48,000 from 1982 to 2007). Maori language immersion schools also exist from primary to tertiary level. Older Maori have often had to learn Te Reo, too, as for those in public life it is the only way to speak on the marae (meeting ground). Maori has several tribal or regional dialects: the official word on vocabulary and new words stems from the Maori Language Commission/Te Taura Whiri i Te Reo Maori.

Te Wai Pounamu

'The waters of the greenstone' is the Maori name for the South Island of New Zealand. An alternative old Maori name Te Wahi Pounamu translates as 'the place of greenstone'. Here, in Westland and south-west Otago, are the sources of the families of greenstone jades. These produced fine tools and ornaments for Maori and the stone was the basis of a trade throughout New Zealand. The Poutini Kai Tahu are a Westland tribe who take their name from the greenstone of which they are guardians. Poutini is the personification of the stone, which is also regarded as sprung from a fish. These people have an older name for the South Island. This is Te Waka a Aoraki, the canoe of Aoraki and his brothers, which came down from the sky and through a mistake in a prayer could not return. Instead the canoe settled on an undersea ridge, tilting to form the Southern Alps. Aoraki and his three brothers sit on the highest thwart as mountains: Mt Cook (Aorangi, or Aoraki in southern Maori), Rangiroa (Mt Dampier), Rangirua (Mt Teichelmann) and Rarangiroa (Mt Silberhorn). These legends were recorded by James Herries Beattie in *Journal of the Polynesian Society*, (1915–1922). See the **Cloud in the Sky**.

Tea Tree

The colloquial name for manuka and kanuka trees. Scrublands of these aromatic plants once covered much of the poor land of New Zealand, particularly in places where Maori had burnt the mature native bush. The British explorer James Cook was first to record making tea and beer from the leaves. Later, gumdiggers and others often made an infusion from the leaves, some preferring it to China tea. Such herbal tea was made from similar plants in Australia, too. Tea tree can be easily confused as a name with the unrelated ti tree. This name is Maori for the family of **Cabbage Trees**.

Ten-acre Blocks

Now, properly, a 4-hectare block, the 10-acre block was for many years the established minimum size for a rural subdivision of land. Increasingly, from the 1970s, New Zealanders with an attachment to the countryside and the growing means to do so bought up farmland adjacent to their cities and commuted by car. The 10-acre block was large enough for a horse for the children, a restful garden, an orchard, and a place to breed coloured sheep for spinning wool, grow grapes or undertake a similar non-commercial activity. The experience often foundered when growing children needed access to the opportunities and recreation of the city. A high rate of marriage mortality has also been ascribed to the lifestyle, where one party had to live isolated in the countryside while the other commuted. The lifestyle has been kinder to the retired, many of them formerly farmers, who want a bit of land for a hobby. For a while, some concerned councils changed the rules about rural subdivision, increasing the minimum area to the metric equivalent of 50 acres, to encourage better land-use, but the demand continues for what have recently become better known as 'lifestyle blocks'. In recent years, vast areas of poorly productive land in many regions have sprouted mansions for commuters and those who work by email, completely changing the character of the countryside.

The Ten Thousand Dollar Cure

The budget-inflated equivalent of the original **Thousand Pound Cure**, undertaken by unhappy British immigrants who could not stand New Zealand in the 1960s and returned home. Things were more boring in New Zealand then, and the culture shock for settlers from traditional Britain could be immense. Some simply 'whinged', a form of homesickness expressed in unflattering comparisons between life 'at **Home**' and 'here in the colonies'. Others acted on their frustration and booked a ticket home to see the relatives. With the hindsight of travel, however, they now saw their 'home country' anew; a place of entrenched privilege, where it was usually winter, overcrowded and still suffering the effects of the Second World War. So they again set sail to return to New Zealand, happier at heart at their decision to emigrate and looking forward to the good side of life Down Under. The cost of the return tickets gave rise to the saying.

Thatcher, Charles, see The Inimitable Thatcher

'The Beach'

Early sailor's name for Kororareka, Bay of Islands. See the **Hell Hole of the Pacific**. Also see **Okiato, Old Russell.**

the bone people

Originally written just like that; no capitals. Keri Hulme's rambling novel, first published by the Spiral Collective of women in 1985, became the first New Zealand novel to win the prestigious Booker McConnell Prize for Literature (now the Man Booker). Her story involves a woman alone, a wild man and an abused child, mixing Maori and English perceptions, evoking the atmosphere of remote Westland and Moeraki in a haunting stream of consciousness. Mentioned here for its pervading, mythic visions of place: tradition in the making. Read *the bone people,* by Keri Hulme (Spiral in association with Hodder & Stoughton, Auckland, 1985).

'The 151 Days'

Duration of the waterside workers' strike (or the Waterfront Lockout) of 1951. Prime Minister Sid Holland broke the impasse by deregistering the waterfront unions and bringing in troops to work the wharves. See the **Waterfront Strike**.

The Thousand Pound Cure

The pre-inflationary version of the **Ten Thousand Dollar Cure**.

Threatened Species

New Zealand has more rare, threatened and endangered species of animal than any other country listed by the World Conservation Union. This is in part due to the very ancient nature of our wildlife, evolved in isolation from the rest of the world and including some plants and creatures that are known elsewhere only as fossils. The other major threat has been the depredations of people and their introduction of foreign animals and plants. The first Maori are believed to have arrived here around 800 years ago, but were shortly responsible for the extinction of several species of giant flightless birds called moa. Other birds were also hunted out. The introduction of guns and the rapid spread of European farming caused another rush of extinctions. Many of the flightless birds could not sustain the onslaught of introduced predators, such as cats and mustelids (stoats, ferrets and weasels), until then unknown in New Zealand. Other creatures, such as deer, goats, rabbits and possum, destroyed the subtle natural balance of forests and grasslands. Fire and the draining of wetlands destroyed further habitats. New species of birds occupied the new landscape: introduced fish such as trout took the place of native fish in the rivers. Weeds smothered and choked areas of natural vegetation. This radically changed landscape provides fewer niches for creatures and plants that have evolved over millions of years in isolation from wild animals, weeds and people. An attempt by the Department of Conservation to rank New Zealand's threatened species listed 70 (or 42 per cent) native birds, 27 reptiles and amphibians, six freshwater fish, 51 land snails, 31 species of insects (0.2 per cent of an estimated 20,000) and 93 plants, some five per cent of New Zealand's indigenous flora. (Statistics from Department of Conservation's Species Priority Ranking System.)

Three Days up the Harbour

A southerly blow, with blustery rain, lashing Dunedin. Such weather is not uncommon elsewhere in southern New Zealand.

'The Making of a New Zealander'

New Zealand writers of the 1930s and 1940s worried a lot about their place in the South Pacific, so far from the centres of culture back 'Home'. Where did they really belong? Frank Sargeson was one of the new breed who deliberately asserted their New Zealandness in the face of critics of the English school. In a refreshing break from the sensitive English character at odds with the New Land, Sargeson takes the example of a lonely Dalmatian immigrant to describe 'The Making of a New Zealander': 'Nick and I were sitting on the hillside and Nick was saying he was a New Zealander, but he knew he wasn't a New Zealander. And he knew he wasn't a Dalmatian any more.' The short story 'The Making of a New Zealander' is published in the *Collected Stories of Frank Sargeson* (Blackwood and Janet Paul, Auckland, 1964).

Thermette

A fire base and water jacket for boiling water, while safely containing the flames. A New Zealand invention attributed to John A. Hart about 1928. Ideal for use by the roadside in dry areas (water can be carried in the water jacket until needed), and swift to boil using small twigs as fuel. New Zealand soldiers serving in North Africa during the Second World War called it a 'Benghazi burner'.

'Think Big'

The policy of the National government in the early 1980s, which wanted New Zealand to take the great leap forward from dependence on agriculture to an industrial base. There was huge State investment, for example in energy and fuel-related industry: 'Think Big' produced the Clyde Dam and other power schemes, the electrification of the North Island Main Trunk railway, Maui gas, a world first in converting gas to petrol, and a plant for making urea from gas. The State also bought a substantial interest in making steel from iron sand. The enterprises have now been largely sold off to private enterprise.

Three Kings Islands

Only the largest was named Three Kings Island, by the Dutch explorer Abel **Tasman**, in honour of the Three Wise Men who visited the baby Jesus in Bethlehem on the 12th night after his birth. Tasman's expedition encountered the islands, just off the far north of New Zealand, on Twelfth Night on January 4, 1643. The seas were too rough for Tasman's men to land, so they sailed on northward and refreshed themselves at their next discovery, Tonga. See also the **Giants of the Three Kings** and *Abel Tasman in Search of the Great South Land*, by Gordon Ell (The Bush Press, Auckland, 1992).

Tin Kettling

After the honeymoon friends and relatives visit *en masse* to interrupt the young marrieds at home. Sometimes tin kettles are carried to rattle out a warning of the approaching party.

Tohunga

The Maori priest class. Their knowledge and incantations pro-
foundly affected many early settlers who recorded tales of their
power and influence. Tohunga were blamed for the placing
of makutu curses on settlers who offended Maori proprieties.
The influence of tohunga was such that the government passed
a Tohunga Suppression Act in 1907. The law remained on the
statute books for more than 50 years, despite Maori objections.
Tohunga are still consulted in traditional areas.

Toi and Whatonga

These two Maori navigators are given major roles in the
settlement of Aotearoa by scholars of the Victorian period. Indeed
the once-popular theory was that Toi was the first to settle New
Zealand in AD 1150. Such theories have since been dismissed by
scholars such as D.R. Simmons, who identifies several different
Toi and Whatonga traditions belonging to various tribes and
demonstrates how they were cobbled together into one, largely
by Europeans anxious to construct an historical record of Maori
settlement in New Zealand. The traditions are outlined in *The
Great New Zealand Myth*, by D.R. Simmons (A.H. & A.W. Reed,
Wellington, 1976).

The Tops, The High Tops

South Island high-country stations often run up to the snowline
of the Alps. Most of this country is unfenced open range, and the
movement of sheep is controlled only by the elements. In early
autumn, **Musterers** on horseback and foot would walk these
high hills to drive the sheep down to the comparative safety of
the **Winter Country**. This exercise was known as 'mustering the
tops'. Trampers, hunters and climbers also refer to the Tops, an
expression that summarises the new habitat of rock plant and
barrens that emerges when you walk above the bush line into
the montane world. Writer Maurice Shadbolt, working with
photographer Brian Brake, gave the tradition expression in
a documentary film about high-country farming entitled *The
Snowline is their Boundary*.

Tramping

A New Zealand version of the British hill-walking and Australian bush-walking. More rugged, however, with the constant threat of getting lost or injured in the bush, suffering from exposure in the highly changeable weather, or having to risk rapidly rising rivers. A network of tracks penetrates national parks and reserves while the Walkways Act provides a mechanism for declaring routes across private land with the owners' consent. The recreation has many adherents, prepared to hump a heavy pack with wet weather gear, tent, sleeping bag and food into the back country. Great tramping routes include crossing the ice-covered Copland Pass by Mt Cook, the easier Heaphy and Kepler Tracks, and the Abel Tasman Coastal Track, which attracts about 28,000 overnight visitors a year. A one-day crossing of the volcanic summit of Mt Tongariro has been described as the greatest one-day walk in the world. The tramping tracks are well-used by foreign backpackers who according to tourism figures may spend up to three months walking the back-country. Their major complaint: the number of their compatriots they encounter in the overcrowded back-country huts.

Tramping Huts

Most date from the days of the old Lands and Survey Department and the Forest Service, which were disestablished in 1988. Basic accommodation along bush trails usually includes a fireplace and bunks, often 'Maori bunks' where several have to roll onto sleeping shelves or mattresses together. Often overcrowded, as tourist numbers swell; trampers are advised to carry their own tent and gas cooker in case they are too late at the hut. Many back-country huts were built by volunteers from the tramping and mountain clubs: the tendency today is for the State to fund a better class of hut and charge more for its use.

Tramps *see* Swaggers, Swagmen

Treasure, Lost and Found *see* General Grant's Gold, Elingamite Treasure, Niagara's Gold

The Treaty of Waitangi, Te Tiriti o Waitangi

The ultimate icon, signed in 1840 by representatives of the British Crown and the chiefs of many tribes, it is regarded as the founding document of New Zealand. Notably absent from the signatories, however, are the senior chiefs of Waikato and Tuwharetoa at that time. At the signing at Waitangi, Bay of Islands, in February 1840, Governor Hobson told the chiefs 'He iwi tahi tatou' – 'We are now one people.' The subsequent definition 'two people in one land' has proved more apposite. In recent years there has been renewed talk of 'honouring the Treaty'. This in essence has revolved around a more literal interpretation of the Maori version of the Treaty that includes guaranteeing chieftainly control of such resources as fisheries, land and forests. The mechanism of the Treaty of Waitangi Tribunal was set up in 1977 to settle outstanding grievances between the Crown and the tribes. The claims really took substance when the field of review was made retrospective to 1840. A 1987 Court of Appeal case, the New Zealand Maori Council versus the Crown, gave a landmark judgement defining a special relationship between Maori people and the Crown, describing this as a partnership and requiring those partners to act reasonably and in utmost good faith with each other. Those principles enshrined in such Acts as the Conservation Act and the Resource Management Act have had a profound effect on how governments and authorities generally deal with issues, particularly those touching on land management and the sea. There has been some backlash from those who consider themselves being treated as a third party on a broad number of issues, and who argue that the Crown today is simply the expression of the will of the people and should be more accountable to them. See the Treaty on display in the refurbished Parliament Buildings; pick and choose from the library of books about the Treaty and related issues, which proliferated about the time of the Sesquicentennial of its signing, in the year 1990.

The Tree Nettle

The tree nettle or ongaonga (*Urtica ferox*) is regarded as a killer tree in the New Zealand bush. Dogs and horses brushing against it along a bush trail have suffered badly, and some are recorded as dying. H.E. Connor in *The Poisonous Plants of New Zealand* (Government Printer, Wellington, 1977), gives details of two young men stung by tree nettle while shooting in the Ruahine Ranges in 1961; one of them died. Strangely, the red admiral butterfly generally relies on the tree nettle as a place to lay its eggs, right on the tips of the stings.

Trench Warfare

New Zealand soldiers, particularly in the First World War, were often engaged in 'trench warfare'. In this way thousands died as they rose from their defensive ditches to race across the mud, wire and mines that separated them from opposing forces, which were also sheltering in trenches. The technique led to armies becoming deadlocked in the French countryside for months. The introduction of bomb-carrying aeroplanes, heavy shelling and tanks was the only way to advance when infantry soldiers were bogged down in trenches. Some military historians have noted that the use of trenches to defend a position could stem in part from the experience of British troops in the **New Zealand Wars**. There, they admired and recorded the Maori system of ditch defences around **Pa,** where warriors sheltered underground when attacked by guns, bayonets and cannon.

Trout at Taupo

The Taupo trout fishery was once believed to be the greatest in the world. During the 1960s rainbow trout still averaged five pounds and the brown trout between seven and eight pounds. Yet at the turn of the 20th century these would have been considered tiddlers as the virgin lake was populated by fish of prodigious size. The first English brown trout were liberated in Taupo in 1886 and North American rainbow trout in 1897 into the Tongariro River. Within 20 years, brown trout of 20–25 lbs were being caught. The rainbows averaged eight and three quarter pounds in 1910 and were preferred for their superior fighting ability. Taupo-moana, a sea of a lake covering 650 sq km, had no eels and a plenitude of small native fish and crayfish for the burgeoning trout. Yet within a decade the trout ate it out, the weight of rainbows falling to three and three quarter pounds. Remote Taupo had too few anglers to keep the trout numbers in check so commercial netting was introduced. Although the fish size recovered to an average of 10 and a half pounds in 1924, the population again deteriorated until the introduction of smelt from the Rotorua lakes increased food and stabilised the population. Recent breeding programmes, using eggs from outsized wild fish, have now produced a super strain of rainbow trout, released largely in Lake Tarawera, which has become the popular place to catch a trophy. The famous Tongariro River fishery, the lake itself and the other rivers in which Taupo trout breed, however, remain a major attraction for visiting anglers from around the world. Note: fish weights in pounds always sound more impressive than when metricated. The sceptical may find the conversion tables at the front of this book.

Tutira

Possibly New Zealand's least read well-known book, named for the Hawke's Bay sheep station it documents. A distinguished naturalist, H. Guthrie-Smith (1861–1940) wrote this lengthy description of the natural history of his property, in the manner of White's *Natural History of Selborne*. The book, published in 1921, traces in great detail the history of a piece of land from its creation, through settlement by Maori, and the sad sequence of its conversion into marginal farmland. The detailed descriptions of weather, weeds and introduced pests are rivalled only by those of farm stock and their effects on the land.

Twenty-first Birthdays

The 21st birthday party once celebrated accession to the adult world, including the expectation of assuming the title Mr or Miss, though in the 1950s Mr was sometimes reserved for those who were married. The age of majority was a substantial rite of passage in the days when it represented the right to vote and it was illegal to buy liquor if you were under 21. The age of majority (and the drinking age) has been subsequently lowered to 18; no one is called Mr while a Ms would be insulted if called Mrs or Miss. The age of 21 is still often taken as something to be celebrated, however.

The Ulster Plantation

Bay of Plenty settlements of Ulstermen were organised by George Vesey Stewart (1832–1920). The expression Ulster Plantation was applied to the Katikati Settlement that began with Northern Irish aboard the *Carisbrook Castle*, which sailed from Belfast in 1875. A second expedition sailed aboard the *Lady Jocelyn* in 1878. Stewart sold his Te Puke block to Irish and British settlers in 1880. Some 4000 settlers were brought to New Zealand under Stewart's schemes. See *Ulster Plantation: the story of the Kati Kati settlement*, by A.J. Gray (A.H. & A.W. Reed, Dunedin, 1938).

'Uncle Scrim'

A charismatic figure of the pioneer radio waves, the Rev. C.G. Scrimgeour was also controversial. His populist broadcasts, tinged with socialism, outraged the conservative government of the time. 'Uncle Scrim' was at the height of his popularity during the 1930s **Great Depression**, broadcasting from his Friendly Road radio station, now called 1ZB. Pioneer film-maker Rudall Hayward based his first 'talking picture', *On the Friendly Road*, on Scrimgeour's work. 'Scrim' used radio to help the people and the government did not like his messages. Almost on the eve of the 1935 election 1ZB was electronically jammed during 'Uncle Scrim's' Sunday chat. 'Uncle Scrim' accused the government of putting him off the air and a political witch-hunt for those responsible ensued. When the first Labour government romped into power an official enquiry forced a former Minister, Adam Hamilton, to accept reponsibility for the jamming. 'Uncle Scrim' was appointed State Director of Commercial Radio and broadcasting was socialised. In time he fell out of favour with the Labour government, too, and was dismissed. Moving to Australia, after the Second World War, 'Uncle Scrim' was successful in radio and television there, before playing a key role in the introduction of television in mainland China. See also **Aunt Daisy.**

Universal Penny Postage

Alas no more; but the principle of cheap penny postage for first-class mail anywhere in the world largely originated in New Zealand. Through the Universal Postage Union, New Zealand persuaded other countries to carry its one penny letters and indeed others matched the service as well. The postage rate fell from 2.5d to one penny, internationally from January 1, 1901. Thus was born the universal postage stamp that for 25 years appeared in various shades of magenta red. The female figure is **Zealandia**, symbolising New Zealand. The steam ship near Mt Egmont (Taranaki) and the globe also give national identity to the stamp. According to Laurie Franks in *All the Postage Stamps of New Zealand*, (Reed, Auckland, 1981), the New Zealand Post Office tried to lead the world in those days, introducing the first slot machines for selling stamps. Mechanised franking was another New Zealand invention.

Universal Super *see* Old Age Pensions

The University of Life

People of finer sensibility have been known to avoid the obviously working-class connotations of education in the **School of Hard Knocks** by claiming graduation from the University of Life.

Up the Boo-ai

The **Back of Beyond** is widely defined as being 'up the Boo-ai'. The phrase is said to have developed from a reference to the once isolated Puhoi settlement north of Auckland, where the **Bohemians** substituted 'B' for 'P' in their local accent, and was a traditional response to the question 'Where is so-and-so?': 'Way up the Boo-ai, where the ducks fly backwards to keep the dust out of their eyes, chasing bokakas with a long-handled shovel.' Traditionally Boo-ai is Puhoi and bokaka is the local name for the pukeko bird. See **Cooking a Pukeko.**

Vegetable Caterpillar

This mystery of the bush looks like a caterpillar that has given rise to a plant. In fact it is both, having begun life as a porina moth caterpillar that has become the host of a fungus. Porina caterpillars grow underground as grass grubs. The fungus takes over the body of the caterpillar, then sends up a rhizome above ground. Maori burnt the vegetable caterpillar to a black powder that could be mixed with oil and used to stain their traditional skin tattoo.

Vegetable Sheep

This alpine shrub has leaves so tightly packed against the elements that it looks more like a growth of moss or lichen than a tree. The plants root on the rock face at high altitudes in the South Island. From a distance its softly haired silver cushion resembles a lost sheep.

Verandah

A feature of colonial architecture now enjoying a resurgence in popularity. The name is Indian and the verandah is useful in hot climates to provide a cool place to sit out and to shade the interior of the house. A verandah end creates shelter from drafts and often provides a sheltered sun-room for lying out. Jeremy Salmond, in his *Old New Zealand Houses 1800–1940*, records that the verandah was an idea imported to Britain from the colonies of Jamaica and India, then re-exported in the form of pre-fabricated houses for hot climates. In the warmer parts of New Zealand it soon proved popular and over the years became a decorative feature, too, with iron or wooden lacework. The shelter from direct sun provided by the verandah made it less popular in cooler districts, where householders preferred large windows admitting as much of the sun as possible. For them the gazebo or conservatory has become a popular addition in recent years. See *Old New Zealand Houses 1800–1940,* by Jeremy Salmond (Reed-Methuen, Auckland, 1986) for a well-illustrated account of New Zealand housing traditions.

Votes for Women

New Zealand is said to be the first country in the world where women could vote. The claim has also been made for a few even more tiny islands elsewhere but New Zealanders claim to be more of a country, less of a dependency of Britain, and therefore claim to be the first place to introduce universal suffrage. The pioneer experience tended to show men and women in a more equal light than in Britain: New Zealand women in some provinces won local voting rights as early as 1867 and many were nationally enfranchised to vote for local authorities before 1893. Women voted for school boards from 1877; ratepaying women for liquor licensing committees from 1881; and for hospital boards and charitable boards from 1885. The franchise superintendent of the Women's Christian Temperance Union, Kate Sheppard (1848–1934), led a determined six-year campaign of letter-writing and petitions, and succeeded in getting the women's cause through Parliament by only two votes. Women's suffrage was achieved under a Liberal government in 1893. Yet, when the Liberals were returned at the first election in which women took part, the effect of the women's vote could not be traced clearly in the result. The right of women to become Members of Parliament was slower coming: the law was changed to allow this in 1919 but it was 40 years after the franchise that the first woman was elected. She was Elizabeth McCombs (1873–1935), elected in place of her deceased husband to represent Lyttelton for Labour in 1933. The Hon. Mabel Howard (1894–1972), Labour Member for Sydenham, became the first woman Cabinet minister in 1947 as Minister of Health. The first Maori woman in Parliament was Iriaka Ratana (1906–1981), who succeeded her husband on his death as Member for Western Maori in 1949. Other landmarks of women's suffrage included the appointment of the Rt. Hon. Helen Clark as Deputy Prime Minister in the 1989 Labour government and Leader of the Opposition in 1993. The first woman prime minister was the Rt. Hon. Jenny Shipley, who headed the Coalition government from 1997 to1999, when she was succeeded by the Rt. Hon. Helen Clark, a Labour prime minister. See also **Women on Top.**

The *Wahine* Storm

A tropical cyclone that wreaked havoc in many parts of the country, including the ripping out of extensive tracts of mountain forests, on April 10, 1968. People still point to changes in their environment, lost trees, etc., as dating back to the *Wahine* storm. The immediate association of the storm, however, is with the loss of the **Inter-island Ferry** *Wahine*, which touched on Barretts Reef and drifted up Wellington Harbour to capsize with the loss of 51 lives.

'Waiata Poi'

Internationally known Maori music by a European New Zealander. Violinist, conductor and composer Alfred Hill (1870–1960) used Maori music as a starting point for many of his compositions, including comic opera and concertos, and the cantata 'Hinemoa'. 'Waiata Poi', dating from around 1904, involves much twirling of poi, with a driving beat and a catchy tune. Once used in the musical montage introducing the BBC World News, 'Waiata Poi' is still among the Commonwealth tunes that bands play as they march to change the guard at Buckingham Palace.

The Waihi Strike

A six-month strike that tore a town apart and cost a man his life also marked the birth of the Federation of Labour as a force in the land. The dispute began as a demarcation, one between two unions. The Waihi Miners' Union left the protection of the Industrial Conciliation and Arbitration Act to join the Federation of Labour and left their companions in the new Waihi Engine-drivers' Union in an industrial no-man's land. While that dispute existed the mining companies would not settle on demands. Lockouts and strikes followed. The streets of Waihi bristled with police. Faction fought faction in a number of riots while the underground mines flooded for want of maintenance. There were frequent charges laid of 'following up', harassing those who continued working. In one riot a man was beaten by the crowd after shooting a policeman. The policeman survived but the striker died of retaliatory injuries. Wildly differing tales of events in Waihi worked their way into the traditions of the labour movement and of the later Labour Party, for several of its influential leaders were 'blooded' as union leaders at Waihi. Mickey Savage and Peter Fraser were in time Prime Ministers of New Zealand, while Paddy Webb, Bill Parry and Bob Semple became senior Ministers of the Crown. See *The Red and the Gold: an informal account of the Waihi Strike 1912*, by Stanley Roche (Oxford University Press, Auckland, 1982).

The Wairau 'Massacre'

The death of 22 Nelson settlers who had laid down their arms after a dispute with Maori in Marlborough was described by settlers as a massacre. It is now more sensitively described as the Wairau Affray since the reason for the killings has been traced to cultural misunderstandings. In brief, surveyors from Nelson were working in Marlborough on land that they believed had been purchased to expand their settlement, though the Maori owners had denied it in court and made it clear the Wairau belonged to them. When argument failed, the Maori owners, led by Te Rauparaha of Ngati Toa, disrupted the work, leading to a charge against them of damaging property. The police magistrate from Nelson and a party of concerned settlers sailed to Marlborough to arrest those responsible, despite warnings from several who were more sensitive to what was involved. Advancing up the Tuamarina branch of the Wairau, the settlers confronted Te Rauparaha and Te Rangihaeata, attempting to arrest them, a situation that deteriorated into an exchange of fire. The New Zealand Company agent from Nelson, Captain Arthur Wakefield, tendered submission by proffering a white flag and his men handed over their firearms. As they sat negotiating, Te Rangihaeata discovered his wife Te Rongo had been killed in the affray and the settlers were attacked to exact utu, the traditional revenge for her death. The Governor, Captain Fitzroy, decided the settlers were in the wrong, and no further action was taken.

Waitangi Day

Formerly known as New Zealand Day, February 6 was renamed Waitangi Day and made a public holiday by the Labour government, in 1975. The day marks the events on February 6, 1840, when Governor Hobson, on behalf of Queen Victoria, signed a treaty with Maori chiefs that is now regarded as the founding document of New Zealand. The site of this event, at Waitangi, near Paihia in the Bay of Islands, was purchased by a former Governor-General, Lord Bledisloe, in 1932 and gifted to the nation. A large **Hui** was held on the anniversary of the signings in 1934 and a major function involving the Navy marked the Centennial in 1940. Subsequently the Navy and northern Maori have traditionally gathered on the lawns of the Treaty House to mark the anniversary of those first signings. (The Treaty was subsequently taken to leaders of Maori tribes throughout New Zealand and the last signatures were appended in Hawke's Bay on June 23, 1840). Naval involvement at Waitangi was curtailed by the government during a period of land-rights agitation during the 1980s, but their central role resumed when in 1990 the tribes granted the sailors the Freedom of Tai Tokerau (Northland), allowing them to march armed and perform the ceremony of Beating the Retreat as the sun sets on the Treaty House lawns at Waitangi whenever they fancy.

Wakefield Settlements

As in Australia, a number of New Zealand's British settlements were born of the colonising entrepreneurship of the Wakefield family. Edward Gibbon Wakefield (1796–1862) initiated the New Zealand Land Company, setting up colonising associations for several settlements with the help of liberal churchmen, Members of Parliament and members of the aristocracy. Members of the Wakefield family were among the leaders of the new colonies. The idea was to transplant a cross-section of British society to new settlements, funding development by the sale of land. Labouring classes were given cheap passage if they qualified as 'useful' settlers. The New Zealand Land Company began purchasing before New Zealand was declared a British colony and tension between company and Crown, over the purchase of land, continued until its demise. The Wellington settlement was first, with an advance party on the *Tory* acquiring land and raising a flag on September 30, 1839, some months before the signing of the Treaty of Waitangi. Led by Colonel William Wakefield (1803–1848), the passengers of the *Aurora, Oriental* and *Duke of Roxburgh* landed at Petone in January 1840 to found Britannia and eventually Wellington. Next was Wanganui, also in 1840, initially named 'Petre' after a director of the New Zealand Land Company. The Plymouth Company merged with the New Zealand Land Company to settle New Plymouth on Wakefield principles in 1841. The Nelson settlement was begun by an advance party sent in 1841, the first settlers arriving in 1842; the company's agent Captain Arthur Wakefield (1799–1843) was among those who died in the **Wairau 'Massacre'** during an expedition prompted by the search for further land for the growing settlement. The Otago Association set up a Free Presbyterian colony at Dunedin in 1848. The Canterbury Association established its colony with the **First Four Ships** arriving in 1850. A lively story of the Wakefields in New Zealand, between 1839 and 1844, is told by Edward Jerningham Wakefield (1820–79) in his *Adventures in New Zealand*, republished many times, more recently by Golden Press. Jerningham was just 20 at the time, but played an active part in making land deals and in the planning of the settlements.

Wakes

Following a funeral, this Irish custom is widespread in New Zealand. People gather at the home of the bereaved, or a hired venue, for light refreshments. Depending on the nature of the deceased and their connections this may deteriorate into an alcoholic occasion; even a maudlin or celebratory release of tension for those less close to the deceased.

Walk Shorts

Before 1987, when 40 per cent of New Zealanders were in public employment, work dress was governed by strict codes. Men in offices were expected to wear ties, but in summer they were allowed to wear shorts instead of long trousers. The combination of the ever-constricting tie with short-sleeved white shirt and shorts was completed by calf-length socks kept up by garters. In summer this clerical uniform can still be occasionally observed.

The War in the North

A series of battles between Maori and British in the Bay of Islands region during 1845 and 1846. The war followed some Maori frustration with government, including the withdrawal of the capital from Russell to Auckland, which had had a serious effect on trade. After **Chopping Down the Flagpole**, Hone Heke and Kawiti attacked Russell on March 11, 1845, and burnt the town. The British responded by attacking Hone Heke's pa at Puketutu, by Lake Omapere, on May 8, 1845. Heke and Kawiti then began a new defensive position at Ohaeawai, where the British lost 40 men in a day during a battle on July 1, 1845. The new Governor George Grey told Maori not to fear for their land and gave them 10 days to stop their actions before moving on Kawiti's pa, Ruapekapeka, the Bat's Nest. The pa was taken on January 11, 1846 while most of its defenders had retired to the forest behind for a church service, believing that the British would not attack on the Sabbath. Both Hone Heke and Kawiti were pardoned for their insurrection.

The Waterfront Strike, 1951

This test of left- and right-wing politics was finally won by the National government abolishing the waterfront unions and setting up new ones. In a state of national emergency, servicemen were used as strike breakers to keep essential goods moving over the wharves and around the coasts. The strike spread from the waterfront to encompass other unions which affected the means of production and distribution: freezing workers, coal miners and seamen. The waterfront workers' leaders, President H. Barnes and Secretary T. Hill, were represented as evil 'commies' by one side but revered by the other. There were street demonstrations with some violence; a railway bridge near Huntly was damaged by dynamite. It became illegal to help a waterfront worker or to speak about conditions brought on by the strike. Labour leader Walter Nash called for conciliation and the return of civil liberties; Prime Minister Sidney Holland insisted on a return to industrial normality first. When Nash finally persuaded Holland to go to the country to test his actions, the government was returned with a big majority. The events shaped the 'them and us' legends of New Zealand unionism for a generation.

'Wayleggo'

The shouted cry of the shepherd to his dog evokes the high-country world of the South Island. 'To the majority the word is meaningless, but to those whose calling takes them where sheep men foregather, it has a fascination of its own,' wrote Peter Newton in 1947, introducing the word as the title of his best-selling book about the musterer's life. 'Pictures are conjured up of green hills and peaceful valleys, rock-bound peaks and misty gullies; white strings of sheep winding away through sunny faces, or disappearing helter-skelter down a dusty spur.' Speculating on the origins of the call, Peter Newton notes it is the command the shepherd uses to 'call his dog off sheep, and is presumably an abbreviation of "come away and let them go." A call stentorian yet with a plaintive note, it carries afar, echoing through the valleys and rolling down from lofty ridges.' See *Wayleggo,* by Peter Newton (A.H. & A.W. Reed, Wellington, 1947 and reprinted many times). Newton's popular accounts of high country life continued with *High Country Days, High Country Journey* and other tales of the high country.

The *Weekly News* (1863–1971)

The pink-covered newsprint magazine, stablemate of the *New Zealand Herald,* became such an institution that after the Second World War people went on a waiting list to get a subscription. Many an early home was wallpapered, over match-lining or hessian, with the shiny, central pages of the 'Auckland Weekly'. In the days before radio, when newspapers, too, might take several days to reach their more distant readers, a weekly news magazine was a popular way to keep in touch with events. Most died out by the time of the 1930s **Great Depression**. The *Weekly News* was rich in human interest, with a country bias, and its picture pages represent a documentary history of New Zealand in black and white. Feature photographers of The *Weekly News* visited distant corners of New Zealand, producing portraits of back-country life, the farming year and the passing of the seasons. The national appeal of the The *Weekly News* saw it outlive The *Weekly Press* of Christchurch (1868–1928) and The *New Zealand Freelance* (1900–60), based in Wellington. Ultimately it failed to attract a big enough share of the advertising dollars being attracted to new media, such as television. Yet its circulation in its dying days was still in excess of 100,000 and the popularity of its documentary record has been reflected more recently in a series of photographic volumes based on its files, called *Those Were the Days.*

The Wellington Cable Car

Running from an alley off downtown Lambton Quay, the Kelburn cable car swiftly rises 122 m to the suburbs above. The system was originally built at the turn of the 20th century to serve land subdivisions uphill. There are two cars, rising and falling from opposite ends of the track. A powerhouse at the top kept the cable revolving and brakemen adjusted the grip to stop and start the cars. Thousands of public servants attending Victoria University part-time used this quick route to and from the campus, making the return journey within their hour-long lecture leave. The original cars ran from 1902 until 1978. They were replaced with a new system using modern Swiss cars in 1979. For more see Graham Stewart's *The Kelburn Cable Car* (Grantham House Publishing, Wellington, 2001). For Dunedin's Cable Cars see the **Steepest Gradient in the Southern Hemisphere**.

Wellington's First Five Ships

The first five immigrant ships, sponsored by the New Zealand Company, arrived in Port Nicholson early in 1840. The *Aurora* was first, on January 22, two weeks before the first signings of the Treaty of Waitangi in the north. The *Oriental* (January 31) also arrived before the Treaty between British and Maori came into force. The *Duke of Roxburgh* arrived two days after the original signing, on February 8, 1840. The *Bengal Merchant* arrived on February 20 and the *Adelaide* on March 7. Maori chiefs of the Wellington area did not sign the Treaty of Waitangi until April 29. See the **Founding of Britannia**, **Wakefield Settlements**.

When XYZ Vanishes the Rain Is Coming

A prominent nearby hill substitutes for XYZ. When the rain clouds engulf it then rain is imminent. This folk wisdom may be heard in several parts of the country. It sounds obvious enough but with a centralised meteorological service, such 'look and see' methods can be more useful than the forecast when deciding whether or not to hang out the washing.

Whingeing Poms

A stereotype, not a tradition, though the expression does reflect on the New Zealand character, too. This expression may in part have been Kiwi backlash to the surge of immigration from Britain from the mid-1950s. Certainly any tendency to complain of anything, in the accents of Britain, brought on a charge of 'whingeing'. Unfavourable comparisons, even those deserved, between 'things here and things at **Home**' would shortly excite the charge of 'whingeing Poms'. The Australians had the same perception of their British immigrants. The condition was often mollified by immigrants taking the **Thousand Pound** or the **Ten Thousand Dollar Cure**, a return journey back home to 'see just how lucky we are'.

'Whitby Cats'

The nickname for a class of vessel chosen by Captain James Cook and the British Admiralty for the explorations of the South Seas. The ships were Yorkshire-built coastal colliers, sailing vessels of great seaworthiness and good hold area, which could be converted to house men and stores. The shallow draught of such vessels made them less likely to run aground. Their flat bottoms meant they could be run gently ashore to be repaired, or careened of the marine life that proliferates on hulls at sea and impairs their sailing. 'Such qualities are to be found in North Country built ships, and in none other,' Cook wrote after the first voyage. The Whitby cats were little ships; *Endeavour* was only 32 m (105 ft) long, but her beam, at 8.8 m (29 ft), was broad. Such vessels could not sail into the wind as modern sailing ships do, which meant they were often swept off course and could not beat directly back. Sailing with the wind following, they could make speeds of up to eight knots. Cook's first Whitby cat was the *Endeavour* (1768–71 voyage), followed on the 1772–75 voyage by the *Resolution* (462 tons) and the *Adventure* (340 tons). See the **Earl of Pembroke**.

The White Chief

There are several examples of Europeans being tattooed in the Maori fashion, if only to hide their true identity, in the days when quite a number of escaped prisoners from the Australian colonies found their way here. John Rutherford is perhaps the most famous for he recounted the story of his experiences of 10 years among the Maori, published in *The New Zealanders* in 1830. Rutherford went to sea at age 16. His travels in the East and the Pacific led him ultimately to the shores of New Zealand, where his ship was attacked while taking on supplies and all but a handful of crew murdered. The survivors were tattooed and accepted into the tribe. Rutherford's description of being tattooed is graphic:

'The whole of the natives having then seated themselves on the ground, in a ring, we were brought into the middle and, being stripped of our clothes, and laid on our backs, we were each of us held down by five or six men, while two others commenced the operation of tattooing us.

'Having taken a piece of charcoal, and rubbed it upon a stone with a little water until they had produced a thickish liquid, they then dipped into it an instrument made of bone, having a sharp edge like a chisel, and shaped in the fashion of a garden-hoe, and immediately applied it to the skin, striking it twice or thrice with a small piece of wood. This made it cut into the flesh as a knife would have done, and caused a great deal of blood to flow, which they kept wiping off with the side of the hand, in order to see if the impression was sufficiently clear. When it was not, they applied the bone a second time to the same place. They employed, however, various instruments in the course of the operation; one which they sometimes used being made of a shark's tooth, and another having teeth like a saw. They had them also of different sizes, to suit the different parts of the work.

'While I was undergoing this operation, although the pain was most acute, I never either moved or uttered a sound; but my comrades moaned dreadfully. Although the operators were very quick and dexterous I was four hours under their hands; and during the operation Aimy's daughter several times wiped the blood from my face with some dressed flax. After it was over she led me to the river, that I might wash myself, for it had made me completely blind, and then conducted me to a great fire …

'We were now not only tattooed but what they called tabooed, the meaning of which is, made sacred, or forbidden to touch any provisions of any kinds with our hands. This state of things lasted for three days, during which time we were fed by the daughters of the chiefs, with the same victuals, and out of the same baskets, as the chiefs themselves, and the persons who had tattooed us. In three days, the swelling which had been produced by the operation had greatly subsided, and I began to recover my sight; but it was six weeks before I was completely well.'

Subsequently, Rutherford took two wives and became a chief, claiming to have seen the great battle of Te Ika a Ranganui where Ngapuhi defeated Ngati Whatua at Kaiwaka in lower Northland. Then, in 1826 he made his escape, by means of a trading vessel that returned him to Britain.

The White Feather

The honourable symbol of passive resistance, worn by the followers of Te Whiti Orongomai (1831–1907) in his campaign to recover confiscated lands in Taranaki. Te Whiti sought self-government and established a town at Parihaka in Taranaki. Here he gathered an industrious community that believed that on the day of reckoning all the Europeans would leave New Zealand, so there was no point in fighting them. Instead, confiscated land allocated to the Europeans was ploughed up, roads were fenced off and survey pegs pulled out. In response dozens of his followers were arrested. In 1881 the government sent 1600 members of the **Armed Constabulary** and volunteers, along with two Ministers of the Crown, to Parihaka. They surrounded the town, but as the force moved forward to make arrests they were welcomed by women and children. Te Whiti and some of his followers spent two years under arrest in the South Island, but returned to strengthen the passive resistance movement among Maori of the western North Island. Te Whiti's followers split into factions in the early 1890s, between his leadership and that of his brother-in-law Tohu, over the disbursements from the Day of Reckoning Fund to which supporters subscribed. Supporters still wear the white feather when appropriate. The Parihaka story is movingly told in *Ask That Mountain*, by Dick Scott (Heinemann/Southern Cross, Auckland, 1975).

Whitebait, Whitebaiting

The traditions of catching and eating these tiny fish are based on the springtime migrations of the young of inanga, various native Galaxiid species. The fish are netted about estuaries and tidal river reaches as they run upstream in their multitudes to grow into adult fish. Whitebaiters occupy a 'stand', a closely guarded personal position from where they can cast a fine net or scoop up the fish as they run upstream. A few light-coloured stones or a painted board on the riverbed may serve to show up the transparent 'bait' as they 'run'. Mature inanga lay their eggs in tidal reaches on vegetation drowned by the highest spring tides. When water covers them again the whitebait hatch and run out to sea for a period before returning in great shoals as semi-transparent young, each only about 50 mm long. Damage to tidal riverbanks and vegetation has affected whitebait numbers but the 'runs' can still be spectacular, particularly along the West Coast. The price of whitebait can be so high that it pays commercial whitebaiters to hire aircraft to fly their catches out to the cities. The delicacy is often served in patties; the best are heavy on fish and lighter on the binding egg yolk and flour. The result is generally bland.

Wild Horses – Aupouri

Land development and smaller farms have trimmed back the wild country where feral horses once roamed. In farthest Northland a few wild horses still run among the sandhills and pinelands of the Aupouri State Forest.

Wild Horses – Kaimanawa

The romance of wild horses, sweeping across the tussocklands in herds dominated by the strongest stallion, lives on in the high country of the central North Island. The Kaimanawa-Moawhango horse herd is said to have originated from unwanted domestic and military animals released from the nearby Waiouru Army Camp. Another line has been traced by the Hon. Denis Marshall to the Exmoor ponies imported into Hawke's Bay in the 1850s by Major George Gwavas Carlyon, who crossed them with local stock to produce the Carlyon pony. These in turn were mated with Welsh stallions, imported by Sir Donald McLean, to produce the Comet breed; it was Sir Donald who released a stallion and mares to form the basis of the wild bloodline. Hunted by commercial horse-breakers, their numbers dropped to around 170 in 1981, when horse lovers had them protected under an Order in Council. In the 1990s wild horse numbers increased to around 1500 to become the centre of controversy with conservationists who claim the horses damage sensitive native plants. An annual cull that captures surplus horses and auctions them for breaking-in, or pet food, has solved that argument. The current population is to be maintained at around 500 horses grazing 18,000 hectares of the 80,000-hectare tussock grasslands.

Wild Horses – St James

The St James herd of horses is still farmed, though the animals run wild in the high-country valleys of this remote station north of Hamner. There, in glacial valleys below the Spenser Mountains near Lewis Pass, the mares foal and feed off the mountain pastures. Traditionally the horses were brought down every two years for sale in January. Many a South Island musterer's horse was broken in from St James wild stock, and some show jumpers and hunters too, have the St James breeding in them.

Wild Irishman

The tightly woven branchlets and clawing spines of the matagouri shrub are still known to some back-country folk as Wild Irishman. The name perhaps reflects traditional feelings about the Irish Fenians in pioneer days.

Wild Spaniard, Spaniard

A traditional name for the *Aciphylla* family of speargrass, found in the high-country tussock lands. These plants have spear-sharp leaves, a name perhaps inspired by the Spanish grandee with sword ever at the ready.

Winter Country

In the traditions of farming the high country, sheep are mustered down from the **Tops** in autumn and held in paddocks in the valleys during the winter snows. Here root crops and other supplementary feed can be available. This country, fenced and more accessible to the station hands, is known by the name winter country.

Women on Top

The Hon. Mabel Howard (1894–1972), Labour Member for Sydenham, became the first woman Cabinet Minister in 1947 as Minister of Health. Other landmarks of women's enfranchisement included the appointment of the Rt. Hon. Helen Clark as Deputy Prime Minister in the 1989 Labour government and Leader of the Opposition in 1993. Her Excellency Dame Catherine Tizard became Governor-General in 1990, the first woman Head of State. The first woman prime minister was the Rt. Hon. Jenny Shipley, who headed a National/Coalition government from December 8, 1997, until December 10, 1999, when she lost the election to Helen Clark, who succeeded her as prime minister. Margaret Wilson was then appointed Attorney-General. The Rt. Hon. Dame Sian Elias was appointed Chief Justice in 1999. With Helen Clark, and a further woman Governor-General in Her Excellency the Hon. Dame Silvia Cartwright appointed in 2001, women in the early 2000s held all the top constitutional appointments in New Zealand. See also **Votes for Women.**

·Wooden Houses

A shortage of bricks and labour soon led pioneers to improvise in wood. Some sent out prefabricated homes in timber, but most turned to the nearby bush, pit-sawing logs into planks and building modest lean-to cottages. So the forests shrank along with the frontiers. Since the 1950s much of the timber for construction has come from the burgeoning exotic forests, planted from the 1930s. New Zealand pioneered techniques for preserving the softwood pine and creating chipboard floors and linings. Wood has usually been comparatively cheap. It is also more flexible as a building material in a country often wrenched by earthquakes. Top the timber house with **Corrugated Iron** and you have the formula that characterises our lived-in landscape, so distinct from the mellow stone or brick of other countries.

Women's Suffrage *see* Votes for Women

Working Dogs

New Zealand's specially bred sheep dogs are a tourist attraction and the basis of a television show. With good dogs, a shepherd can move and control large flocks of sheep. These are traditionally bred from the border collie. Heading dogs, cast well ahead of the musterer, find sheep in gullies but still respond to whistles from their owner, who may be out of sight. The huntaways, bred to bark, chivvy along the flock and keep the mob moving. 'Backing dogs' may leap on the backs of sheep in the yards to keep the leaders moving down the races. A 'strong-eyed' dog can mesmerise a sheep, holding it from bolting from the flock, turning it back by giving it 'the eye'. Australian kelpies are said to have some dingo in their ancestry, giving a useful belligerence for moving cattle. The beardie or English Smithfield is another favourite for mustering cattle. Working-dog competitions, **Dog Trials**, reputedly began on Haldon Station in the **Mackenzie Country** of Canterbury in 1869. There are nearly 200 dog-trial clubs, and competitions have been shown on television.

Wowsers

People who don't drink alcohol were universally condemned by the 'drinking man' in former times. This sprang largely from the historical conflict over **Prohibition** that marked New Zealand politics from the 1880s until recent years. See **Dry Towns.**

The Wreck of the *Endeavour*

The remains of a sailing ship once reputed to be the wreck of Captain Cook's *Endeavour* can still be seen in the dark waters of Facile Harbour, Dusky Sound, in Fiordland. The confusion with Cook's ship (which was in fact wrecked in Newport, Rhode Island) arises from the common name. This *Endeavour* was an 800-ton East Indiaman abandoned in 1795. In Sydney her captain had heard of a vessel built by castaway sealers at Luncheon Cove in Dusky Sound. The idea was to finish the sealers' vessel and leave the *Endeavour* to rot. Unfortunately the *Endeavour* was found to have many more aboard than expected; as she cleared Sydney, 41 stowaways, likely all convicts, revealed themselves. When run onto the beach, the *Endeavour* left 244 people in Dusky Sound, with their only workable ship a small brig called the *Fancy*, which could carry only 64. A village was built in an area still marked by second-growth forest. The *Endeavour*'s fittings and timbers were stripped away to complete the sealers' vessel. The new ship, called *Providence*, could take 90 people, leaving a further 90 as castaways in the remote fiord. Of these, 55 sailed to Sydney aboard the long-boat salvaged from the sunken *Endeavour*. The remaining 35 lived off the harsh land for 20 months before being rescued by a visiting ship and taken to Norfolk Island. Read the 'Log of Captain Robert Murry', who was a fourth officer with the sealing ship and later with the *Endeavour*, located by Robert McNab in 1906 and quoted in *Dusky Bay*, by A. Charles Begg and Neil C. Begg (Whitcombe and Tombs, Christchurch, 1966). See also the **First European Settlement in New Zealand**.

Yates Garden Guide

The *Edmonds Cookery Book* of the New Zealand garden, *Yates Garden Guide* dates from 1895 and has since been republished regularly. The book is a straightforward handbook of garden techniques, suitable flowers, vegetables, shrubs and trees. Native plants were included for the first time in 1987, along with micro-irrigation and organic techniques. The book was originally produced by seedsmen Arthur Yates and Co and continues to complement the branding of their corporate successors. Cumulative sales reached the one-million mark in 1990. It still sells round 7000 copies a year.

'Yellow Fever'

The excitement brought on by the discovery of gold, which prompted the **Gold Rushes** and **Duffer Rushes**.

The 'Yellow Peril'

Also described as the 'heathen Chinee', goldminers from Southern China were the butt of racial discrimination in early New Zealand. In 1881, as economic depression threatened, the government introduced a poll tax to discourage Chinese immigration. One who particularly disliked the Chinese was Lionel Terry, an otherwise gentlemanly figure, who wrote a book, *The Shadow*, to express his fear of the 'yellow peril'. One evening in 1905, he walked into Wellington's **Chinatown**, along Haining Street, and shot an old Chinese man. The next morning he handed himself and his weapon into the police. He claimed his crime was to draw attention to the dangers of immigration and the mixing of races. Terry's life sentence ended in a psychiatric institution when he died in 1952 at the age of 85.

Zambuck

A popular name for St John's Ambulance volunteers who attend sports games and public events in New Zealand. Zambuck arises from the first-aid practice, decades ago, of rubbing a product called Zambuck Oil onto the injured at football matches. The nickname, if not the oil, stuck. Now 'Magic Water,' poured on liberally, is the permitted panacea.

Zealandia

The romantic figure of a gowned woman was a popular national image around the beginning of last century. Similar in grandeur to her contemporary figure, Britannia, Zealandia appears on the **Postage Stamps** of the period. Zealandia was occasionally addressed in nationalistic poems. Her role today is largely limited to holding a New Zealand flag, and facing a Maori chief, across the national coat of arms.

Acknowledgements

Putting together more than 700 entries on New Zealand traditions requires a lot of detailed work and checking. The original text editing of this book was handled by my daughter, Sarah Ell, to whom I owe particular thanks for her persistence and constructive criticism; thanks also to Ruth Ell for finding time to check proofs and above all for continuing encouragement. For the rest, both friends and officials helped with their recollections and by providing details from their special expertise. I must thank them all for their advice and absolve them from any blame for errors of omission or commission. The illustrations in this book have been largely drawn from my own library of old books about New Zealand, particularly from Australasia Illustrated, (1892), and from books previously published by Bush Press. The Auckland Institute and Museum Library and the Alexander Turnbull Library in Wellington also gave permission for the reproduction of some images. I would also like to thank the librarians at Takapuna Public Library in Auckland for patiently helping me to use their computer system, from time to time.

G.C.E.